SECURITY STRATEGIES, POWER DISPARITY AND IDENTITY

Security Strategies, Power Disparity and Identity
The Baltic Sea Region

Edited by

OLAV F. KNUDSEN
*Swedish Institute of International Affairs, and
Södertörn University College, Sweden*

LONDON AND NEW YORK

First published 2007 by Ashgate Publishing

Reissued 2018 by Routledge
2 Park Square, Milton Park, Abingdon, Oxon OX14 4RN
711 Third Avenue, New York, NY 10017, USA

Routledge is an imprint of the Taylor & Francis Group, an informa business

First issued in paperback 2018

© Olav F. Knudsen 2007

Olav F. Knudsen has asserted his moral right under the Copyright, Designs and Patents Act, 1988, to be identified as the editor of this work.

All rights reserved. No part of this book may be reprinted or reproduced or utilised in any form or by any electronic, mechanical, or other means, now known or hereafter invented, including photocopying and recording, or in any information storage or retrieval system, without permission in writing from the publishers.

A Library of Congress record exists under LC control number: 2006025033

Notice:
Product or corporate names may be trademarks or registered trademarks, and are used only for identification and explanation without intent to infringe.

Publisher's Note
The publisher has gone to great lengths to ensure the quality of this reprint but points out that some imperfections in the original copies may be apparent.

Disclaimer
The publisher has made every effort to trace copyright holders and welcomes correspondence from those they have been unable to contact.

ISBN 13: 978-0-815-39695-6 (hbk)
ISBN 13: 978-1-138-62049-0 (pbk)
ISBN 13: 978-1-351-14952-5 (ebk)

Contents

List of Figures *vii*
List of Tables *viii*
List of Contributors *ix*
Acknowledgements *xi*

1 An Overall Perspective on Regional Power Strategies
  Olav F. Knudsen 1

2 Power Disparities and the Avoidance of Confrontation
  Olav F. Knudsen 9

3 Events and Ideas in the Region: An Overview 1980s–2000s
  Olav F. Knudsen and Christopher Jones 29

4 The Conditionality of Security Integration: Identity and Alignment Choices in Finland and Sweden
  Regina Karp 45

5 Power Disparity and Epistemic Communities: The Paldiski Case
  Michael Karlsson 73

6 Threat Images and Socialization: Estonia and Russia in the New Millennium
  Erik Noreen 97

7 Power Disparity in the Digital Age
  Johan Eriksson 123

8 Generalizing About Security Strategies in the Baltic Sea Region
  Stephen G. Walker 149

9 Looking to the Future: Security Strategies, Identity and Power Disparity
  Olav F. Knudsen 177

References *187*
Index *215*

List of Figures

2.1	Range of Resistance/Avoidance Behaviors	15
2.2	Small State Strategies	19
6.1	Threat Image Trends	110
7.1	Types of Digital Powers	145

List of Tables

5.1	Members of the Working Group on Nuclear and Radiation Safety	80
5.2	Three Views on How Power Disparity Affects the Role of Epistemic Communities	91
7.1	Network Society Rankings	141
7.2	Assertions on Power Disparity in the Digital Age	146
8.1	Grand Strategy Typology	151
8.2	Families of Grand Strategies	152
8.3	Power Equality Games with Symmetrical Strategies	157
8.4	Power Equality Games with Asymmetrical Strategies	158
8.5	Power Disparity Games with Symmetrical Strategies	161
8.6	Power Disparity Games with Asymmetrical Strategies	162
8.7	Power Relationships and Baltic Security Strategies	164
8.8	Security Strategies for Estonia and Russia	166
8.9	Sweden's Security Games with the EU and NATO	168
8.10	Bandwagoning for Profit Strategy and EU Strategies	169
8.11	Bandwagoning for Safety and Balancing Toward NATO[a]	170
8.12	Three Kinds of 2 x 2 Ordinal Games	175

List of Contributors

Johan Eriksson is Associate Professor of Political Science at Södertörn University College, and Research Fellow at the Swedish Institute of International Affairs, Stockholm. He has produced five books, including *International Relations and Security in the Digital Age* (Routledge, 2006). Articles have appeared in *Cooperation and Conflict, Foreign Policy, International Political Science Review, International Studies Perspectives*, and *Journal of Contingencies and Crisis Management*.

Christopher Jones is a lecturer in International Relations and a member of the '*Threat Politics*' project at the Swedish Institute of International Affairs during 2002-2005.

Michael Karlsson is Associate Professor of Political Science at the Södertörn University College, Stockholm. His interest in transnational relations is reflected in *Transnational Relations in the Baltic Sea Region* (2004) and 'Epistemic Communities and Cooperative Security' (*Journal of International and Area Studies*, 2004).

Regina Karp is Associate Professor and the Director of the Center for Regional and Global Study at Old Dominion University in Virginia. She is a specialist in the topics of arms control, weapons proliferation, and international security. She has published books and articles on the issues of the Strategic Defense Initiative (SDI) and European security and defense procurement of the former Federal Republic of Germany, before becoming involved in the present project.

Olav Fagelund Knudsen is Professor *Emeritus* of Political Science and International Politics, previously at the University of Oslo and Södertörn University College. He has published on small state security and Baltic regional affairs in *Chaillot Papers, Cooperation and Conflict, Journal of Peace Research, International Politics, Security Dialogue* and *the Journal of International Relations and Development*, as well as editing the volume *Security and Stability in the Baltic Sea Region* (Frank Cass 1999). He has served as Research Director and Director of the Norweigian Institute of International Affairs. From 2003 until his retirement in 2006 he was Research Director at the Swedish Institute of International Affairs.

Erik Noreen is Associate Professor of Peace and Conflict Research. He has published studies on foreign and security issues focusing on the Baltic Sea area, *inter alia* in *Journal of Peace Research*. He is currently head of the Department of Peace and Conflict Research at Uppsala University.

Stephen G. Walker is an Emeritus Professor of Political Science at Arizona State University. He has published papers on conflict resolution, foreign policy analysis, and political psychology in *Cooperation and Conflict, Journal of Peace Research, Journal of Conflict Resolution, International Studies Quarterly*, and *Political Psychology.*

Acknowledgements

We gratefully acknowledge the support of the Foundation for Baltic and East European Studies for the research project 'Power Disparity, Identity and Cooperative Security in the Baltic Sea Region' during the years 2002-2006. Södertörn University College has contributed office space and excellent modern facilities for our work. A number of our seminars and meetings have been hosted by the Swedish Institute of International Affairs. We thank both of these institutions for their hospitality.

We also wish to acknowledge the numerous colleagues who have participated in our work in guest roles and helped by their comments or services in other ways. As external reviewers we have been privileged to have Clive Archer, Anders Kjølberg, Andrey Makarychev, Patrick M. Morgan, Jan Trost, Raimo Väyrynen, and Stephen Walker – the latter subsequently joining our team as a co-contributor with his own chapter. Their time and their willingness to offer their reflections are deeply appreciated. Colleagues in Political Science at Södertörn have gone through our various chapters in repeated readings at research seminars. A special supporting role has been played by Jan Softa, our Russian language specialist. Fredrik Doeser, Johnny Rodin, Roxanna Sjöstedt and Kristin Ljungkvist have provided invaluable and cheerful assistance at various stages. Background support by Gunilla Reischl, Jenny Wahren, Åsa Fritzon and Margaretha Dufwa has helped tremendously.

Finally, we wish to thank our loved ones in all generations for their patience with our reckless waste of family time.

On behalf of all,

                      Olav Fagelund Knudsen

Chapter 1

An Overall Perspective on Regional Power Strategies

Olav F. Knudsen

Analytical Aims

This book is motivated by a desire to learn more about unequal power relations between neighbouring countries – *in casu* the Baltic Sea region. In particular we look into how governments deal with the consequences of power disparity and its possible effects on cooperative security and integration. We assume that differences in power can have beneficial effects as well as undesirable ones, and seek to understand how such consequences come about. Power as such is conceived in terms of shared assessments among decision makers of other governments' capacity to act. An especially intriguing aspect of such assessments is whether they are associated with perceptions of threat.[1]

The Baltic Sea region has long been marked by a pronounced difference between what decision-makers have recognized as great powers and small states, differences most clearly visible from the 1930s onwards and reaching a peak during the Cold War years. Subsequently, a great power shift occurred around 1990. We want to know whether threatening power disparity is now a thing of the past in the Baltic Sea region. The experience of a decade of new, relaxed international relations in the region could lead some to conclude that power differentials are of little importance today – or that their threat aspects have disappeared because of Russia's new profile and the integration of its former allies and all of Germany in European and Transatlantic structures.

Our working hypothesis has been that power differentials are still politically significant. We have been especially concerned to understand the nature of the cooperative security relationships which have been promoted by the governments of the region, with Sweden and Finland in the lead, and with the expansion of the EU and NATO as important elements. The relationship between power differentials and threat is ambiguous, in that threats need not be made to be perceived. Is power disparity between Russia and its regional neighbours in itself an obstacle to better relations? The opposite possibility will also be explored: Great powers have

---

1   More on concepts below.

been known to provide resources and opportunities for better relations with their neighbours. Is Russia gradually taking on this kind of role in the Baltic Sea region?

Another factor to which we want to pay attention is the possible change – weakening or strengthening – of state structures relative to integration processes and other transnational phenomena. In this connection, identity aspects of states have particular relevance in the Baltic Sea region, where so many fundamental reorganizations of political units have taken place and are still going on: the experience of the Baltic states in regaining independence and moving on to European integration, the recreation of a federal Russian state, the process and consequences of German reunification.

We want to see the region from a comparative perspective and are conscious that the dimension of time must therefore also be kept in mind. Other eras have seen different power relations in the Baltic Sea region. Historically there have been periods of approximately balanced power in the region, for instance when a stronger Denmark and a stronger Sweden existed alongside an emerging Russian great power and a fragmented Germany. The massive change that took place in 1989-1991 had consequences that must be assessed in a broad historical perspective.

Our broadest questions, then, are the following: Under what conditions may unequal power prevent or encumber the emergence of cooperative security? Can progress towards cooperative security help overcome the threat perceptions often engendered by power disparity? Could strong group identities intervene to determine whether integrative rather than disintegrative effects take place? What is the role of concrete conflicts and specific interests in this connection?

Regional security studies have blossomed during the 1990s and beyond (e.g. Mack and Ravenhill 1994; Lake and Morgan 1997; Adler and Barnett 1999; Knudsen 1999; Buzan and Waever 2003. From older studies (Etzioni 1965; Fox 1977) it is well established that unequal power may have constructive and beneficial effects by providing leadership and resources, and because great power often attracts (Nye 2004), thus giving regional integration an extra boost. However, those studies have not fully examined the simultaneous potentially negative effects, and some of the empirical cases they drew upon (e.g., early European integration, Caribbean integration projects of the 1960s, US-Canadian relations) were inconclusive. Our working hypothesis has been that cooperative security is hampered by power disparity in itself, as well as by concrete conflicts of specific interests, but power disparity is the more serious obstacle.

This working hypothesis is pursued along several avenues of research by individual chapter authors. The project as a whole has left room for both constructivist perspectives, realist perspectives and more eclectic perspectives. In our work we have still held to a common core of concepts, which will be further specified in the following.

Concepts and Assumptions

Here our central concepts are defined and further clarified by supplementary explications.

Actors and agents

Leaders of large organized groups – here mostly states – are conceived as key actors. The individuals are agents, in the sense of principal/agent reasoning – the organized group is their principal. Other actors are sub-national territorial units, others yet again are non-territorial units. In the region, direct societal contact between individuals of the different groups is ongoing routinely across a wide range of activities. At the same time, actors maintain contact at leadership levels, in 'collective mode', and in so doing are agents acting on behalf of their collectivity.

Relationships

Regional politics can be exceedingly diverse. According to a simplified representation, we conceive governments as pursuing their relations alternately in two modes: a) anarchical – without universally reliable, orderly procedures for resolving differences; b) cooperative – according to established traditions and agreements, with conflict resolution undertaken by joint agreement. It is worth noting that as seen here the same actor may deal with some interlocutors in the cooperative mode and with others in the anarchical mode.

In the anarchical mode, actors resort to a wide range of improvised methods to have their way and promote their interests. Some of those methods involve the threat or use of military means or other forms of organized mass violence, other methods are more sophisticated, but all are geared to assuring and asserting the collectivity's will in the face of uncertainties seen to have been brought on by conflict with other collectivities.

In the cooperative mode, actors' conceptions of self-interest are pursued within the frameworks and constraints of intergovernmental institutions. In the resultant combinations of cooperation and confrontation, the more long-term strategies for cooperation are of particular interest here.

Power

The concept of power is here defined in terms of actors' understandings[2] of the presumed relative capacity of group leaders (one's own as well as others') to affect

---

2 Understanding involves elements of cognition, evaluation against endogenized value standards, and analysis based on experience as well as situational anticipation. These understandings of actors are the foundation for the emergence of power relationships when actors meet and deal with each other.

the political landscape within which all actors function. Actors' interpretations in this regard are taken to be approximate and 'fuzzy', seldom explicitly stated or shared between colleagues. Such assessments contribute to the shaping of each actor's behaviour and her strategies regarding future action. The role of power is thus causal, indirect and subjective, and socially based. It may or may not be associated with perceptions of threat.

It is also contingent on context, which renders it in a certain sense 'multidimensional'. The distribution of (perceived) power relations for a given actor over different contexts is in some cases rather similar (all strong, or all weak), in which a cumulative effect reinforces an overall image of a 'strong' or a 'weak' state. In the case of other actors, power varies from context to context.

It follows from the above that power should be seen as a social relationship dependent on mutual readings of past relations, present capabilities and future intentions. By taking this analytical stance, we approach the related idea that power may be conceived as socially constructed, flowing from sources that are part subjective, part intersubjective or objective. We emphasize power relations that are played out in situations where actors have to cope – in contexts of confrontation as well as cooperation.

Power relations are here hypothesized to be linked to conceptions of *identity*.[3] Following Wendt[4] but taking a slightly different course, we suggest that between actors who see each other as roughly equal in power, identity often becomes linked to rivalry and competition. When power relations are seen to be distinctly unequal, we suggest that a different kind of stereotyping of self and other begins about which Wendt is relatively silent. The experience of facing an apparently overwhelming power has, for instance, in many cases led to the use of simplifying identifications like 'great power' (or just 'stronger') for the other and 'small state' (or just 'weaker') for the self.

---

3   Leaning on Wendt, we conceive identity as '... rooted in an actor's self-understandings' which can be of at least four different kinds: '(1) personal or corporate, (2) type, (3) role, and (4) collective' (Wendt 1999: 224). The first has a material base and is only applicable to persons or corporate entities – being unique for each actor. A state has a corporate identity in Wendt's conception. The second – type identity – is based on shared social characteristics thought to somehow typify particular groups of people: for example teenagers, speakers of particular languages, heterosexuals (Wendt 1999: 225). The third identity category – role identity – is based on shared expectations linked to a position in a social structure. To be recognized as a state is in Wendt's view a role identity because of the shared norms of sovereignty (Wendt 1999: 228). Finally, the fourth kind of identity – collective identity – involves the process of identification, Self's identification with the (generalized) Other. 'Collective identity, in short, is a distinct combination of role and type identities, one with the causal power to induce actors to define the welfare of the Other as part of that of the Self, to be "altruistic".' (229) See also pp 96ff, 106-07.

4   See his discussion pp 246 ff which emphasizes the role identities of enemy, rival and friend. See also pp 327, 331. I am grateful to Stephen Walker for helpful comments on roles and identities.

Cooperative security

The term 'cooperative security' refers to policies of governments or organized groups to handle conflict by the conscious use of confidence-building or 'confidence-preserving' measures. Cooperative security policies thus (a) reflect the attitudes of former or potential adversaries to the present and future relationship between them, policies which (b) they seek to shift from a more to a less conflictual mode (Knudsen 2003). By proposing confidence-building measures – i.e., moves which would expose the initiator to potential exploitation (even danger) on the part of the adversary – the initiator demonstrates a willingness to put a corresponding measure of trust in the other side. Cooperative security policies seek to develop such first steps into a self-sustaining, longer-range process.[5] Hence, cooperative security is different from the long-term strategy that Rapoport first called tit-for-tat (Axelrod 1984, viii), in that tit-for-tat involves immediate retaliation when the other side does not cooperate. Cooperative security avoids retaliatory moves.

Progress in the long-term may lead to the emergence of a security community (Deutsch et al 1957; Adler and Barnett 1998). In the interim, while trust is not entirely certain, cooperative security moves will have enabled governments to cooperate in their own interest and even in the joint interest of all involved. Presumably the experience of joint satisfaction in such ventures will increase the likelihood of the emergence of a full-fledged security community. At the same time, the long-term progress from initial cooperative security moves (here also called phase 1) via cooperation (phase 2) to a security community (phase 3) cannot be taken for granted.[6]

The Baltic Sea region

This term refers to a cluster of geographically proximate countries in Northern Europe bordering on the Baltic Sea. At the same time that specific area is here conceived as an instance of a more general phenomenon: regions of interacting state-societies. As such the region comprises – *inter alia* – a range of unequal power relations. The political and economic viability of the younger state units in the Baltic Sea region has recently been confirmed by their membership in the European Union. A lingering perception of existential uncertainty nevertheless remains. It involves the identity aspect in the collective mode: Individuals conceive of themselves as part not just of a social system, but of a social body, coexisting with other bodies of the same collective kind. Such relationships involve actors – i.e., individuals acting in formal

---

5   The concept of cooperative security is here an idealized and simplified description of policies, some of which were only proposed while others were actually tried out in various phases of the Cold War and its aftermath. Nordic governments have typically preferred such policies. See also Knudsen 2003; Knudsen and Jones Ch 3 in this volume.

6   I am here combining the reasoning of Deutsch et al (1957) with my own. Adler and Barnett (1998) follow a parallel line of reasoning couched in constructivist terms.

roles on behalf of collectivities, the latter often being governments of state units, but at times also international organizations, lobbying groups or private business firms (see Walker 1987; on identities also Neumann 1992; 1996).

Security

This concept is used here in a manner traceable to Haftendorn (1991), who gave what she called '… a very elementary, "generic" definition of "security" as *value and/or system maintenance over time*, and the absence of threats to it.' (1991, 5; emphasis added, see also Wolfers 1962). Haftendorn emphasized international over national security, yet remained otherwise a 'traditionalist' in the eyes of subsequent constructivist theorists like Buzan et al (1998). Inspired by Haftendorn, Knudsen later offered a somewhat more concrete specification to the effect that 'Security … has to do with how one deals with conflict so as to limit the harm it brings to the physical and social well-being of individuals and the political and economic well-being of societies.' (Knudsen 1999, vii) Thus were listed the policies, the subject matter and the referent groups of security. In the present volume, security complex theory (Buzan 1991; Buzan et al 1998) is seen as potentially relevant, along with security community theory previously referred to.

Power disparity

Unequal power relations and uncertain viability bear on the security of the units. Power plays are moves by actors to assert themselves vis-a-vis and at the expense of other actors. The power context – the issue at hand – determines the salience of a particular power disparity. The maintenance of cooperative relations in the region is an assumed goal. If actors seriously aspire to it, they need to cope with conflict so as to keep power plays within limits (Knudsen 1999).

At present there is little established knowledge on the experience of combining power disparity and integration. Preliminary examination of cases of great powers like the USA, Russia and China and their respective neighbours suggests that more research is needed concerning the conditions under which cooperation and integration are advanced rather than hampered by power disparity.

Power relations undergo continual change over time. Economic and technological dynamics may leave contextual power less clear-cut than conventional notions might suggest. Current processes of change especially relevant to these particular regional power relations are:

a. the integration, expansion and development of the EU;
b. the integration and development of Russia;
c. the development of regional cooperative practices / institutions and the role of smaller or weaker units in them;
d. the relationships between sub-regions and supra-regions;
e. the role of extra-regional states/units.

Structure of the Volume

Chapter 2 further explores the concepts of power and power disparity, while Chapter 3 by Olav F. Knudsen and Christopher Jones surveys the policies pursued by the countries involved in the period covered. Against this general background, each of the book's remaining chapters examines the region from a different angle and asks how its actors coped with the new situation facing them after 1991. The contributors look at how governments defined their new circumstances, and thus how they dealt with the opportunity to shift to a new mode of coexistence and collaboration. A key underlying question is how they tackled the challenge of peacefully converting their region to a security community. To the extent they have realized the ideal of a security community, have the actors arrived at new understandings of power and identity in the process? To the extent they have fallen short of that goal, what went wrong and what can be learned from the experience?

The book is not organized according to a traditional country-by-country lay-out. Instead, regional problems and functions are at the center of attention. Disparities of power are pursued and illustrated in various contexts.

Chapter 4 by Regina Karp compares policymaking in Finland and Sweden from the perspective that regional policymaking has come under increasing pressure by global change. After 10 years of membership in the EU and extensive relations with NATO, why have Sweden and Finland stayed militarily non-aligned? The chapter argues that these two Nordics have not remained inert; they have rather – each in their own way – adapted significantly to structural changes in their security environment. In doing so they have reinterpreted their power position and launched new 'authoritative' readings of their basic policy orientations. Yet these national adaptations have had to be tempered by the enduring strength of national identity. The outcome is a strategy of balancing between remaining Swedish and Finnish, and institutionalizing national security as international.

Chapter 5 by Michael Karlsson offers a case study of a process of cooperative security at its inception. It considers the joint regional decision-making on the question of dismantling the former Soviet Nuclear Submarine Training Center at Paldiski in Estonia. In this process a transnational expert group on nuclear safety – conceptualized as an epistemic community – eventually managed to break a Russian wall of secrecy, leading to an agreement to dismantle. The study found that Russia's control of information and territory set initial limits for the expert group, but the power disparity was not sufficient to stop the experts from eventually breaking the secrecy surrounding the Paldiski site. The chapter concludes that power disparity represents an open structure setting certain limits for the functioning of epistemic communities, but this structure is at the same time also developed by their activities.

Chapter 6 by Erik Noreen further illustrates cooperative security at work and the effects of power disparity. Noreen examines how processes of regional change also register – and work through – the way regional actors express their thinking. He analyses the threat images of Estonian and Russian political elites and finds that in the views expressed by Estonian decision makers, Russia is – unexpectedly – nearly absent as a threat. Likewise, NATO is rarely brought up by the Russian policy makers as a threat. Instead, in both countries, issues like international terrorism, organized crime and drug trafficking are framed as severe threats. Thus, there are striking similarities in how the language of threat has developed in Russia and Estonia. This change of security discourses might indicate that policy-makers in Moscow and Tallinn seek to develop a common understanding of not only what is threatening, but also of what is threatened in terms of values and identities. The study therefore argues that it might become possible to develop cooperative security towards a security community even between such unequal cases as Russia and Estonia in the Baltic sea area.

Chapter 7 examines the role of alternative dimensions of power by contextually confining the analysis to the issue area of *information technology (IT)*. Johan Eriksson explores power and security in the digital age, comparing the policies of Estonia, Russia, Sweden and the US. The author argues that complete information dominance is not only unlikely but also counterproductive – soft power (Nye 2004; 1989) depends on the opponent's continued ability to communicate. Access to cyberspace potentially provides actors with a global reach, and thereby broadens the domain of both foes and friends beyond the region. Against the background of the four countries' policy profiles, the chapter argues that the scope of digital power depends on whether a government perceives IT as a means of online attack on critical infrastructures, as a booster of offline-technologies, as a means of soft power, or as any combination of these.

Chapter 8 draws on the preceding diverse analyses. Stephen Walker uses contrasting theories of power, interests, and identities to offer rival explanations for when states pursue cooperative strategies of appeasement and bandwagoning, or coercive strategies of competition and balancing. These strategies are associated with the equilibrium outcomes of settlement, submission, domination, and deadlock. Sequential game theory models in this chapter synthesize and specify generalizable distributions of power, interests, and identities to predict dyadic security strategies and equilibria. These models are then compared to selected dyads in the Baltic region to see if the antecedent conditions, strategies, and equilibria specified in the models fit the antecedent conditions, strategies and equilibria reported in the cases of other chapters.

The closing chapter reexamines the working hypothesis in the light of the patterns observed and looks for lessons learned.

Chapter 2

Power Disparities and the Avoidance of Confrontation

Olav F. Knudsen

Introduction

This chapter[1] seeks to provide a foundation for the use of the power disparity concept in the present volume. While the message is ultimately empirical – a claim that power at work is as much a matter of confrontations avoided and unobserved as of confrontations won and observed – the thrust of the chapter is on how to conceptualize this feature of power as seen 'from below'. A central point in the analysis is that confrontations avoided are mostly to be classified as unobservables – they cannot be seen.

I shall here first discuss the power concept in order to identify those versions that may be said to be leading in the study of International Relations. Next I examine some of their antecedents in order to better understand how the problem of unobservables in power relations has been dealt with over time. Power disparity being a key notion in this volume, it has its own section next, with subsections on identity and the time dimension. From here I go into a discussion of avoidance behaviour in two typically different classes of cases: those of large power disparities, and those of small.

The Power Concept

Power analysis is well known as a conceptual jungle. To make headway in this *maquis* I have found it necessary to transcend particular definitions and take a broader view. Thus, instead of working from a strict definition of power, I start from a primitive notion and explore a number of alternative specifications.[2]

The primitive notion at my departure – one of the broadest conceptions of power in sociology and political science – is that of the ability to confront someone else and

---

1 I gratefully acknowledge comments on earlier drafts from David Baldwin, Linus Hagström, Joel W Simmons and other colleagues at a 2005 ISA panel, from colleagues in research seminars at the SIIA and Södertörn and from partners within our project.

2 Which is to say that for the sake of discussion, I do not start out with the definition offered in Ch. 1.

win, to sway others, to overcome resistance.[3] It is worth noting that this perspective allows a wide range of specifications and many different empirical applications.

The criterion of overcoming resistance has both a conceptual and an empirical foundation. Conceptually, Weber included this criterion in his definition of power about a century ago.[4] It reflects a conviction that power should be seen as an active contest of wills – undertaken in a social setting – in which one side prevails. Since Weber's time, writers on the subject have tended to shift their attention away from the resistance aspect. Some writers in the field of IR – such as James Rosenau – have discarded the notion of power entirely;[5] others, like John Mearsheimer, point out its elusive and subjective nature as a reason for looking merely at capabilities (Mearsheimer 2001). Many more have concentrated instead on conflicting preferences. The range of views based on conflicting preferences is now the predominant one. Dahl and Lukes illustrate the span: while Dahl assumes preferences are maintained in confrontation and then watches what happens next, Lukes asks why they are so often abandoned or never even consciously entertained by the weaker side (Dahl 1957, 201-215; 1961; also Lukes 1974, 22-23; 2005).[6]

Empirical studies of power are required, but all encounter serious obstacles. Two alternative empirical applications of power are common in the study of International Relations. A simple method, also the least reliable, is that of equating power and capabilities.[7] The other is to look for winners and losers in actual confrontations. Though not often thought of in such terms, I argue that both of these empirical applications rest on an assumption of conflicting preferences. The implicit idea of using capabilities is that in case of future conflict, assessed capabilities will influence action. The method has uncertain foundations; it could rely on a deduction from a logic of 'accumulated booty' ('one must have been powerful to have gained all those resources'); yet, it could also rely on the postulated effectiveness of the capabilities in hypothetical confrontations ('the greater your resources, the more likely you are to win in case of conflict.')[8]

The alternative to relying on capabilities, to focus on the actual occurrence of confrontations, or on the analysis of scenarios of confrontations, within their

---

3   Going back to Weber (Gerth and Mills 1948), and subsequently Dahl 1957, 1961. See even Lukes 1974, 22-23, second revised edition 2005.

4   'In general, we understand by "power" the chance of a man or of a number of men to realize their own will in a communal action even against the resistance of others, who are participating in the action' (Gerth and Mills 1998, 180). This was one of several definitions Weber offered, though arguably the most precise one. See also Bendix 1959.

5   James N. Rosenau, personal communication, February 2005.

6   Though Lukes is now deemphasizing conflict.

7   Often without any reference to Weber. For a thorough analysis see Knorr 1970.

8   This convenient hypothesis has survived many waves of attack. Both Waltz and Mearsheimer argue that the capabilities solution is superior to any other (Waltz 1979; Mearsheimer 2001).

specific contexts – is the relational approach.⁹ In Baldwin's recent discussion, the two approaches appear as rivals (Baldwin 2002). However, in my view, these two rival perspectives are not really rivals; on certain conditions, they are both tenable and compatible.

If power is conceptualized as flowing from the actors' own assessments, the appearance of power becomes the guide to understanding action in the relational approach – action flows from interpreted appearance. At the same time, the appearance interpreted is the image of capabilities. Capabilities become images of apparent power, not merely signs for political scientists to read, but also signals between potential opponents. This linkage transcends the often deeply drawn distinction between the 'capabilities school' and the 'relational school' in IR power analysis.

In the following, I proceed with a discussion of conceptual and theoretical antecedents, before examining more closely the role of confrontations avoided in international power relations. Power disparity is the starting point. One part of the discussion will deal with power under conditions of marked inequality, power disparity, more specifically the strategies of small states in handling confrontations with a superior power. A second part will deal with power disparity under conditions approaching equality (or balance) – great power relations and the confrontations involved in the balancing of power.

Antecedents and Unobservables

Unobservable aspects of power were dealt with early on both by Friedrich and by Lasswell and Kaplan (Friedrich 1937, 16-17; Lasswell and Kaplan 1950, 56). However, the discussion of these aspects came into its own with the non-decision-making debate in the 1960s, triggered by the work of Robert Dahl. Dahl insisted on a relational type of concept. Power was not a possession, it was a relationship tied to a political context. It could change with the context, and was closely linked to decision-making. The ensuing debate, spearheaded by the critique of Bachrach and Baratz, later followed by Lukes (Bachrach and Baratz 1962, 947-952; 1963, 632-642),¹⁰ turned on the problem of non-observable aspects at the receiving end of power relationships – what occasionally appears as non-behavior (inactivity, passivity),

---

9   It is worth noting that the capabilities approach opens up for the analysis of avoidance behavior – you calculate your options after assessing the other's potential strength in a putative confrontation. When actual confrontations are studied, obviously, much if not most of the avoidance behavior is defined out of the analysis.

10 Lukes (op.cit. 1974) also objected to the focus on struggle and resistance, a view he reinforces in his last chapter of the 2nd edition.

sometimes as behavior that is evasive, conformist or 'non-deviant'.[11] Subsequently these non-visible aspects have not been much in focus in the literature.[12]

Broadly speaking, such cases of invisible responses to power reflect a whole spectrum of different underlying phenomena – some exemplify the acknowledgement or accommodation of power, others illustrate the effects of authority more than power, and yet other cases boil down to pure consent. Since my interest is in power, which I prefer to distinguish from other, related phenomena, this requires an initial sorting of concepts, in particular authority and power.[13] The criterion of legitimacy offers a useful borderline, a test of what is authority – when compliance is seen to be right, experienced as being just, even if inconvenient, costly or painful. Moreover, I would argue that unthinking obedience, honest agreement, habitual conformity, and deference to tradition, origin or law, are best seen as aspects of authority.[14]

The problem of observability is relevant to some crucial dimensions of power, one of them intentionality, but above all causality. If we begin with Russell – 'power is the production of intended effects' (Russell 1938, 35) – as the broadest statement that includes both of these aspects, his umbrella covers not just the relational school of Dahl, Emerson, Baldwin and others (even Lukes – except on intentionality), but also structural perspectives (Dahl 1957; 1961; Emerson 1962, 31-41; Baldwin 1969, 425-47; 1971, 19-38; also 2002). Yet, Russell is somewhat elliptical. The others are more explicit about what produces the intended effects, and how. Intentionality is usually observable. Actors express their aims and intentions, or demonstrate them through their actions. The cases where intentionality becomes problematic in the present context is limited to two cases: 1) in so far as intentions are not shown, but are guessed or inferred by the target who proceeds to fulfill the anticipated wishes (Friedrich 1937) (which amounts to a power relation only if the target has other preferences); 2) the case of power structures. Both illustrate the avoidance of confrontation. Emerson, like Lukes after him, highlights the weaker side, linking power to dependence, defined as aspiring to goals one cannot achieve without the

---

[11] Voter apathy and related phenomena such as political fatigue, hostility to government, and other apolitical trends are mass phenomena in politics that are outside my focus, which is, rather, trained on actors who are self-consciously acting out political roles and who under certain circumstances simply choose to follow a line of non-confrontation, evasion, lying-low.

[12] A major exception is Scott 1990. The second edition of Lukes (2005) is also strongly focused on such aspects in its new chapters.

[13] Lukes usefully provides a graphic illustration of how these concepts may be sorted, 1974, 32; 2005, 36. While he retains a considerable overlap between authority and power, I find it more useful to keep these concepts distinct.

[14] Krieger 1968, 141-162, especially in reference to '... the crucial problem of establishing a basis for government beyond the specific punishments its organs could impose, and the specific benefits it could deliver.' (146) This is compliance without specific incentives. Though Roman practice is referred to, the limited utility of sanctions is a timeless fact, witness the analysis of Baldwin 1971, 19-38. For an alternative view placing compliance without incentives under the heading of structural power, see, e.g., Haugaard 2000.

intervention of others. Emerson thus points the way out of dependence: Avoid confrontation by reducing your 'emotional investment' in goals mediated by others, or shift to other goals that are not so much tied to others. Lukes, pursuing his differences with Dahl, shows how structural tendencies can follow from persistent power differentials.[15]

I regard the notion of power structures as a useful device in certain kinds of power analysis. As I see it, intentionality is also compatible with structuration, if power structures are defined as social structures that render certain groups more favoured in the eyes of others, and whose individual favoured members therefore exert themselves, whenever challenged, to maintain and reproduce their advantages over time. In the present context – the avoidance of confrontation – a power structure might also be described as a set of recurrent patterns of apparent acceptance of apparent power positions.

Causality is the larger problem in analyzing the avoidance of confrontations. The causal element has a strong tradition in analyses of power, boldly reasserted as recently as 2002 by Baldwin (2002). It takes as its point of departure assumed cases of successful influence relations and seeks to explain the sources of advantage involved in them, their range and scope, and so on. Even other concepts of power – including that of Lukes (1974, 27, 31)[16] – build on putative cases of power exercised, evidenced by some chain of events or pattern of behavior. The concept of power (or influence) then is the name given to the explanation or the account given for the phenomenon in question. It describes one event as being brought about by another. In this sense, as often noted, power is about causality.[17] Observable phenomena therefore easily come to play a prominent role in this kind of power analysis.[18]

In short, repeatedly we find ourselves facing the problem of observability. Not only are many ways of exercising power invisible, even some of the most characteristic responses to the exercise of power are not easily observable. Thus – provided we put aside as irrelevant the effects of socialization or brainwashing and the actual use of force – most forms of political power hinge crucially on acts of non-opposition, submission or acceptance at the receiving end, all of them acts

---

15 On power structures see Lasswell and Kaplan 1950, 200-239, esp. 205; also Guzzini 1993, 443-478; Haugaard, 2000; Lukes 1974, 22. Note that in his 2nd ed. Lukes rejects the attribution of power '... to structures or relations or processes that cannot be characterized as agents.' (2005, 72).

16 In his 2nd ed Lukes – while repeating the analysis of the first edition – later adds the comment that such a view of power, while in and of itself valid, is too narrow; 2005, 60-61. See also Singer 1963, 420- 430.

17 Nagel's approach is based entirely upon causal analysis as the way to study power (Nagel 1975).

18 While Dahl is usually closely associated with this type of analysis, there is no necessary fixation on observability in Dahl's conceptualization, as one can see from Dahl's later presentations of his ideas. See (e.g.) Dahl 1991, 25-41. I am grateful to David Baldwin for his reminder on this point.

that are sometimes invisible or difficult to discern. Indeed, acceptance, subjection or submission are acts that do not usually advertise themselves, but are nevertheless essential ingredients that give the idea of power meaning – as long as they are not seen to be right, or just.

Proceeding now from antecedents to empirical specification, the cases to be examined more closely in the following are instances of 'tactically conscious compliance' (labeled patterns 1 and 2 in the introduction); that is, a pattern of deferring[19] to specific perceived demands without ceding autonomy.

Power Disparity

The notion of differentials of power has a central place here. Power analysis often takes as its point of departure cases when the relationship is far from equal; indeed, marked power disparity may be more the norm than the exception. In Robert Dahl's well-worn definition of influence,[20] a relationship of disparity is lurking underneath the surface. The gist of the definition is that influence is present to the extent A prevails over B, hence there is also some degree of disparity present. Power analysis à la Dahl is about what made B give in. The sanctions are his standard, posited answer. Dahl's initial story is that by skilful use of available sanctions, A has 'made' B do what A wants.

Dahl may be right that power depends to a considerable extent on A's available sanctions, but it should not lead our attention away from B's reasoning. B is in many ways the key to the relationship, as much as or even more than A. Indeed, the more independent B appears to be from the outset, the more intriguing is the question of why his behaviour in a particular context conforms to A's wishes. Dahl, however, does not go into this; his purpose is different. He is analysing confrontations. Yet, the more common practical effect of power disparity is for the weaker side to avoid confrontations if at all possible. Actors are rarely new to confrontations; in most cases they have experienced them before.

It is argued here that instead of selecting confrontations for closer study, one should more usefully conceive of power relations in terms of series of contemplated confrontations. What actually happens as a potential confrontation becomes actual depends partly on how available alternatives for action (resistance/avoidance

---

19 Lasswell and Kaplan actually define power in terms of deference. 'Deference values are those that consist in being taken into consideration (in the acts of others and of the self). Most important of the deference values, for political science, is *power*.' (56-57) While the authors emphasize (56-73, 77ff) the aspect of deference in relation to power, in a footnote they make it clear that 'It is not necessary, however, that those over whom power is had consciously defer to the power holders; indeed, they may not be aware of who the power holders are.' (77n) This comes close to the view later argued by Mills (1956) and antecedes Lukes by more than two decades.

20 'A has influence over B to the extent A can make B do something he would not otherwise have done' (Dahl 1957).

options) are assessed at the moment, partly on how actors view themselves and others (identities). Resistance/avoidance options may be illustrated by the Ethiopian proverb 'When the great lord passes the wise peasant bows deeply and silently farts.'[21]

Possibilities may be ranged on a scale like the following:

1. Complete compliance in thought as well as action
2. Compliance demonstrated by required physical action (e.g. payment of tribute), mental reservation, no visible counteraction
3. Compliance demonstrated by symbolic action only (e.g., bows his head, flies the flag); mental reservation
4. Compliance demonstrated by inaction, complete passiveness; mental reservation
5. Deception: compliance by overt obedience undermined by secret counteraction
6. Symbolic protest: compliance demonstrated by incomplete fulfillment (foot dragging, deliberate mistakes)
7. Opposition; active resistance

Figure 2.1 Range of Resistance/Avoidance Behaviors

Behavior patterns are not necessarily chosen deliberately; they will vary with context and may be mediated by whatever combination of context and identity happens to be operative.[22]

On Identities

This subsection argues that identities carry with them notions of implied power and that some identities common in international affairs express assumed power positions. In other words, power relations are often (not always) played out through conceptions of collective role identity. The role conception of identity is a generalized idea of collective self in given contexts. Some identity conceptions common in international affairs express postulated power positions ('great power', 'small state'). An important question is whether such identities are adopted and internalized by political leaders. If so, are they confined to role conceptions for specific contexts or do they become more comprehensive identities covering all policy contexts? Moreover, to what extent are they shared across political dividing lines in any particular country?

Governments acting on behalf of states do not suddenly find themselves in that position; they consist of individuals who have been gradually socialized into their positions; they have had predecessors and have been working with colleagues of an older generation who pass on their values and role conceptions. Hence most

---

21 Quoted by Scott on the frontispiece of his book (1990).

22 A contemporary example of symbolic protest: Sovereignty groups in Hawaii are flying the state flag upside down (observed in numerous locations at Big Island, notably at a public institution like Hilo airport, February 2005).

governments have a shared conception of the collective self which even extends to power terms: the roles of small states and great powers are only the best known.

Power relations are thus linked to conceptions of identity. Yet, these are complex identities, and, in international relations, strongly context-bound. This bias towards contextuality comes from the intercultural nature of international affairs, which reduces the effects of social constructions.

What in one understanding would be 'inherited' is on the constructivist view continually being reconstructed. Herrmann refers to '... the conventional wisdom that [collective identities] are social constructions.' (Herrmann 2001, 131). However, constructions may be deep, or they may be shallow. Mercer shows convincingly that any group, regardless of socialization or pre-existing ties, unites when encountering an outside group and shows a common front (Mercer 1995). Such shallow identities, if that is the appropriate term, go beyond any cultural boundary. They are contextual in an immediate sense and support only an interpretation congruent with role identities narrowly constructed.[23]

When a particular collective identity is *assumed*, it becomes the enactment of a role. It 'works' to the extent it is taken seriously by other elites representing other collectivities – in some cases only then. As an obvious illustration, '... the fact that the sovereignty of the modern state is recognized by other states means that it is now also a *role* identity with substantial rights and behavioral norms' (Wendt 1999, 228.)

Among role identities commonly encountered in international affairs are – as already mentioned – those of 'great power' and 'small state'. Another example is that of the 'neutral state' or the 'non-aligned state', exemplified in Europe by Switzerland and Sweden, respectively. The 'small ally' is another one. All of these entail some kind of consequence for their government's comportment in international conflict; they indicate a preconceived position in a relationship of power disparity.

When a government conceives of itself as a small state in a conflict situation with a more powerful interlocutor, it assumes a particular role and a specific pattern of action.[24] It is then likely to choose the path of tactically conscious evasion, a semblance of compliance. In the conceptualization adopted here, few governments, however, would assume for themselves a constant identity of a small state.[25] This would only occur occasionally, when the shadow of vastly disparate power falls over its relations. The predominant pattern would presumably be to reserve for themselves as much autonomy as possible, and to single out certain areas of activity where they have some particular advantage, which they would then emphasize in their international dealings. Yet, when 'power role' conceptions are triggered the

---

23 Much of the writing on identities in international relations describes them as properties of collectivities that generate 'we-feeling' (Adler 2001, 104). In Wendt's words, 'The state is a "group Self" capable of group-level cognition' (Wendt 1999, 225).

24 In a discussion of 'The Prestige and Power of the Great Powers', Weber emphasizes self-assumed (subjective) role conceptions of power as typical of great powers of his day (pre-1914), as well as of the small states and the neutrals. Gerth and Mills 1948/1998, 159-161.

25 Indeed, as we shall see in Ch. 9, they probably very rarely do so.

ideas of great power or small state status will come into play and corresponding behaviors be taken.

On Time and Structuration

The time dimension is an indispensable element in understanding power disparities. Deference endures. Cases of compliance behavior must be viewed over time, as sequential moves in long-term power relationships. We cannot look merely at isolated episodes of confrontation. Social memories link the encounters where the relationships arise, are recreated, redefined, or reproduced, as the case may be. Obviously, power as deference should be conceived as the result of potential struggles as much as of actual struggles. We must not exclude episodes that never became actual struggles because one side shied away.

The factor of time therefore plays a central role in power relationships. It works differently, however, in cases of near equality and cases of distinct power disparity. When power is nearly equal, new encounters may offer opportunities for redefinition. When power is manifestly unequal, new encounters tend mostly to reproduce previous experience, thus producing or cementing structure. Intermediate cases may be less clear-cut.

Consider the case of what appear to be drastic power differentials. Initially, a few encounters may stimulate resistance. Ultimately, however, repeated encounters of overtly unequal assessed power are likely to set off tendencies towards the structural. If actors see each other as too different or unequal to be potential rivals, then tendencies for structuration will come to predominate. Lukes states very succinctly that '... evidence relating to the Indian caste system can ... be adduced which supports the claim that the internalization of subordinate status is a consequence of power.'[26] On the other hand, Scott emphasizes the likelihood that even in strongly repressive structures like slavery, resistance will always be present under the surface, though its 'script' is usually hidden – partially hidden even to the participants themselves.[27]

In contrast, smaller power differentials presumably produce temporizing patterns. Many encounters where one side yields involve only the yielder's implicit concessions of temporary advantage vis-à-vis the other, not her relinquishing the ambition to somehow later prevail. Such cases of ostensibly effective power relationships easily come to make the winner appear more effective than he really is, because the relationships are observed merely in brief glimpses of confrontations, not during the longer intervening periods when confrontations are tactically avoided or 'postponed'. While the yielder in such cases is obviously the weaker party, her

---

26 Lukes 1974, 49; 2005, 52. It has been suggested to me by Joel W. Simmons that structuration is at odds with a subjective notion of power. Ultimately, it seems to me that this is an empirical question. On this point Lukes in his 2nd ed is ambiguous since after repeating what he says in the first edition, he later adds his rejection of the ascription of power to structures, 2005, 72.

27 This is the dominant theme of the book, Scott 1990.

strength is easily underestimated. Examples may be seen in relations between the five permanent members of the UN Security Council. Actors who do not see themselves as equal to others in the political arena tend to keep a low profile and refrain from advancing their views – and if they have political ambitions will simply bide their time, in order to return stronger in the future. This kind of attitude is deeply engrained (e.g.) in Swedish culture.

There is obviously a major empirical problem here, that of documenting what does not occur. Lukes has shown that even in strongly structured cases the problem can be overcome.[28] Keep in mind that Lukes does not do away with the requirement of B's preference to be different from A's. Lukes shows that in the Indian case Untouchables, when given options, decide to go for change, and concludes generally that 'One can take steps to find out what people would have done otherwise.'[29] Hence, though much harder to substantiate than visible conflict, I take the position that many confrontations avoided should still be possible to trace.[30]

If what I have said so far is tenable, I am very close to drawing the conclusion that power, in this subjective sense of self-definition and self-assessment compared to others, has a possessive aspect. I am not here referring to power as a possession in the manner of something the powerful can seize or take into his control, but as being something the weaker party gives away – especially in the shape of confrontations evaded. When control is seized, it is a matter of force, or violence. As a possession, political power – as distinct from coercive power – can only be given by the one who submits, not taken by the other.

The patterns of evasive responses to power identified above will now be discussed in relation to two common phenomena in international politics – one being cases of marked power disparity, here, the conduct of small states in the face of conflict; the other being cases of near power balance, the moves of great powers in relation to their perceived rivals under conditions of near-equality.

Power Disparity and International Relations

In the following I shall go more concretely into illustrations of these kinds of behavioural patterns in small states and great powers.

---

28 Lukes retains this optimistic view of the methodological possibilities in his 2nd edition, 2005, 64.

29 Lukes 1974, 50, cf also 41. Scott emphasizes the natural secrecy of much of what goes on with relevance to power relations. His evidence is largely from Southeast Asia, but probably has much broader validity.

30 Publicly diverging positions may be traced over time to see whether confrontations occur and what becomes the ultimate outcome.

Power Disparity and Small States

Let us look more closely at established empirical generalizations about small states. Remember that 'small state' is here taken to be a role conception, not an objective phenomenon. The classical foreign policy orientation of a small state has long been that of nonalignment in peacetime and neutrality in times of war. It was developed during the classical periods of great power supremacy, the 18th and 19th centuries, when it was not necessarily assumed that a smaller state would abstain from war. The rationale of neutrality, of course, is to avoid confrontations, to make every effort to keep a distance from close involvement with a superior power that would allow the latter to put its superiority into play. Over the centuries, therefore, nonalignment or neutrality has developed a highly formalised and institutionalised way of coping with power disparity.

However, small states have not just one way of coping, nor are they necessarily resigned to submission. Using Figure 2.1 as a template their strategic choices may schematically be outlined thus:

---

1. & 2. Complete compliance / Demonstrative overt compliance:
    Bandwagoning for profit ('Pilot fish')

3. Symbolic compliance: Accommodation
    Bandwagoning for survival

4. Inaction, complete passiveness
    Avoidance
    a. isolation
    b. nonalignment / neutrality: non-preference among others; (balanced closure)
    c. balanced openness ('Maastricht neutrality')

5. [Deception]

6. Symbolic protest: Voice opportunity

7. Opposition, resistance
    Assertion
    a. seeking impregnability: fortify, arm
    b. alliance: external security guarantee
    c. guerrilla war

Figure 2.2 Small State Strategies

Beginning at the bottom, with the theoretical ideal for a country seeking to protect its independence, the last category is a strategy of assertion and resistance (category 7), such as seeking impregnability by internal armaments, or ultimately by guerrilla warfare. A much-preferred alternative has been for small states to seek security guarantees in alliance with a great power, usually one that has no apparent motive to dominate the internal affairs of its smaller partner. NATO has been the main example in our time.[31]

A notch down from active resistance is symbolic opposition. In the face of inevitable loss in settings marked by potential gain, 'voice opportunities' is a strategy well described and analyzed by Grieco, drawing on Hirschman (Grieco 1996, 261-306, Hirschman 1970).[32] In settings where their long-run expectations are positive, actors who foresee the possibility that they will be overruled or fail in part to achieve their goals, will insist on voice opportunities – occasions to be heard. Formal occasions for voice are secured, and repeatedly utilized, for this express purpose. This has been typical of small state roles in the EU. Here, a special pattern of relations between small and large members can be discerned. All indications tell us that even in the EU, power politics is as common as ever. EU great powers expect EU small states to acquiesce in great power demands, and many EU small states on the contrary expect 'equality' to be the norm. In the sandbox world of European Union issues, old-fashioned power plays – only stripped of military content – continue to be a reality, while voice opportunities soften the experience.

Corresponding to the general category of 'inaction, complete passiveness' is the small state strategy of avoidance. The actor avoids contact with the more powerful as much as possible, and avoids confrontation in interaction when contact cannot be avoided. A supplementary strategy is to balance between interested great powers. If geopolitical circumstances permit, a strategy of balanced closure keeps both or all great powers at arm's length. Ideally, the doctrine of neutrality is based on such reasoning. Subscribing to it officially adds the legitimacy of international law to the otherwise implied power logic of this strategy. In practice, true balance is hard to maintain, as most European neutrals learned during World War I – and as Sweden learned during World War II, and Finland thereafter.[33]

A somewhat different way for a small state to balance between interested great powers is to conduct a policy of 'balanced openness'. In this case all interested external powers are allowed to participate and pursue their interests within the weak state, provided none of them gets privileges that are not available to others.[34] In the 1920s, Norway solved the problem of outside powers' interests in the arctic archipelago of

---

31 But cases of bandwagoning for security have often masqueraded as alliances, most prominently in the Soviet-led Warsaw Pact from 1955-1991; also the Fenno-Soviet Friendship and Mutual Assistance Treaty of 1948.

32 I am grateful to Regina Karp for pointing out the relevance of this article.

33 e.g., as analyzed by Fox (1959).

34 I here exclude the forced openness that European great powers imposed upon China, Turkey and others during the imperialist era before World War I. The policy considered must be self-chosen.

Svalbard in this way. Svalbard continues even today to be run under an international regime (the Svalbard Treaty of 1925) of equal access in the exploitation of natural resources and other economic activities. Similarly, Armenia currently conducts what it calls a policy of 'complementarity' that fits the same basic description, inspired by the principle of the same name in the Maastricht Treaty (Martirosyan 2004).[35]

However, territorial location and topography sometimes make isolation or resistance unlikely to succeed. In such cases, accommodation (symbolic compliance) is an alternative: The weaker side adapts to the extent it has to, and does its best to retain autonomy. Denmark from 1864 to 1918 vis-à-vis Germany, and Finland from 1944 until 1991 illustrate the policy (Mouritzen 1988). By pursuing this kind of policy, these countries' governments at the same time preserved their autonomy in almost all other substantial areas of government.

In contrast, the last strategy referred to above is one of active collaboration with the powerful in order to share in whatever spoils materialize (categories 1 and 2).[36] Hungary and Romania during World War II illustrate this type of strategy, as well as its dangers.[37] The two strategies of accommodation are typical of small states in the geopolitical quandary of territorial contiguity.

What is the empirical record? That is to say, comparing the strategies to tackle manifest power disparity, which ones appear to be more prevalent? In research on the foreign policies of states neighbouring the USSR, Germany, China and the US during the 20th century the theme of accommodation is more of a common refrain than that of resistance and assertion.[38] While NATO in its formative years may look like a resistance strategy for small members, few were genuinely exposed. Of the eight small European states that joined NATO during the early Cold War, only three

---

35 The Maastricht Treaty, of course, enshrined this principle at the core of the conditions for the Single European Market, i.e., a principle of economic rather than foreign policy. Yet, to countries like the Nordic ones, which have had the discouragement of foreign ownership as a key part of their foreign economic policies, the Maastricht Treaty required a fundamental retreat and reconstruction of their legal frameworks.

36 In international relations, the difference may be hard to distinguish.

37 The literature on bandwagoning is relevant here, describing cases in which small states ally with the great power in their neighbourhood who is their most immediate source of threat. Some confusion has been caused by Kenneth Waltz's writing on the subject, which does not distinguish between threatening and non-threatening neighbours, leading to a conflation of the motive of greed and the motive of fear behind this kind of move. This has led to two kinds of usage, one broad (both greed and fear, see Schweller 1994, Mouritzen 1998, and Walker, Ch. 9 in this volume), the other narrow (fear only, see especially the excellent clarification by Walt 1987).

38 Eight cases of European small states are covered by Fox 1959; a crucial part of Norway's experience is dealt with by Riste 1965; more general patterns are spelled out by Keal, 1983; while Moon, 1983 offers a quantitative perspective repeated in several subsequent studies. An in-depth study of extreme cases of accommodation is offered by Mouritzen 1988. A number of case studies of mainly Soviet neighbours are summarized in Knudsen, 1992a.

(Denmark Norway, and Greece) could be said to be under direct threat from the Soviet Union. Still, they all experienced that exposure.

The two European states that opted for neutrality – Sweden and Finland – clearly were under considerable pressure to accommodate the Soviets. Sweden performed two additional acts of flat-out submission when the Swedish government after World War II, on Moscow's request, handed over hundreds of Baltic refugees who had been resistance fighters, and shipped back the gold from Baltic treasuries which had been transported to Stockholm for safekeeping during the war. It was not that the Soviet government threatened military reprisals – the fact was simply that Sweden acted out of a motive hard to explain as anything except fear.

In a longitudinal study (mid-1960s to 1990) of military ground force deployments along the Soviet borders of Norway and Turkey, this author demonstrated that Norway maintained a consistently low-profile presence along its border, with just a symbolic force stationed there and several hundred kilometers separating it from the next back-up, while the Russian side all along kept a strong force on its side close to the border. The Soviet policy never changed despite Norway's repeated declaration that that was the purpose of its self-restraint. On the Turkish-Soviet border, the Turks never tried any such accommodative stance, yet the Soviets responded not much differently here than they did in the Norwegian case, if anything their deployments were more modest. The pattern that appeared to explain Soviet deployments was the protection of military assets on the Kola peninsula, to which there was no corresponding parallel in the Black Sea area (Knudsen 1992b). Norway in this case did two important things simultaneously: (1) it satisfied its own collective sense of identity as a small, nonaggressive state and (2) it made a strategic move to ensure that nervous Soviets defending their bases would not be triggered into war by an offensive Norwegian posture. It is worth noting how the first explanation fits a constructivist interpretation while the second fits a rationalist interpretation. Norway avoided confrontation even on behalf of NATO.

The Turkish case, while its deployment patterns are also possibly explainable by the Kurdish issue, offers a different demonstration of accommodation when Ankara silently bowed before the anticipated anger of Moscow by allowing Soviet aircraft carriers to pass through the Turkish Straits on two occasions in the 1980s and 1990s, despite the text of the Montreux Treaty that expressly forbids such passage. Even here, then, accommodation was preferred by a state that defined itself in the circumstances as an underdog.

While clearly examples of yielding, these are not cases of yielding to strong pressure. In peacetime and in the absence of overt pressure, circumstances have commonly been perceived as sufficiently restraining on many small states – Sweden, Finland, Denmark and Norway during the Cold War are notable examples – to dictate an accommodating strategy rather than one marking autonomy, recalcitrance or resistance.[39] What we have seen since the collapse of the Soviet Union in relations

---

39 It may be a quite different matter if one considers conflict within hierarchies of small states, such as in Lemke's study of Latin America. See Lemke 1996, 77-91.

between Russia and its neighbouring states in the CIS seems to bear out this broad pattern. In other words, self-conceived small states prefer to handle power disparity by accommodating early and avoiding confrontation.[40]

Confrontations Between Great Powers

Now let me shift to the theme of confrontation avoidance among great powers.[41] My argument is, as before, that non-confrontation and evasion tend to be overlooked even in studies of great power politics and the balance of power. These tendencies are present even in great power relations, and their pervasiveness is linked to the continuous process of power assessments. When to confront and when to evade, these are the perennial questions.

The essence of the balance of power is presumably to oppose superiority in others – alternatively seek to attain and maintain superiority oneself, leading in either case to what may be described as an endless repetition of confrontations between leading states and their coalitions.[42] As (e.g.) Waltz describes it, 'The theory depicts international politics as a competitive realm. ... The fate of each state depends on its responses to what others do' (Waltz 1979, 127).

The relevance of this line of reasoning to the present paper lies in the assumption that confrontations will take place; they will not be avoided. For balance to be maintained confrontations have to occur in opposition to any attempt by a leading state to get an advantage.[43]

However, while historically a group of leading powers usually can be discerned as standing out from the greater mass of polities, these states should not necessarily be assumed to see each other as equal or nearly equal in power. Power differentials are usually present and noted by those involved. Indeed the original idea of Organski, later developed further by Kugler, of a hierarchy of powers, seems a more realistic assumption (Organski 1958; Organski and Kugler 1980. See also Kugler and Lemke 1996). If differentials of power are common – and commonly

---

40 Estonia, Latvia and Lithuania made a different choice, one of recalcitrance and alliance with a remote power. Their choice was premised on the experience of having tried the other option – submission – for fifty years.

41 Again, we are dealing with self-defined great powers. The literature on great powers is vast, and no attempt will be made to recite it here. Kissinger 1994 gives a good overview. See also Mearsheimer 2001. Bull 1977 covers great power roles well, as did Wight before him (1978).

42 Assumptions in defensive and offensive versions of realist thinking differ. See, e.g., Mearsheimer (2001) compared to Waltz (1979). Vasquez lays out a broad and critical perspective in the APSR (1997), which spurred a debate in the same issue of the journal.

43 The penetrating discussion by Vasquez (1997) illuminates the multiple problems of the balance-of-power theory, many of which have to do with exactly the tendency to avoid confrontations (esp. 904-908).

perceived – confrontations are also less likely to be forthcoming. In the absence of urgent threat, they will be postponed.[44]

Hence, a complementary aspect of any power balancing or power maneuvering in practice is that it is also about non-confrontation. The point of balancing in a balance-of-power system is not war, but the avoidance of war. However, paradoxically, according to the reasoning, war can only be avoided by threatening to go to war – the old Roman adage of 'si vis pacem, para bellum'.[45] The practice of the classical balance of power is thus a careful combination of diplomacy and military posturing. It involves interminable feints and threats, attempts to gain advantage or to block such moves by others, while actual engagement in violent conflict is comparatively rare. Going to the brink is sometimes necessary, but to go beyond that into war itself – while occasionally unavoidable – is not the point. The key ingredient here is restraint, actors maintaining a careful watch on each others' behaviour, imputed intentions and presumed capacity to act. The watch they keep boils down to some rather crude and subjective assessments of potential power in presumed opponents.

Moreover, the way great power politics plays out in practice often breaks the rules of balance-of-power theory. No great power came forth to confront Japan, Italy or Germany in the 1930s until a very late stage. Britain, France and the US avoided those confrontations. In the end they had to take them on nevertheless.[46] Hence evasion and non-confrontation are a full-fledged and normal part of the power games among great powers.

Classical descriptions of balancing power, however, usually one-sidedly emphasize the offensive, even aggressive nature of the interaction. Different literatures also branch into the more ideological, on the one hand the lamentations of the balance of power as a major cause of wars; on the other its adoration as a mechanism to preserve the peace. The cases when confrontation is avoided tend to be overlooked.

Part of the problem is the narrow focus of most balance of power conceptions on military confrontation. Here we are moving on to the capabilities aspect referred to at the beginning of this section. This is a main point in the critique put forward by David Baldwin (Baldwin 2002, 181-184). He takes the implication of measurement in the term 'balance' as his point of departure, and contrasts it with the relational school:

---

44 According to Organski and elaborated by Kugler, power disparity between great powers entails stability while equality leads to challenge. In conventional balance-of-power thinking, power disparity is a spur to balancing or compensating efforts. The present account of balance of power reasoning differs from many others in that I describe it more as a pattern of behavior, a tendency, rather than as a body of theory about a type of system.

45 Now, although its critics in the power transitions school argue that this type of pattern is more likely to result in war, whether war occurs is not the point here. The point is that assessments of power is an ongoing activity on the part of participants in any power contest, whether hierarchical or not. See Lemke and Kugler, 1996.

46 ... arguably vindicating the prediction of balancing only at the last moment.

The analytical perspective of relational power prompts one to ask, "Power to get whom to do what?" One of the benefits of bringing this perspective to bear on balance of power theories is that it brings to light the underlying assumptions that: (1) military force is the measure of power; and (2) war-winning is what matters most. Only after these assumptions have been made explicit can fruitful debate as to their wisdom occur. (Baldwin 2002, 182)

Underneath this critique, with which I agree, two questions may be identified for clarification: What place should there be in power theories for measurement or estimations of power? Is the balance of power in itself a workable conception to understand power? The point about measurement ties directly into my overall argument here concerning the non-observability of evasion and avoidance.

Power over others works through the 'measurement' or assessments made by those others. The victims decide to whom they will give power. That is, such relationships are entirely based on subjective assessments made by the actors themselves. As researchers we can only seek to retrieve those assessments, but attempts at objective measurement will miss the point.

Baldwin – who is not making this point – is nevertheless relevant here because he raises these matters in his critique of neo-realism, taking issue with Waltz for saying that '... states devote "a lot of time to estimating one another's capabilities, especially their abilities to do harm"'. Baldwin calls this statement '... unsupported and contestable' (2002, 183). His critique is that abstract estimation is not what governments do: '... it is unlikely that they [defence ministries] spend much time estimating each other's capabilities in general or without reference to actual or postulated situations' (2002, 183).

The target of Baldwin's critique, then, appears to be chiefly the notion that there is such a thing as 'power in general' and that it can be estimated from military capabilities. I share with Baldwin the rejection of such an idea; indeed, I have elsewhere demonstrated this point empirically (Knudsen 1979).

However, I believe Waltz made an important point in emphasizing the process of estimation[47] – what he did not emphasize was above all the uncertainty of such assessments. The consciousness of uncertainty tends to instil caution in a decision-maker.[48] And caution often precedes evasion and non-confrontation.

Waltz also in my view bypasses something else here: the ubiquity of such assessments in relations between governments. As the author of this chapter sees

---

47 In a different part of his book Waltz actually rejects the entire conception of power on which this paper is based – the one emphasizing results – because in his view results are always due to many other factors besides power. 'Power is one cause among others.' (1979, 191-192). In the context where he makes the remark about estimating capabilities, however, he also says 'A country becomes a superpower if we treat it like one. We create other states in our image.' (130) What is pertinent to my argument here is still that the subjective factor is a crucial element.

48 In a comment on the power transition theory Bueno de Mesquita develops this uncertainty point in a number of examples; see Bueno de Mesquita 1996, 277, 280.

it, crude 'power assessments' are made in all sorts of issue contexts, regarding all kinds of 'capabilities'.[49] It is probably true that actors do not make very accurate assessments of putative power in contemplated confrontations, but they very likely do make them, rather than wait for 'results' to determine their course of action.

In other words, in all that large domain of international politics where results – outcomes – are most of the time indeterminate, the power of a government is what other governments THINK it is. This apparent banality is nevertheless crucial in each specific context. What decision-makers estimate is the ability to cause trouble, make mischief, combined with an imputed interest to do so. This is not just a matter of thinking about war. It is a much more general phenomenon, and governments pay a lot of attention to avoiding such difficulties. It is empirically illustrated every week in the Security Council of the United Nations – the veto gives sufficient weight to the positions of all permanent members to endow that game with a realism that it would not have if it were played 'outdoors'. Appearance becomes reality, to paraphrase Waltz (1979, 130).

For this reason confrontations are often avoided in many issue areas. For this reason power results are usually not clearly visible – measurable – in many issue areas. For this reason, also, even the balancing of power in military affairs may be part of our living experience, in spite of all the missing evidence. It is therefore also likely to be part of the everyday life of all governments, not merely of those near the top or the bottom of the scale of self-esteemed power in international affairs.

So, is the balance of power in itself a workable conception to understand power? Taken as a theory of balancing in the manner presented by Waltz and others, and evaluated by Vasquez, it is clearly not supported by the evidence. If, however, we take the term to mean a tendency or a pattern of behavior of compensatory reaction to perceived power differentials, I would say yes. But it does not mean counterpoising power.

More broadly speaking, therefore, I argue that the balance of power in the sense of a pattern of behavior is a phenomenon that is 'real' – i.e., empirically researchable. Moreover, it ought to be less than sensational to claim that a basic tendency on the part of political actors to assess relative advantage is found in all issue areas. Confrontations are sometimes sought – but more often avoided – based on rough assessments in which situations and contexts are given considerable weight. In some areas, this tendency leads to patterns of 'balancing' – compensatory action of some kind – and group formation.

If this line of argument is pursued further, and the emphasis shifted from measuring power to understanding how it works, one will find that it removes the

---

49 Knudsen 1979. This point is also central to the argument of Grieco about relative gains, which notably extends an argument parallel to mine to a broad scope of international relations, including matters of trade. See Grieco 1993. Baldwin, in a personal communication, adds that 'I quite agree with you that actors are probably constantly making estimates of the capabilities of others with respect to a wide variety of capabilities.' (Correspondence Baldwin to Knudsen, October 2004.)

perceived gap between the relational tradition in international power analysis[50] and the capability-focused tradition of IR realism, which after all are the two main schools of IR power analysis.

Assembling the Strands ...

In this chapter, I have argued that if we conceive of power as overcoming resistance – or overcoming conflicting preferences, then we need to revise the way we conceptualize it to take account of a broad tendency on the part of self-defined weaker actors to avoid confrontations. More specifically, I have made the following points:

a. Power is best conceived as a subjective phenomenon, partly as self-identification and self-assessment, partly as the assessment of putative opponents in potential conflicts.
b. Power relations are played out as much in confrontations avoided as in clashes taking place. Assessed power disparities guide behaviour.
c. Cost considerations in the broadest sense make the tendency of confrontation avoidance a common pattern in all social affairs, including world politics, producing tendencies towards hierarchy and structures of power.
d. Basing empirical studies on non-occurrences raises a methodological challenge which may be overcome by following cases over time.

Ultimately, we need to reintegrate power structures conceptually into our work as part of a larger family of social control phenomena that include relational aspects and capabilities assessed. In principle, all lend themselves to empirical study. In this way, power would emerge more clearly as both a long-term, durable if unstable phenomenon and as a short-term, situationally contingent phenomenon, in both cases resting – somewhat shakily – on the evaluations made by the weaker side.

---

50 Dating back to Baldwin's early work and to the outstanding volume by Cox, Jacobson et al., 1973.

Chapter 3

Events and Ideas in the Region: An Overview 1980s–2000s

Olav F. Knudsen and Christopher Jones

This chapter[1] offers essential background to the chapters that follow. In two parts, it deals first with the events that redefined the Baltic Sea region as the Cold war came to an end – the security context; secondly, it deals with the ideas that accompanied the historical developments, as political leaders adjusted and searched for new, long-term orientations.

The Security Context

The Baltic Sea region was eminently secure during the Cold War: Hardly anyone thought about challenging the invisible wall separating Warsaw Pact territories from the rest. Long-term strategies were apparently set in stone. As we shall see, while the seeds of change were indeed in place in the East during the 1980s, their possibility to sprout and grow was hastened by ideas that came in part from the West. While Poland's early democratization through Solidarity provided a strong impetus for change, the Baltic states – reduced to 'republics' encapsulated in the Soviet Union – were at the centre of the subsequent developments in the Baltic Sea region which from the mid-1980s were to completely overthrow the old order and force neighbouring countries to think anew. Ideas and events were closely related, but rarely went hand in hand.

During the late 1980s, the countries outside the Soviet sphere were essentially content with the growing stability of their security, especially after the INF (US-Soviet) missile treaty of 1988 and Gorbachev's announced troop withdrawals from Eastern Europe. However, the Nordic countries were still in a special geopolitical situation. The development of the Russian Kola Peninsula as a major base for the building, equipping and stationing of Soviet nuclear submarines (SSN), and ballistic missile carrying nuclear submarines (SSBN), together with a high level of ground, naval and air defence forces, were factors that added to the strategic importance of the

---

1   In the division of labour of this chapter Christopher Jones has been responsible for the section on ideas.

region. The close proximity of these forces to Norway's and Finland's north-eastern borders had a considerable impact on the respective policies of these countries.[2]

On the Eastern side political change was brewing nearly everywhere. Environmental movements had already started challenging Soviet authorities in Estonia and Latvia from 1986. A process aiming for more fundamental political reforms was initiated in 1988 with the formation of politically all-embracing 'Popular Fronts' in all three Baltic states that year. The Popular Fronts demanded political freedom.

In the spring of 1990, elections that were basically free were held all over the Soviet Union. Those elections brought the Popular Fronts to power in Lithuania, Estonia and Latvia. Faced with a Lithuanian declaration of (re-established) independence and similar noises from Tallinn and Riga, Gorbachev responded in April 1990 with the declaration of a blockade backed up by military force. A stand-off followed during the period April-October 1990, while the new Baltic governments sought to establish a makeshift diplomatic service and approached Western governments for help.

The Paris CSCE Summit in November 1990 – the first since 1975 – was called against the backdrop of the 'fall of the Wall' and the unification of Germany, to activate cooperation across the old dividing lines of Europe. Given the 1975 Helsinki Summit guarantee of the then existing borders of Europe, the first revision of those borders had just been effected with the merger of the GDR and the FRG. The Baltic states now saw their chance to ask for the same. However, at the Paris Summit Mr. Gorbachev was unshakeable in his resistance to further change. The Baltic leaders never even made it into the conference rooms.

During the subsequent nine months Soviet military and interior ministry (OMON) forces harassed the three Baltic countries repeatedly, on Mr. Gorbachev's direct orders, with numerous innocent lives taken. These tense times ended with the fiasco of the failed coup against Gorbachev in Moscow in August 1991. Shortly thereafter, the Congress of People's Deputies in Moscow, on behalf of the Soviet Union, recognized the independence of Estonia, Latvia and Lithuania. The dissolution of the USSR in December 1991 moved Russia into the central position as successor state and main interlocutor for the Baltic states in their new international relations.

With independence secured, the next step for Vilnius, Tallinn and Riga was to rid their territories of occupying forces. This turned out to be an even harder nut to crack. Russia seemed in no hurry to pull out, their recent undertaking to withdraw several hundred thousand troops out of Eastern Europe explaining at least some of their reluctance. There was simply not room in the officers' quarters on Russian territory, it was argued. Moreover, the bases in the Baltic states were forward strategic positions that were attractive from a military standpoint.

---

2   The major Soviet naval bases of Polyarny, Murmansk and Sevoromosrk are approximately 100 miles (150km) from the Norwegian border. For a compelling study of the military strategic significance of the Kola Peninsula in Cold War Soviet military planning, see Ries and Skorve, 1986.

There was also the situation of the ex-Soviet citizens to keep in mind. Their hoped-for automatic naturalization as Baltic citizens happened only in Lithuania.³ The Russians tried repeatedly over the next three years to link troop withdrawal and the status of the Russian-speaking populations in Estonia and Latvia (Simonsen 2001). The summit of the CSCE at Helsinki in July 1992, however, unconditionally demanded the withdrawal of Russian troops from the Baltic states (CSCE 1992, 8):

> Even where violence has been contained, the sovereignty and independence of some States still needs to be upheld. We express support for efforts by CSCE participating States to remove, in a peaceful manner and through negotiations, the problems that remain from the past, like the stationing of foreign armed forces on the territories of the Baltic States without the required consent of those countries.
>
> Therefore, in line with basic principles of international law and in order to prevent any possible conflict, we call on the participating States concerned to conclude, without delay, appropriate bilateral agreements, including timetables, for the early, orderly and complete withdrawal of such foreign troops from the territories of the Baltic States.

Although the rights of minorities were frequently referred to in the document, there was no specific reference to such issues in connection with the Baltic states. Obviously, however, the presence of these large non-citizen populations were a minus in the political scorebook of the Baltic states in other countries. The special circumstances of their origin were poorly understood by other – especially Western – European governments. Providing for CSCE missions to monitor the situation of non-citizens in Estonia and Latvia was therefore probably a wise decision, if not particularly popular in Tallinn and Riga. The CSCE mission in Estonia was proposed by Sweden and decided in December 1992 at the Stockholm CSCE ministerial. The Latvian mission was established a year later (see CSCE documents archive at <www.osce.org>; Fredén 2006, 125-27).

The slow start of the troop withdrawal negotiations led others to seek ways to back up the Baltic side and ensure a more expeditious process. The so-called 'Stockholm Group'⁴ was formed by interested Western governments, including the Nordics and the UK, providing advice by MFA officials for the three Baltic governments. At the same time the Swedish government under Carl Bildt undertook a unique campaign of high level diplomacy on behalf of the Baltic states, which lasted for the duration of his time in office (November 1991-October 1994). The effort involved Sweden's top political leadership as a virtual channel of communication between, in particular, the

---

3   There was nothing automatic about naturalization in Lithuania, however; one had to show up at the appropriate office and request Lithuanian citizenship, on the sensible reasoning that respect for the citizenship would otherwise be undermined.

4   The Stockholm Ad Hoc Group on the Baltic States, formed in 1992 at the initiative of the UK. Sweden chaired the group and all meetings were held in Stockholm. Members included representatives of the governments of Denmark, Finland, Norway, Canada, France, Germany, Italy, UK, USA and the EC Commission, in addition to Sweden (Fredén 2006, 61-62).

Estonian and Latvian governments, the Russian government and the US government. One of the participating diplomats concluded in the end that the Russian Ministry of Foreign Affairs actively sought to undermine the process (Fredén 2006, 362).

In the most critical phases, Sweden on several occasions secured support by President Clinton for Baltic positions in direct talks with President Yeltsin. At the same time Sweden worked to clarify and perhaps at times moderate Baltic positions (Fredén 2006).

This patient and intensive diplomatic effort paid off.[5] Moreover, Russian resistance proved part sham when it emerged that withdrawals were already taking place, slowly but surely, from the Russian bases in the Baltics.[6] Soon the Russian side decided to pull out of Lithuania earlier than requested (by August 31st, 1993) – possibly a 'reward' for a more generous citizenship policy.

Despite Western backing and de facto Russian withdrawals, Estonia and Latvia were left with little or no progress in the negotiations until spring 1994, sticking points being the status of officers who wanted to retire and stay, the Paldiski nuclear training facility in Estonia (see also Ch. 5) and the Skrunda long-distance radar in Latvia. Ultimately, the US government interceded in the negotiations[7] and secured the termination of the process where these sticking points were concerned. Amazingly, in the end the Russian troops were pulled out on time by August 31st, 1994, after a presence of 54 years.

Only at this time did Estonia, Latvia and Lithuania face a situation where they could start thinking more freely and seriously about their future security. They had obviously had their thoughts along the way. Early on, a future as neutrals or non-aligned seemed like the right approach. That alternative probably died along with the Warsaw Pact in 1991. A possible alternative security constellation of the Baltic states and the Visegrad Group was another scheme bandied about in the early period. That notion even had its supporters in Moscow. However, events of 1993 in Moscow – especially the October bombardment of the parliament – served to jell the thinking of East European politicians. The EU and NATO would be their solutions.

The Copenhagen Summit of the EU in 1993 had raised hopes and expectations with the declaration that in principle all European countries were entitled to membership, provided they satisfied the basic criteria of democracy, rule of law, and market economy. Still, security was an open question in the minds of sceptical Balts and Central Europeans. The suggestion of NATO membership had occasionally been aired before,[8] but 1993 brought impulses together to move further on this issue.

---

5   Although Sweden was at the centre of these efforts, all governments represented in the Stockholm group supported the efforts in other ways. A heavy input of aid from the Nordic countries was a significant supplement, to Northwest Russia and Poland in addition to the Baltic states.

6   A fact that was never publicly admitted by Russia.

7   Which were otherwise conducted separately by Russia with the three Baltic states.

8   Asmus relates entertainingly from a 1990 Rand seminar in Poland, where the eagerness to join NATO probably exceeded realistic possibilities (2002, 13).

In Washington, despite early caution in the untried Clinton administration (Talbott 2002, 92ff), the NATO decision began to take shape, prodded especially by Poland. A scheme for the expansion of NATO's membership was put together before the end of the year, but with the added feature of a 'waiting room', the Partnership for Peace, to avoid rushing things and to prevent the early division of 'membership candidates' from 'non-candidates'.

Russia had already declared its opposition, in no uncertain terms, in late August 1993.[9] Nonetheless, NATO decided in January 1994, in principle, to open up for new members. The invitation for Russia to join the PfP, when it subsequently came, hardly softened the blow. On a more positive note, Russia and the European Union had negotiated a ground-breaking political agreement. Then Chechnya occurred (December 1994). To other Europeans, Russia was back on a war path. From then on, two mutually rejecting sides could once more be discerned in Europe. As planning for NATO expansion proceeded to a new step in 1995,[10] the Russia-EU agreement was put on hold for the time being – which turned out to be three years.

All along, the Nordic countries had not only offered substantial amounts of bilateral and multilateral aid to Russia, Poland and the Baltic States, but also made efforts to provide basic defence assistance to the Baltic States. Denmark was the first to offer bilateral defence agreements. Finland was the first to offer 'lethal aid' – shooting weapons. Over this issue, Norway, like Sweden, had a serious soul-searching. The thought of moving guns into an unsettled political situation was contrary to established Scandinavian principles, regardless of who was involved at the receiving end. Swedish lethal aid was decided in principle in autumn 1994, after the Russian troop withdrawals had been secured (see Fredén 2006).

These honest but faltering attempts from the Nordics to side with the Baltic states, without giving the security guarantees that Britain and the US encouraged them to offer, left a less-than-good atmosphere on all sides. The Balts felt they were getting secondary treatment. The Nordics felt the great powers of the West were passing the buck.

---

9 The Yeltsin incidence during his visit to Warsaw on August 23, 1993 brought the Russian position to clarity with sudden drama. In Warsaw, President Boris Yeltsin stated that Poland was free to join whatever alliance it wished; then, within days, he publicly withdrew that statement in a letter to Western governments. The anti-expansion statement was subsequently reissued on various occasions: 'NATO expansion to countries in immediate proximity to our borders will elicit a negative reaction from public opinion and promote undesirable sentiments in civilian and military circles and could ultimately lead to military and political de-stability' (Zhdannikov 1994). Yeltsin repeated this sentiment in his letter to President Clinton, prior to the visit of the Presidents of the three Baltic States in July 1996. In it he repeated Russian objections to Baltic membership of NATO – 'There can be no question of even the hypothetical possibility of extending NATO's sphere of operation to the Baltic countries. Such a prospect is categorically unacceptable to Russia, and we would regard steps in that direction as posing a direct challenge to our national security interests and destroying the fundamental structures of European stability,' (Eggert and Yusin 1996).

10 ... with a study of criteria for membership.

Under the circumstances, a project hit upon by the Baltic governments themselves proved a useful device in the interim, to encourage defence cooperation while keeping it slim and close to the Baltic states themselves. BALTBAT, a Baltic peacekeeping battalion trained in cooperation with Danish and other Nordic peacekeeping contingents, was a concept that quickly spawned others – BALTRON for naval forces, BALTNET for air surveillance, BALTDEFCOL for perhaps the most durable idea: a defence college for the new armed forces of the Baltic states.[11] These projects successfully continued until past the turn of the Millennium and kept a number of Western defence ministries involved with their Baltic counterparts, for instruction and training.

The effect was probably more morale-building than anything else, but the projects also reflected the need for some more solid structure in which to embed Baltic security. The most comprehensive European security structure at the time was the CSCE, in which the memberships of Estonia, Latvia and Lithuania were certified in late autumn 1991.

During 1992-94 the institutionalization of the CSCE/OSCE proceeded rapidly. Within the decade, however, aspirations for the reconstituted OSCE to take on the broader role of a 'security council' for Europe proved vain. Russian ambitions met Western scepticism. Due to remaining political divisions this forum did not provide sufficient further guidance – at least not for Baltic regional security strategies. This became clear in the first preparation for EU membership (1993-95) by East-Central European countries, with the Balladur plan, requiring neighbouring states to resolve outstanding disagreements between themselves under the aegis of the CSCE/OSCE. The end product of this marathon of negotiation processes was the Stability Pact of Paris of March 1995, a compact of bilateral agreements. To support the effort to achieve these agreements, multilateral ('sub-regional') discussion groups were formed within the CSCE/OSCE – so-called 'regional tables' – of which one on the Baltic region (1994-95). Most of the regional tables proved to be good working instruments, but the Baltic regional table was an utter failure. The complete lack of connection between Russian and Baltic views on border issues was apparently the reason.[12]

Against strong advise from Western supporting governments, Estonia and Latvia made border revision demands on Russia as soon as their independence was secured. While entirely understandable considering the 1920 Treaties with Russia that first formalized their independence and specified their borders, the demands were politically insensitive and created unnecessary irritation in Moscow. While the troop

---

11 Each of these projects originally had an external (Baltic regional) sponsor state and an international oversight committee consisting of MOD officials from the Nordic countries and West European NATO countries. Numerous sources, especially in the Nordic countries, official (defence ministries) and unofficial, can relate further details of these projects.

12 The Baltic regional table for the OSCE has been kept out of public view; a subject for historical research to come, no doubt.

withdrawal negotiations were going on the border issues were mostly kept out of the way. After September 1994 the border issues were back on the Baltic agenda.

All three Baltic countries conducted border negotiations separately with Russia 1994-96. They got nowhere beyond the status quo. Draft agreements were ready for signature in 1996-97, but only Lithuania got the complete ratified end product. As of June 2006 the other two agreements with Latvia and Estonia are not yet ratified.

While the long-term bilateral strategy thus partly had failed, not least due to the Baltic governments' own political ineptitude, Estonia, Latvia and Lithuania moved in accordance with parallel multilateral strategies towards the 'euroatlantic structures'. Lithuania's membership bid for NATO was launched in early 1994. All three Baltic states signed EU agreements for prospective members in June 1995.

From then on, future membership in these two structures – NATO and the EU – became alpha and omega in the practice of Baltic diplomacy. Despite repeated rebuffs from NATO and even once from the EU, the Baltic governments were not discouraged and ultimately succeeded on both counts in 2004. No doubt, their persistence was part of the explanation, but other factors may have been more important. In the EU case, Nordic and British support within the EU was probably crucial in prevailing over French aloofness. In the NATO case, the US position in favour of Baltic membership ultimately overcame the resistance of key countries like Germany,[13] whose appetite for NATO expansion appeared to have been satisfied with the case of Poland.

For a while, the two structures were posited as alternative security strategies. It suited the general drift of European political debate over security before 9/11 – especially on the social-democratic side – to represent the EU as a 'demilitarized' option. On the other hand, NATO seemed to many to have the advantage over the EU in hard security terms that it included the US. The Baltic states rejected this discussion of alternatives. In Estonia, Latvia and Lithuania the two structures were widely seen as complementary.

As things turned out, debate did not resolve the issue. Events did. Gaining EU membership took its time and again shifted attention towards NATO as the quicker route. The shock of 9/11 brought NATO's second round of expansion out of the doldrums. While President Bush had already stated his readiness to take Estonia, Latvia and Lithuania in as new NATO members, Russia responded to 9/11 by dropping its earlier opposition to Baltic NATO membership.

For a while, at least, the issue was depoliticized. With Poland, Germany and Denmark there were, as of 1999, already three Baltic coastal states in NATO; adding Estonia, Latvia and Lithuania would leave only Sweden and Finland as non-

---

13 The French case was different. As early as spring 1998, when Baltic NATO memberships seemed to have been put off for the foreseeable future, a high-level French policy-maker envisioned NATO expansion in the somewhat strained metaphor of a train with many carriages, one for each candidate country, and while the Baltic carriages were among the last, the whole train would ultimately reach its destination. (Knudsen interview at the Quai d'Orsay, May 1998.)

members in the Baltic Sea region. As Ch. 4 will show, both of the latter are deeply and peculiarly divided over the NATO issue. The peculiarity has to do with a split between the public at large and political elites: the general public in both countries is strongly opposed to NATO membership (more than 70%), while the political elites are probably more evenly divided for and against.[14] The strategy that more or less offers itself under such conditions is what may be called 'hedging'; keeping it open – cooperating with NATO without seeking membership. As strategies go, this one may well be a non-strategy.[15]

Germany's role in the region has shown a definite penchant for the geopolitical grand view, combined with a concern to avoid repeating old mistakes. In the region, the formula Germany + Russia instantaneously recalls Messrs Ribbentrop and Molotov. Germany has interpreted the moral of that history as requiring a strategy of not breaking with Russia when relations get difficult, not letting Russia down – which in matters concerning the Baltic Sea region translates into 'Russia first'. Under Chancellor Schröder, of course, this close bilateral link was further developed into a tight energy partnership, culminating with a new Russian gas export pipeline along the Baltic sea-floor to which only Germany would be connected.

Does Russia have a long-term strategy to deal with the Baltic Sea region as a separate part of its security environment? While the practice of distinct policies for different regions along its borders have marked both Russia and the Soviet Union, to Moscow its north-western area has been a headache ever since 1990. The experience of loss and defeat being prominent and other business more pressing, Russia has only half-heartedly developed a 'north-western policy'. The broader European scene is more attractive, more important, and Germany has become Russia's bridgehead into the Baltic Sea region as well as the EU. (See Lo 2003 for further analysis of this trend.)

Well aware that the Baltic Sea region has indeed been stabilized, even Moscow has shown its readiness – up to a point – to join in the cooperative efforts flourishing around the Baltic Sea. The limit to cooperation alluded to shows itself in actual Russian bilateral conduct vis-à-vis the Baltic states – still rather confrontational – and in the Russian way of dealing with the multilateral institutions of the Baltic Sea region – the CBSS and HELCOM: selectively cooperating in good faith, selectively evading these bodies when Moscow's convenience so dictates. In the CBSS and HELCOM cases, the best example of non-cooperation is the designation of the Baltic as a Particularly Sensitive Sea Area (Knudsen 2006, also Ch. 9 in this volume).

---

14 ... although this latter point cannot be corroborated by actual opinion studies.

15 Sweden and Finland both at this time refer to their policies by the term 'military nonalignment.' Abstinence from membership of security alliances is held to provide Sweden and Finland with a degree of political and military freedom, in that they are not constrained by the conditions of membership, nor policies adopted by such alliances. In addition, it would allow them to choose to be neutral (i.e. non-participatory) in a conflict given the absence of a pre-determined agreement to fight. It should be noted that Finland's freedom of action and decision during the Cold War was limited by the Agreement of Friendship, Co-operation and Mutual Assistance (FCMA Treaty) with USSR, concluded in 1948.

Yet, like many of the other governments in the Baltic Sea region, Russia sees the outside as the 'real world', while the Baltic circumference remains a mere backyard. There is thus an appearance of diffuse incompletion over Russian policy.

The context of Baltic Sea regional security thus sketched, we shall proceed to the ideas about security that have taken hold during the same period.

Ideas of Security

In the years since the fall of the Berlin Wall, the end of Communism in Eastern Europe, the collapse of the Soviet Union and the passing into history of the Cold War, one of the major projects in European security has been the idea of extending the zone of security enjoyed by the countries of Western Europe and the North Atlantic area to the countries of Central and Eastern Europe. Throughout this period of building and rebuilding Europe, a number of texts have been written on the extension of the European 'security community'[16] to the east (Wallensteen 1994; Gambles 1995; IFSH 1996; Hallberg 2000; Mouritzen 2001; Peou 2001; Goodby 2002). Deutsch et al defined a security community as 'a group of people which has become "integrated"' to the point that 'there is real assurance that the members of that community will not fight each other physically, but will settle their disputes in some other way' – what Deutsch termed 'dependable expectations of peaceful change' (1957, 5). The members of this community[17] would not even contemplate or prepare for violent armed action against other members. In this sense, Western Europe and the trans-Atlantic Area is a security community. Similarly, the Scandinavian countries were cited in the original work of Deutsch as a key example of a pluralistic security community[18] (Deutsch 1957: 7-8). The hope in extending the European security community to the countries of Central and Eastern Europe is the discontinuation of the threat and use of armed violence in political intercourse, and the amelioration of the security dilemma,[19] reflecting 'a genuine desire to reduce

---

16 Karl Deutsch et al developed the theory of Security Communities in the book *Political Community in the North Atlantic Area* (Deutsch 1957). See also Deutsch 1978. For a more recent work on the theory, see Adler and Barnett, 1998.

17 Wæver notes that the achievement of a security community in Western Europe has come about 'primarily through a process of "desecuritization," a progressive marginalization of mutual security concerns in favor of other issues.' In referring to Deutsch's definition as a security community being one without war, he uses the term non-war community, as 'security problems can continue to unfold within it' (1998, 69).

18 Deutsch et al differentiated between an amalgamated security community, meaning '... the formal merger of two or more previously independent units into a single larger unit, with some type of common government after amalgamation', of which the United States is an example, and a pluralistic security community, which 'retains the legal independence of separate governments', of which Iceland, Norway, Sweden, Denmark and Finland would be an example. Deutsch's specific reference was to Sweden and Norway (1957, 6).

19 For more on the security dilemma see Booth and Wheeler 1992, 29-60.

security anxieties of Central and East European states by including them in a broader security community' (Ruggie 1997, 109).

Simultaneous to this expansion of the European security community has been an expansion of the concept and understanding of security. With the end of the Cold War and the removal of nuclear deterrence as the predominant strategy for ensuring peace and stability, a reassessment of our understanding of what is meant by security has taken place, chiefly in academic circles, but also at an official and organizational level in the 'new' thinking of Europe's political and security organizations (Bitzinger 1990; Booth 1991; Jalonen 1993; Weiss 1993; Downs 1994; Wæver 1995; Butfoy 1997; Baldwin 1997; Krause and Williams 1997; Mutimer 1997; Walker 1997; Buzan et al 1998; Solomon 1998). While some of these 'new' concepts have their origins in the Cold War, it was not until the 1990s that they came to the fore, in what Nossal has termed the 'adornment of security', modifying the term 'by tagging the word with a variety of adjectives (most of which, coincidentally, happen to begin with a "c").' This 'c-ing' of security, as Nossal calls it, refers to the related concepts of Common, Comprehensive and Cooperative security[20] (1995, 34-36).

Nordic and Baltic Thinking About Security

This section looks at the Nordic security discourse during and after the Cold War, and the prevalent ideas and concepts of security that featured in the Nordic nexus of ideas, such as Common Security and Cooperative Security.

Checkel defines ideas as

> broad concepts and basic beliefs that can play a central role in organizing politics and shaping public policy. For decision makers, ideas provide a policy paradigm or road map for interpreting international politics and shaping preferences, as well as a sense of the proper instruments to use in promoting state interests (1997, 5).

The metaphor is important here – organiser, road map, a guide to instruments. Ideas, as defined here, help one to organise one's actions, to decide a broad course of action, and to choose the most suitable instruments. Goldstein and Keohane discuss this use of ideas as road maps further (1993, 13-17). In essence, they see ideas as playing this vital role of a 'map' in the process of policy formulation, or the making of decisions particularly in times of uncertainty. Goldstein and Keohane categorize ideas into three types: *worldviews, principled beliefs* and *causal beliefs*.

The first category, *worldviews*, describes the way in which a group of people look at their environment, the world around them, be it from a cultural or sociological perspective, or a political one. Any given religion or 'Western civilization' provide examples of a worldview. They are the lenses through which the world and all things in it are viewed.

---

20 These three concepts contain many similarities. Indeed, Dewitt argues, "any attempt to differentiate between them runs the risk of drawing artificial boundaries" (1994, 1).

One could argue that the worldview of the three Baltic States is defined, in part, by their geography - small territories on the borders of Russia, along the south eastern shore of the Baltic Sea – and their history of conquest and defeat by successions of invading armies from Denmark, Sweden, Germany, Poland, and Russia/Soviet Union. Their history gives them today some small element of attachment to the Nordic countries (most applicable to the relationship between Estonia and Finland), the basis for differentiation from Russia to their east, and thus a strong determination to ally themselves with the Western world through membership in NATO and the European Union.

In a similar fashion, the brutal attack on Finland by the USSR in 1939-40, and the 'war of continuation' waged by Finland upon the Soviet Union from 1941-44, (Jakobson 1984; Ries 1988) have largely shaped the present-day older generation's worldview. The isolation of Finland during its war with the Soviet Union forced Finland to look to itself alone for defence, an experience which has helped to fashion Finnish foreign and defence policy ever since, up to and including the present. More generally, Scandinavian worldviews derive from similar influences, with the possible addition of a religious element, that of Lutheran Protestantism, which has lent a certain moralist element to the Scandinavian attitude to the world around them.

These fundamental positions are likely to impact upon discussions of foreign policy, defence and security. Decision-makers probably approach such questions with an established set of values and priorities, even though the initial factors that conditioned those views, or at least their relevance to the situation in hand, may have changed over time.

Goldstein and Keohane continue their classification of ideas with *principled beliefs*, normative understandings of what is right and wrong. In the field of international relations such subjects as slavery and human rights instantly command attention as matters of principle in most Western countries. In addition to these one could add democratic beliefs. Such ideas can thus be seen as the more specific component elements of a particular worldview, in that the basket of normative principled beliefs one holds will, to a degree, be determined according to the former. Goldstein and Keohane write that 'principled beliefs mediate between worldviews and particular policy conclusions; they translate fundamental doctrines into guidance for contemporary human action' (1993, 9).

There is a certain measure of principle to Nordic foreign policy, seen in their almost altruistic views on the Third World and the support they have given to the development of poor countries. Though not clearly a matter of principle, Nordic relations with the Baltic States since their reforms began have, with only minor exceptions,[21] supported the establishment of these principled beliefs in the re-

---

21 Indicative of the mixed reactions to the early stirrings on the other shore of the Baltic Sea, Sten Andersson, then Swedish Minister for Foreign Affairs, stated in March 1988 that '... he had no intention of bringing up the status of the Baltic republics at the CSCE ...', fearing that '... a demand for immediate independence would be counter-productive ...' (Karlsson and Knudsen, 2001, 182-184).

emerging Baltic societies. Much of the so-called 'sovereignty support' given by the Nordic countries to the three Baltic States has been tailored to the realization of such principles as the rule of law, respect for minority rights, and the freedom of an elected government to determine its own policy.

The third category used by Goldstein and Keohane is that of *causal beliefs*.[22] Beliefs of cause and effect relationships may derive from scientific sources, from political or economic observations, or they may derive from a shared consensus (e.g., that peaceful mass protest can change repressive political regimes). Whatever the source, in providing the two ends of an equation, causal beliefs suggest the strategies necessary to achieve that goal. Changes in causal beliefs can facilitate major changes on the ground.

The most significant shift of causal beliefs during the Cold War period was the emergence of the idea of a non-zero sum security relationship, particularly between the West and the Soviet Union. Contrary to the popular notion that, in measuring security after changes in defence and security policy and/or practice, only one side won and the other consequently lost,[23] the non-zero sum equation meant that both sides could benefit from a change on one or both sides of the equation. At least, the other side would not lose any security.

Certainly, as the idea of Common Security came to the fore in the early 1980s, this causal belief became more prominent, being one of the critical elements of the new thinking on security. Security *with* one's adversary's interest in mind was the driving tenet of this concept, and had been practiced to a degree by the Nordic countries well before Common Security developed as a concept of security. They were well aware of the strategic significance of their region in any future European war, especially as nuclear strategies and weaponry developed from the 1960s to 1980s. Arguably the 'base and ban' decisions[24] by Norway and Denmark exemplify this belief, in that their decisions not to accept the peacetime stationing of NATO troops on their territory, nor the peacetime deployment of nuclear weaponry, were taken partly out

---

22 This category of knowledge is akin to Alexander George's notion of 'generic knowledge', which he describes as 'conditional generalizations (or laws, as they are often referred to in discussions of theory)' (George 1993, 120-122).

23 The 'I win – you lose' logic of a zero-sum relationship drives the power-security dilemma. Following an attempt by one side to increase its security vis-à-vis a second party, the second party perceives that it has lost ground, that its security has diminished as a result. It will then seek to redress that imbalance through implementing its own increases, thereby repeating the cycle of insecurity for the original initiating party (Booth and Wheeler 1992). It continues to mark the thinking of Russian and Baltic leaders as well as the general public (cf. Lo 2003).

24 This refers to the policy of reassurance vis-à-vis the Soviet Union whereby both Norway and Denmark imposed restrictions on certain elements of their participation in NATO. No Allied troops were to be permanently stationed in the two countries (base), nor would they accept the presence of Allied nuclear weapons (bombs, missiles or other munitions) in their territory during times of peace (ban) (Archer 1984; Borch 1995).

of consideration of its likely consequences for Finland, given likely Soviet responses to the presence of NATO troops and nuclear forces on its north-western borders.[25]

Russian opposition to the eastward expansion of NATO, previously discussed, may have been based on the *causal belief* that the location of NATO forces along Russia's borders would be a threat to Russian security. At a deeper level, it may also have resulted from a continued belief in Russia's right of 'influence' in the Baltic States (Godzimirski 1998; Svennevig 1998; Simonsen 2001, cf. Neumann 2005).

On the other hand, the stated foreign policy goals of Estonia, Latvia and Lithuania to become members of the European Union and NATO may be attributed to a *causal belief* that non-membership would be an appeasement of the local hegemon – Russia. The *policy outcome* of this belief is thus the persistent pursuit of membership of those two organizations. Failure to secure membership of these organizations would have the effect, as they saw it, of relegating them to the political influence of Russia. With that in mind, these respective causal beliefs provide, as Goldstein and Keohane state, 'strategies for the attainment of goals, themselves valued because of shared principled beliefs, and understandable only within the context of broader worldviews' (1993, 10).

Writing on the origins of the US-Canadian security community, Sean M. Shore stated that:

> ... the level of threat in a given interstate relationship is a function of the quality of prior interaction; where those interactions are peaceful, states can internalise positive images of one another, and come to expect friendly behavior in the future. They can *learn* to trust one another, in the sense that their theories about the "Other" can be revised in the light of new evidence (1998, 34).

In light of this statement, it is easy to understand that the Baltic States continue to harbour *negative* images of Russia even into the present. Their 'prior interaction' has led them to expect unfriendly behaviour from Russia. Former Estonian Minister of Foreign Affairs, Toomas Hendrik Ilves, stressed this *causal belief*, when asked by a Swedish participant to comment on the apparent paradox between the benefits of membership of the European Union, which would provide possibilities for cooperation at the level that could provide true security for the region, and the belief that possible NATO membership by Estonia (as for the other two Baltic States) would decrease security, as a result of worsened relations with Russia. He responded in a manner that was characteristically succinct and blunt:

---

25 Initially, the Norwegian base policy was formed in response to a Soviet official query before Norway joined the Washington Treaty in 1949. Denmark later followed suit. However, domestic political reasons and inter-Allied issues were more prominent in the decisions to adopt these policies (Archer 1984; Brundtland 1985; Brundtland 1966; Noreen 1983; Andrén 1977). Finnish politicians argued both then and later that this reasoning was misleading, in that there was no necessary single interpretation of the policy moves involved in Nordic balance thinking.

> If you haven't been invaded for 250 years, then it's understandable that NATO seems like a ridiculous organization. If you have been invaded, if you've had ethnic cleansing carried out in your territory, then you might think that NATO is not such a bad idea.

He continued by saying that

> ... the threats to the security of the Baltic area are, by and large, not tied to hard security issues but rather to soft security issues. I do not think any of us has the kinds of concerns we had when we had foreign troops on our soil. We do not think about troops being involved in any kind of action on our territory any longer. Rather the issues are more related to soft security issues, which nevertheless can present real threats.

He then pointed to the role played by the European Union in meeting these challenges, but concluded with the telling statement that 'the problem, of course, is that working with soft security issues is not enough.' While the prospect of EU membership and the adoption of its standards and norms 'tremendously increases our sense of security in the soft security areas – *the hard security issues remain*' (emphasis added) (Ilves, 1999).

Alternative Ideas About Security

Having solved security issues between them, to the extent that, as Joeniemmi (1996; cf. Wæver 1998) argues, the Nordic region became one of 'a-security', the focus for the Nordic countries became alleviation of the worst extremes of the 'overlay' (Buzan *et al* 1991b, 31) of superpower rivalry present in and around the region, which increased in intensity from the 1970s. An 'alternative' to nuclear deterrence and 'security against' the enemy was developed, in pursuit of an overall understanding of security as non zero-sum. The 'C' concepts of security (Common, Cooperative and Comprehensive) were all based on this notion, in stark contrast to the mainstream thinking of the Cold War.

Though not exclusively a 'Nordic' idea, the concept of Common Security was widely discussed, and arguably practiced by some of the Nordic countries during the Cold War. The concept is most widely attached to the work of the Independent Commission on Disarmament and Security Issues, also known as the Palme Commission, after its Chair, the late Olof Palme, then Swedish Prime Minister and leader of the Swedish Social Democratic Party 1969–1986. The concept received its widest exposure in the publication of the *Report of the Independent Commission on Disarmament and Security Issues,* having begun with initial discussions on security amongst Social Democratic parties in Western Europe, most notably in West

Germany, to later become an important contribution to the security dialogue that developed in Europe during what were to be the latter stages of the Cold War.[26]

The core insight conveyed by Common Security is that the security of states is fundamentally interdependent. Security is not a divisible commodity – all are either all secure or all insecure.

With the end of the Cold War, a general 're-think' on the nature of security took place. The term broadened in its scope and definition, encompassing many threats and challenges outside the realm of traditional military security. Furthermore, the nature of security between states in Europe changed from being largely adversarial to being chiefly cooperative.

It may be argued that the concept of Common Security has metamorphosed into its contemporary expression, Cooperative Security (see Ch. 1). It has allowed the Nordic countries to provide the Baltic States in particular with an expanded 'menu for choice' (Russett and Starr 1995) in the area of defence and security policy. In this sense, cooperative security in the Baltic Sea region is less about the relationship between, say, Sweden and Latvia, than about an approach which the Nordic countries, *inter alia*, have encouraged the Baltic States to take up, particularly in their relations with Russia.

As NATO redefined its role in 1990s Europe, and as the European Union began to develop a security identity, the resulting concepts echoed ideas from the Nordic countries. The coincidence between Nordic ideas on security and those now entertained by NATO is striking. NATO has to all intents and purposes adopted cooperative security in the sense used in this volume as the basis of its relations with non-member countries to the east, and above all with Russia. NATO has initiated a range of political and military cooperative ventures to foster understanding, facilitate agreement, and coordinate responses to the issues and challenges in European security.

In the process, candidate member countries were increasingly exposed, and thus socialised, to a widened approach to security akin to the ideas of security espoused by the Nordic countries, albeit founded on the bedrock of 'hard' military security.

It may well be that the evidence of the Baltic States at least considering, if not adopting, these ideas has more to do with presenting to NATO, and primarily to the United States, the image and speech that is required of a NATO member country. That is to say that the acceptance of these ideas may only be superficial, for the purpose of political presentation and accepted rhetoric.[27] Be that as it may, the socialising effect should not be underestimated.

---

26 It should be kept in mind that the Palme commission and its report were products of the international Social Democratic movement, and was received as such in the ensuing debates of the 1980: favourably on the left; unfavourably – or passed over in silence – on the right of the political spectrum.

27 Gambles writes that the Central and Eastern European states '… have been so anxious to avoid a "loose cannon on the deck" label which might harm their prospects of integration into Western institutions that they have often seemed to slip the other way. This can lead to the rather unreal kind of conformity expressed in the emollient rhetoric of official communiqués,

How does one explain why the ideas and concepts of so-called 'alternative security' took such a firm hold on Nordic security and defence policies? In a general sense, the understanding or definition of security in the Nordic countries was much broader than the more widely held view that equates security with military force.

The rejection of the pursuit of power in its traditional understanding goes a long way to the development of a security community. While the Nordic, Baltic and other European countries enjoy such a 'community', in their relations with Russia they do not. The current situation does not comply with Adler and Barnett's first initial phase in the development of a security community – the *nascent* phase, wherein

> ... governments do not explicitly seek to create a security community. Instead, they begin to consider how they might coordinate their relations in order to increase their mutual security; lower the transaction costs associated with their exchanges; and/or encourage further exchanges and interactions (1998, 50).[28]

The crucial problem is that Russia and the Baltic States in particular have demonstrated little or no interest in doing so. Both sides seem to entertain a *zero-sum* understanding of their mutual security.

Closing Remarks

We have traced the development of events and ideas relating to security in the Baltic Sea region before and after the end of the Cold War. Estonia, Latvia and Lithuania have now achieved the two major foreign policy goals they set out in the early 1990s, namely full membership in the European Union and the North Atlantic Treaty Organization. The assurance of their identity[29] and place as (Western) European states has been given, and their troublesome history with the Soviet Union is placed far behind them. Their security, as they see it, will be much stronger and more resolute than at any time in their history. The open questions in the region mainly concern Russia's new profile and the future responses of Finland and Sweden.

---

which can conceal real and legitimate conflicts of interest' (1995: 96). Further discussion of this question is in Ch. 9.

28 For a somewhat different perspective on this point, see Ch. 6 in this volume.

29 On the reshaping of Estonian identity, see Noreen 2001. For other works on the subject of identity in the Baltic States see Miniotaitė 2001; Lehti and Smith 2003.

Chapter 4

The Conditionality of Security Integration: Identity and Alignment Choices in Finland and Sweden[1]

Regina Karp

Introduction

Within the European security environment Finland and Sweden are institutional oddities. Their continued adherence to military non-alignment appears at odds with the structural changes brought about by the end of the Cold War. The collapse of the Soviet Union eliminated the strategic rationale for military non-alignment in Europe and NATO enlargements in 1999 and 2004 highlight the dynamics of intensified security integration. Seemingly impervious to structural changes and institutional growth in their immediate neighbourhood, Sweden and Finland have not abandoned policies crafted decades before. Whatever credibility military non-alignment had during the Cold War, such policies are puzzling today.

With membership in the EU and extensive relations with NATO, why have Sweden and Finland stayed militarily non-aligned? I argue that Sweden and Finland have adapted to structural changes in their security environment and that these national adaptations are both encouraged and limited by the respective strength of national identity. Both countries have an established record of navigating their security environment and its institutions. This record reveals a strategy of balancing between remaining Swedish and Finnish and institutionalizing national security.

The purpose of this chapter is to explain the apparent peculiarities of Swedish and Finnish approaches to security institutions within the context of theoretical debates on security integration. Departing from the dichotomy of competing rationalist and constructivist approaches, I argue that rationalist *and* constructivist perspectives have explanatory validity. The cases of Sweden and Finland show that neither the structure of the international environment nor national identity acts as a single consistent variable. Previously understood only as unique cases, the Nordic neutrals illustrate a general principle about the complex relationship between structure, on

---

1 My project colleagues have extensively commented on earlier chapter drafts and I thank them all for their many insightful comments, especially Olav F. Knudsen. I also wish to thank the many Finnish and Swedish officials and academics who have guided my research through interviews and discussions.

the one hand, and identity on the other. Structure and identity serve as independent variables and policy-makers relate to both to fashion policies. Hence *security choices are reflections of the interplay between the demands of structural adaptation and the demands of identity preferences*. Foreign, security and defence policies in Sweden and Finland reflect carefully orchestrated efforts to regulate how and where the demands of adaptation to structural change and identity preservation interact. Bringing these influences together to respond to the dual demands of adaptation and identity and keeping them apart when the demands of one threaten the credibility of the other, is the story of Swedish and Finnish post-Cold War foreign policy, integration into Europe and relations with NATO.[2]

These cases show that theorizing about security integration cannot rely upon compelling evidence in support of either rationalist or constructivist approaches. Finland and Sweden do not act in a purely calculative and instrumental fashion. Nor, however, do they act solely out of a sense of obligation to domestic or international norms. Hence this chapter explores the growing conviction among theorists of international politics that the two opposing poles of constructivism and rational choice can no longer be legitimately kept apart. To better understand how states react to incentives and disincentives in their environment, I do not separate rational choice from constructivism but aim to show that constructivism and rational choice inform one another (Adler 2002, 103). I argue that what motivates states is a rich combination of material and ideational interests. These emerge from a socially constructed context serving as backdrop to the analysis since it is within this context that we observe calculating and self-serving behaviour as well as norm appropriate action.

To promote norms and interests, states craft policies that promise success. Indeed, recent scholarship on European integration suggests that states, in the pursuit of normative goals, can act instrumentally even in an institutionalized, normatively dense, environment. States do not merely abide by rules and norms because it is the right thing to do. They also use these rules and norms to pursue interests (Schimmelpfennig 2000, 109-139; 2001, 47-80; 2003; Checkel 2001, 553-588; Cowles et al 2001). This research has made an important contribution to clarifying the relationship between interests and norms. It shows that states argue, compete, bargain and compromise on the basis of interests and norms, in order to promote them or resist them. They do this within an environment that they interpret according to established beliefs of what their interests and obligations are.

Examining the examples of Finnish and Swedish security policy since the end of the Cold War sheds light on the broader question of *how* interests and identity

---

2   Security integration is defined here as encompassing all intergovernmental and European level initiatives that lead states to institutionalize security cooperation or, at least, lead states to expect longer term reciprocal commitments to security cooperation. This definition builds on Wallace's distinction between 'formal' and 'informal' integration where integration is the result of deliberate steps taken at the national level, or emerges through a high degree of interdependence (Wallace 1990).

interact. While the issue of identity is the subject of debate in the foreign policies of many countries, it is on the European and transatlantic security context that the most intensive debate has focused. Here states are uniquely challenged to define their relations with the institutions that dominate their immediate environment. Much can be learned from studying how states shape institutions and, in turn, are shaped by them.

There is no predetermined course states take to assure their security in an institutional context. We cannot assume that states act purely to balance or abate threats, as realism would suggest (Walt 1988). Institutions offer more than augmentation of national capabilities. They also provide opportunities to share in the values and expectations existing members already hold. States might therefore want to join for reasons other than security. Neither can we assume that domestic interests determine incentives to seek security in institutions, as liberals would argue (Keohane and Martin 1995, 39-51; Moravcsik 1998). Such interests undoubtedly can play a role but they should not be equated with security concerns. While institutions help to spread the cost of security among members, economic savings may not be decisive when states consider institutional membership. Conversely, we cannot assume that states evaluate security integration only in terms of sharing a community of values, as constructivist would argue (Wendt 1994, 384-396) or out of a sense of obligation (Finnemore and Sikkink 1998). Though these values hold attraction, sharing them in an institutional setting might conflict with other important normative concerns. Questions of identity, for example, might gain in saliency and challenge states to consider the connections between security integration and identity preservations.

The Finnish and Swedish cases suit our purpose well. These two cases are examples of how states choose among the incentives and disincentives of security integration within an established framework of values and interests. The empirical evidence suggests that determining security choices involves complex processes of balancing between responding to changes in the security environment and maintaining a preferred security identity. As policy, such balancing of objectives ranks material and ideational goals equally. The material and ideational benefits of security and institutional belonging are as important as the material and ideational benefits of autonomy and identity.

The Finnish and Swedish case studies illustrate that security choices in a highly institutionalized and norm governed environment may neither be purely norm confirming nor purely egotistic. On the contrary, they reflect an intricate mix of motivations. We can therefore hypothesize that the socialization processes involved in security integration are conditioned by the interaction of normative and rationalist behaviour and that theoretical advance needs to focus on the *conditionality* that produces this interaction. In other words, how can we determine the extent to which states are willing to share in a security integration process? There are no obvious theoretical models that explain how security integration choices translate into policy.

Moreover, these two cases help illuminate different ways in which security choices and identity are connected. Though both countries have policies of military non-alignment, each has different motives. For Finland, military non-alignment is about *preserving* the option of joining NATO as part of an ongoing national debate on the meaning of its Cold War legacy of neutrality, its relationship with Russia, and its place in Europe. For Sweden, military non-alignment expresses resistance to change and an effort to *eliminate* alternative options. The Swedish focus is on strengthening links between non-alignment and the credibility of the country's international role. Membership in NATO is seen as compromising the sincerity of Stockholm's commitment to such global causes as disarmament, justice and development.

Thus the conditionality of security integration in these two countries varies considerably and serves different goals. Whereas Finland remains undecided on the longer-term merits of military non-alignment, Sweden has not embarked upon redefining the principal connection between autonomy and international engagement. As shown below, however, both countries have taken important steps to alleviate the cost of their current position vis-à-vis security integration.

Finally, these case studies point towards the need for more modest theoretical goals. Instead of trying to resolve fundamental, philosophical differences of ontology, much theoretical insight can be gained from empirical evidence (Walt 1999, 5-48; Schweller 2003: 311-347; Snyder 2003, 349-377; Duffield, Farrel, Price and Desch 1999, 156-180). As Fearon and Wendt (2002, 52-72) and Snidal (2002, 73-94; Katzenstein 1996) have argued, the strength of theoretical explanations rests not on demonstrating the presumed weaknesses of one theory vis-à-vis another but on how well different theories can accommodate empirical evidence typically only reserved for or associated with any one particular theoretical approach.

A more pragmatic rather than doctrinal approach to theory allows us to explore how much any one theory can explain. Our goal should not be, in the first instance, to explain all security behaviour, nor even to explain all variations of security behaviour within one individual issue area. Rather, our goal should be to develop mid-range theories that capture some of the key factors that inhibit or promote state choices. With regard to security integration, the cases of Finland and Sweden provide an opportunity to demonstrate the rich diversity of the empirical record. In turn, we gain a more informed understanding of how states weigh the costs and benefits of security integration, how they view incentives and disincentives, and how all these come together in policies. Theories used to explain these policies need to reflect their complex genesis (Laudan 1977, 41-43, 111).

Though Sweden and Finland are small states on the northern periphery of Europe, their persistent choice of military non-alignment shows that small states can achieve trade-offs between security integration and identity preferences. Power disparities need not translate into abandoning identity. Even in the security field, where low national capacities make a compelling case for military alignment, small states can maintain considerable autonomy and institutional choice. They need neither rush to embrace institutions nor suffer the drawbacks of marginalization. If small states can successfully negotiate between the demands for structural adaptation and identity preservation, larger states can be expected to use their much greater capacity to develop policies that reflect conditionality. Hence the examples of Finnish and

Swedish security integration are of both theoretical and practical relevance to advancing the broader inquiry into how states balance national identity and security choices and their impact on the future of European security integration.

The remainder of this chapter is divided into three parts. The first part presents the individual country case studies. It explores the relative strength of Finland's and Sweden's current military non-alignment stance and how they have translated material and ideational preferences into policy.

The second part examines the role of the institutional environment within which Finland and Sweden make their security choices. A distinction is made between an institutionally permissive and non-permissive environment and it is argued that the slow evolution of the European Union's security profile has allowed Finland and Sweden to pursue security policies that have not challenged military non-alignment. Recently, however, as part of the Union's deliberations on a constitution, the EU's security focus has sharpened. As a result, the erstwhile bargains these two countries had struck between integration and military non-alignment have reached a critical point. The greater the EU's institutional definition in the area of collective defence, the less tenable the military non-alignment stance becomes.

In the concluding part of the chapter, I explore the theoretical implications of identity and security integration. The section argues that questions of identity decisively shape the security choices of Finland and Sweden. Membership in the European Union and a focus on crisis management are goals both countries have pursued in an instrumentally rational fashion. This approach has avoided, or at least, postponed, decisions on identity change. Both countries have successfully balanced the twin needs of adaptation to their security environment and the preservation of identity. I find that state behaviour is more complex than neo-realists allow and more interest determined than constructivists credit.

If actual state behaviour reflects a synthesis between change and status quo, theory needs to recognize this. Constructivist approaches need to be more attentive to rational, goal-seeking state behaviour, especially if, as in the cases under consideration, such behaviour is identity-based. Rationalists, as realists, would benefit from better understanding the normative basis for security choices and how identity issues condition the interpretation of security options and resulting policies.

Identity and Non-Alignment: The Finnish and Swedish Cases

What is interesting in the study of Swedish and Finnish security choices is that both trends in environmental transformation and identity matter *equally*. Policy-makers respond to both with the aim of averting rivalry between them. If non-alignment were only about the preservation of identity, it would not explain active participation in EU and NATO crisis management operations. A policy focus on identity alone would render security policy not merely odd, but decidedly absurd. Sweden and Finland would not have integrated into the EU, nor cooperate as closely with NATO as they evidently do. Hence partial responsiveness to a changed environment has occurred. A 'non-alignment-live-or-die' attitude would quickly condemn both countries to marginalization, isolation, and obscurity; the ultimate free riders. It would expose them to strategic uncertainty and geopolitical vulnerability. Holding fast to non-alignment after the Cold War suggests that other, non-security factors come into play.

Likewise, if policy had been about structural adaptation alone, non-alignment would have long given way to membership in NATO. The neo-realist answer to Sweden's and Finland's post-cold War security environment would have led these countries to seek NATO membership at the earliest possible time following the end of the Cold War. They would have recognized the irrelevance of non-alignment. Instead, two rounds of NATO enlargement, in 1999 and 2004 respectively, passed and neither country put itself forward as a candidate for membership (Asmus 2002; Talbott 2002; Larrabee 2003).

These observations should make us cautious. It would indeed be misleading to view non-alignment *a priori* as either a normative or a security choice. The real world is more complex. As we examine the empirical record, we should remain open to the notion that military non-alignment may be an identity choice *and* a security choice and that what it represents is the product of harmonizing identity and security choices. There is no reason to assume that national identity is reflected in all public spheres except security. Nor should it be assumed that security choices exclude identity. In other words, security can be as much of a normative concern as identity is also the product of rationalist, self-interested calculations.

The relationship between identity and security has not been sufficiently explored in the literature. It therefore is not surprising to find the Finnish and Swedish cases primarily analyzed from a security perspective with only scant attention to how national identity impacts security choices and vice versa. Analyses generally focus on national capacities to meet threats, the development of relations with both the EU and NATO, the relative influence small countries have, or do not have, on their security environments. Above all, analyses of Finland and Sweden focus on the seemingly obvious fact that it is better for small states to be "in" than "out" when it comes to security institutions. Invariably, these studies conclude on the puzzle of why Finland and Sweden are such 'bad' realists.

It is my contention that the language of security studies, dominated by realist approaches, falls short of explaining why these two countries so strenuously cling to military non-alignment. Thus the literature debates military non-alignment but its realist focus fails to resolve the puzzle. Phrases such as 'post-neutral' (Vaahtoranta and Forsberg 2000), 'pre-allied' (Vaahtoranta and Forsberg 2000), and 'ambiguity at work' (Ojanen, Herolf and Lindahl 2000) all reflect attempts at fitting these cases into a realist framework.

Including identity in our analysis of security choices provides explanations that broaden the inquiry and resolve the puzzle of military non-alignment. The basic proposition advanced here is that the interplay between institutional security structure and identity can be specifically explained by recognizing that basic alignment choices reflect not only security considerations but also identity preferences. Hence we can postulate that there is an identity dimension to security choice and a security dimension to identity choice. Swedishness and Finnishness, ostensibly an identity choice, is also maintained through a security choice, namely non-alignment. It follows that changes in alignment also attest to changes in identity. The kind of alignment sought is not exclusively determined by the pressures of regional power distribution or the lure of reducing defence cost, it is also significantly influenced by how closely a match can be achieved between national and institutional identity. In short, whether and how to align are questions that go to the heart of how Finland and Sweden see themselves 'fit' into institutional identities.

For Finland, military non-alignment is about postponing a decision on NATO membership while at the same time reducing the cost of not deciding. For Sweden, military non-alignment is about maintaining its current posture while reducing the cost of resisting NATO membership. The interplay between structure and identity can be most clearly observed by studying how these two countries have worked to reduce the cost of not being NATO members. They want to be seen as effectively contributing to stability in their region and Europe at large. They look for opportunities to cooperate in the security field that stop short of collective defence. As active members of NATO's Partnership for Peace and the Euro-Atlantic Partnership Council, they want to be seen as providing security, not as security consuming free-riders. In the process, they have adopted similar policies and focus on crisis management in the EU and NATO as the only institutional arrangement that allows preservation of their identity *and* identification with institutional goals. As both countries examine their security environment, they do not want to remain outsiders and rebuff the rising norm of security integration. Neither, however, are they prepared to revamp their identities entirely and embrace the totality of institutional norms.

Finland

For Finland, the links between identity and military nonalignment are a direct result of the country's Cold War experience. The Finnish-Soviet Treaty of 1948 on friendship, cooperation and mutual assistance (FCMA) contained a provision not to join alliances directed against the Soviet Union. Throughout the Cold War, Finnish leaders adopted neutrality as peacetime strategy, anxiously avoiding policies that might offend the Soviets (Jakobson 1998, 9-48). Finnish caution governed foreign policy not only in the security field. Membership in or association with international organizations were carefully tailored to reflect specific Finnish needs (Ojanen 2000, 89-92).

Emerging from the shadow of the Soviet Union at the end of the Cold War, Finland would appear to have been free to align itself with NATO, following the example of newly independent Estonia, Latvia and Lithuania. Since the circumstances that had led to neutrality had disappeared, Finland could have fundamentally reoriented its foreign policy. It did to a degree. Key to understanding Finnish foreign policy choices is the adaptation of neutrality to military non-alignment.

What had been a political response to the geo-strategic position Finland found itself in between two hostile blocs during the Cold War, subsequently turned into an asset. Though membership in the EU in 1995 necessitated the abandonment of strict neutrality, Finnish leaders saw no contradiction between membership in the EU and non-alignment. As Ojanen (2000, 105) explains,

> It continued to be the best option. It was motivated by a concern for stability in the neighbouring Northern regions. In addition to furthering stability, Finnish security policy aims at avoiding the formation of new dividing political or military lines ... Thus, it is seen, Finland contributes best to stability if it is integrated in the EU but remains militarily non-aligned.

And, as then president Ahtisaari expressed it,

> As a member state of the European Union we are part of a political community of solidarity. If one member state is threatened, the threat is directed against the whole of the community... (quoted in Tiilikainen 2001, 63).

The EU became the core of Finnish security policy. Notably, this core was based on political connectedness rather than alliance membership. The transition from neutrality to non-alignment had made accession to the EU possible and even permitted an emphasis on the security role of the EU. At the same time, it was non-alignment that provided the rationale for staying out of NATO. It served as the security reason for institutional choice. Finland has, however, not finalized its position towards eventual NATO membership. The 1997 Defence White Paper emphasizes that security policy is based on 'prevailing circumstances' and that 'the effectiveness of the policy of non-alliance' is open to reassessment. Hence military non-alignment is not a goal in and of itself, but a pragmatic policy choice (Sivonen 2000, 94).

For realists, Finnish security policy is easily explicable. Rather than aligning itself fully, Finland has taken those steps that transformed its security situation from isolation to connectedness. At the same time, these steps stop short of the more fundamental and, in its domestic and international impact, less controllable move towards NATO membership. With accession to the EU, Finland has gained the 'multilateralization' of its relationship with Russia and decreased its political vulnerability. Since Russia does not pose a territorial threat, the need to do more, that is to join NATO, is not obvious. After all, were circumstances to change, Finland could reassess the NATO option.

On the other hand, realism does not address the issue of Finnish identity. In an otherwise excellent description of a range of Finnish alignment choices, Pursiainen and Saari (2002, 35) conceive of the country's cooperation with the alliance only in an instrumental fashion. Security cooperation appears, they argue, 'as a conscious but concealed preparation for NATO membership'. If not 'bad' realists, since they keep the NATO option open, Finns are seen as 'hidden' realists.

Normative perspectives, too, are offered. Finnish security choices also have roots in national identity (Möttölä 2001, 123). From this perspective, we also see the positive connotations of the Cold War policy of neutrality. 'Neutrality,' Ojanen argues, 'was a synonym for independent decision-making capacity and autonomous policies,' and led to the emergence of 'neutrality as a part of Finland's identity' (Ojanen 2000, 91; Tiilikainen 1998). Archer (2003, 57-70) and Browning (1999) suggest that the longevity of neutrality is underestimated in analyses of Finnish foreign policy. Though neutrality was a policy choice, they argue that the way in which neutrality was domestically propagated led to its internalization. Neutrality, as the dominant narrative, came to exclude all dissent. It '... became part of the identity of Finland, and therefore part of being Finnish' (Archer 2003, 61). How was it possible for policy choice to become internalized?

Joenniemi (2002, 182-213), offering a sweeping historical evaluation of the relationship between state and society in Finland, provides a possible answer. His main proposition is that Finnish national identity is not as firmly established as one might think; hence it is able to accommodate significant flexibility. Joenniemi traces the main features of Finnish identity to centuries of rule by Sweden and Russia which prevented the rise of a territorially defined national identity. Deprived of independence until 1917, the Finnish concept of nation developed around the Herderian idea of *Kulturnation*, a nation defined not by nationalism and statehood but through its cultural attributes, especially its language (Joenniemi 2002,194-197; Jakobson 1998, 12-13). Though a more Hegelian notion of *Staatsnation* emerged with independence and war in the 1930s and 1940s, it was never quite able to displace cultural connectedness as the organizational inspiration of Finnishness. As a result, Finnish identity was never as 'fixed' in nationalist terms as might have been the case had Finns gained statehood before cultural identification had substituted for its absence.

Following this line of argument, we are better equipped to understand Finland's security choices. Internalization of neutrality happened because it did not clash with pre-existing notions of what it is to be Finnish. Similarly, entry into the European Union was accomplished without much debate because there was no nationally defined Finnishness to fall back on. Finland was looking for cultural connectedness. This also explains why Finland could emphasize the security aspect of EU membership before the EU had developed an actual security dimension (Koivisto 1997, 246; Haikio 1997, 83-96). Lingering neutralist tendencies are accommodated by a non-aligned posture. Such tendencies, however, do not appear to stand in the way of further integration into the EU, though they continue to close the door to NATO membership. On the outskirts of Europe, being part of the European Union conveys a sense of ideational grounding believed to offset geographic remoteness. If Finnish identity has become Europeanized, we can expect a strengthening of the country's commitments to deepening integration (Tiilikainen 2000, 62-64).

The choice of military non-alignment thus reflects a complex mix of realist and ideational considerations. Finland's geopolitical situation clearly suggests taking national security seriously (Väyrynen 2003, 29). Yet we also see that Finland has infused its security thinking with normative considerations that preserve the option of joining NATO without making it inevitable. The point is that Finland was not looking for territorial security but for normative anchoring (Himanen 2003, 21-22; Jacobsen 1998, 120). After the Soviet collapse, Finland strenuously avoided being viewed as the fourth Baltic state or any other Eastern European state in need of large scale political transformation. It did not suffer from a security deficit (Möttölä 2001, 124).

For the time being, the 'prevailing circumstances' that form the basis of the Finnish policy of military non-alignment appear stable. Indeed, after NATO and EU enlargement to the Baltic States, regional stability has become the responsibility of these institutions, a development that reduces the urgency for realizing the Finnish NATO option. The more integrated the region as a whole, either in the EU or in NATO, the greater Finland's own connectedness and the lesser the possibility of renewed marginalization. The cost of not being a NATO member has become smaller over time. Bar a resurgence of Russian meddling in Baltic affairs, still a possibility, the distinct lack of urgency to resolve the NATO question will continue.

Though committed to integration, lingering neutralist thinking does shape Finnish attitudes towards security integration in the EU. It is ironic to note that the country that joined the EU for security reasons is not at all sure how it should support CFSP and ESDP now that the Union has made foreign and defence policy its next integration focus. Finland emphasizes the need for joint approaches, lest different national opinions 'risk splitting the Union and thus weakening the CFSP' on such issues as intensified cooperation in the defence field and the transatlantic relationship (Tuomioja 2003). At the same time, Finland is keenly aware that the EU is moving towards greater military capability and autonomy and that its own connectedness with Europe cannot be insulated from calls for more cooperation in security affairs (Tuomioja 2004). Hence Finnish leaders can be seen to carefully balance their own preference for continued military non-alignment with intensified security cooperation in the EU and the possibility of NATO membership in the future (Vanhanen 2004a, 2004b).

Above all, Finland does not appear ready to resolve the question of national identity in favour of any one institution. In fact, it would be a mistake to view the Finnish situation as one merely of policy decisions. As in the Swedish case, there is still a noticeable detachment on the part of Finnish society from issues that have impacted on Finland but for which no discourse space has been created. This leads Vogt (2004, 74) to suggest that Finnish national identity is 'closed' in that it has become locked into unresolved debates about what it is to be Finnish. As a result, Finnish leaders turn political caution into a virtue. 'The most important lesson of history,' says Prime Minister Vanhanen, 'is the principle of cautiousness' (quoted in Vogt 2004, 74).

Such caution is also evident in EU data. 62 percent of Finns, the highest percentage in the Union, identify with their national identity only, compared to the EU average of 42 percent (Eurobarometer 60.1, Autumn 2003). There are no attempts by the government to lead a debate on a broader understanding of identity.

The much anticipated 2004 Defence White Paper was disappointing in this respect. Indeed, it largely avoids raising what many commentators believe to be the three most important Finnish security concerns namely, the transatlantic relationship, the decline of democracy in Russia and the development of the EU's security role.

Together, these issues question the viability of continued military non-alignment (Heikka 2005, 14-16). By implication, they also question the future of Finnish identity. The solidarity afforded by membership in the European Union is no substitute for national security or national identity. The 'stickiness' of its Cold War identity nonetheless inhibits institutional decisiveness for the time being.

Political parties reinforce this indecisiveness. Though the Swedish[3] People's Party supports NATO membership, it is small and thus even when part of the government exerts little influence. The much larger Social Democratic Party and the conservative Centre and National Coalition parties represent a lowest common denominator consensus on foreign and defence policy that prefers the status quo of security cooperation with the European Union. The NATO alternative is firmly ruled out and unlikely to be seriously considered in the near future. As Foreign Minister Erkki Tuomioja explains, 'as Finland does not have any reason to give up its military non-alignment in the present situation, the careful wait-and-see policy [...........] remains a well-founded line of action with respect to NATO membership. This policy line does not hurt anyone, and is not in conflict with anyone's interests' (quoted in Helsingin Sanomat, 23 March, 2004). Finns themselves have overwhelmingly supported the policy status quo with support for NATO hovering around 20 percent mark. Under the earlier leadership of Prime Minister Paavo Lipponen, the Social Democrats had appeared to move towards NATO and it is widely believed that if the Social Democrats had won the parliamentary elections in 2003, Finland would already be a NATO member. Instead, Lipponen lost and though the Social Democrats returned to office, they did so as junior partners to the Centre Party. This outcome empowered the anti-Nato wing of the Social Democratic Party, now also supported by the President of Finland, Tarja Halonen (Dagens Nyheter, 21 February, 2004).

More recently, the National Coalition Party, instrumental for securing popular support for EU membership in the early 1990s, has broken ranks. In December 2004, the party leadership issued a statement arguing for a departure from military non-alignment. With increasing defence cooperation in the EU, it was argued, Finland could no longer credibly refer to itself as militarily non-aligned. Endorsement of NATO membership has also come from former President Martti Ahtisaari who feels that 'for Finland to get out from under the shadow of the Cold War, the country should be involved in all Western organizations, including NATO' (Helsingin Sanomat, 28 February, 2005).

The extent to which a break in the national consensus on security can be translated into pro-NATO policy remains to be seen. To win general elections, any one of Finland's three biggest parties needs to form a coalition with one of the other

---

3 A party seeking its support mainly in Finland's Swedish-speaking minority. (Editor's remark.)

two. Hence, unless the Social Democrats or the Centre Party likewise adopt a more positive attitude towards military alignment with NATO, the National Coalition Party is unlikely to make a decisive difference to Finnish foreign and security policy.

The competition got close, however, when in the run-up to presidential elections in early 2006, the debate on NATO membership came back into focus. In a closely contested election that denied her an absolute majority in the first round, Tarja Halonen faced Sauli Niinistö, the candidate of the National Coalition Party and an outspoken supporter of alliance membership. Returned to office for a second six-year term, Halonen sees no urgency for NATO membership and continues to describe it as 'only an option'. Niinistö, by contrast, believes that Finland should not sit out another round of NATO enlargement and criticizes the credibility of the 'NATO option' as policy. 'From NATO's point of view,' he argues, 'Finland is like a postage stamp on a letter. We are not on the inside, but we are stuck on as tightly as possible' (Helsingin Sanomat, 22 January 2006).

What is significant about this election is that in the run-off against Niinistö, Halonen secured only 51.8 percent of the vote against her opponent's 48.2 percent. With Niinistö having so clearly campaigned on the NATO ticket, we may see the emergence of a refashioned security discourse that links Finland to NATO as a *European* security institution reminiscent of earlier pro-EU arguments that paved the way for membership in the Union. Indeed, Niinistö believes NATO to be increasingly more European as '… the Americans have largely committed themselves elsewhere' (Helsingin Sanomat, 22 January 2006).

A discourse that describes the alliance in non-hegemonial, European terms resonates with Finnish desires to anchor itself at Europe's core. Such a discourse might be able to canvass greater support for NATO membership and create opportunities for shifting a membership debate towards aligning Finnish and NATO identity. In the process, we might see a narrowing of the gap between how NATO is described and how Finland views itself. For the time being, however, close cooperation with NATO does not appear to require resolution of the identity issue. Opinion polls conducted in the fall of 2005 show 67 percent of voters satisfied with Finnish-NATO relations (Ministry of Defence, 2005).

Sweden

For Sweden, military non-alignment is the most recent interpretation of a well established and popularly supported national vision of independence and activism. The Sweden that emerged after 1945 is a country with a long-standing sense of self. Though compromising its historic neutrality through secret cooperation with NATO during the Cold War, Sweden achieved a remarkable degree of independence. The purpose of maintaining independence was to fashion a foreign policy that reflected the most prominent values of the domestic Swedish model – a prosperous welfare state/ society, collective social advancement, social equality, freedom and democracy.

In a seminal rendition of the historical sources of today's Swedish 'model', Trägårdh (2002) traces the development of modern Sweden's reluctance to integrate in security institutions, its need for independence despite its size, the legitimacy of non-alignment, and its seemingly irrepressible international activism, to the development of state-society relations. The onset of a Swedish national identity came with the 15th century rebellion of the peasants, led by Engelbrekt in the region of Dalarna, against their Danish and German rulers. Thus saved from foreign domination, the origins of the Swedish state provide fertile ground for national mythmaking.

Most prominent among the mythmakers was Erik Gustaf Geijer, a 19th century conservative historian. The influence of Geijer, Trägårdh argues, was paramount and the themes of freedom, the *folk* and the independence of the Swedish souls he developed had an extraordinary influence on Sweden's subsequent sense of self. In the 1920s, Social Democrats, among them the later Prime Minister, Per Albin Hanson, evoked Geijer's conservative romanticism and fashioned it into a new social democratic narrative of the *folk*. 'The best of democratic traditions,' according to Hanson, 'can be found among peasants and workers. Just like the peasant class during its struggle for influence protected the *folk*-freedom, so has the working class. Here is a common heritage to administer'. This shrewd inclusion of the workers into the national narrative enabled the Social Democrats to connect their political goals with historic national themes. In the process, conservative liberalism failed to capitalize on the national myth and share in the development of foundational political ideas.

Over time, we see a merging of the ideas of state, nation, and society, a combination that came to full fruition after World War II when Swedes began to translate political cohesion into national projects of modernity, welfare and internationalism. The Sweden created after 1945 embraced modernity and turned it into a social ideology of collective advancement, equality, freedom and democracy. To many, the social experiment that had weaved historical narrative with rational and functional ideas of modern life had become quintessentially Swedish.

At the international level, the self-confidence created at home translated into unprecedented activism. Under the leadership of Olof Palme, the belief took hold that international divisions, rivalries, and self-serving ideologies could be transcended similarly to Sweden's own domestic success story. Sweden began to speak out on issues that far exceeded its own capacities to bring about change. Capacities were, however, not the motivating force. Rather, the driving force behind Sweden's focus on development, disarmament and conflict prevention was the idea of setting examples.

Swedish leadership was used to bringing to the international agenda – otherwise dominated by superpower competition – those problems of international welfare whose resolution would benefit the international community at large. Sweden would make it its international mission to speak out against the arms race, against human rights violations, against North-South divisions, and speak for the strengthening of the rule of law and peaceful resolution of conflicts. Where others only see difference, Sweden would seek commonalities. The 1982 Palme Commission Report on

Common Security illustrates the Swedish mission and approach perfectly (Palme Commission 1982).

The parallels between Sweden's domestic achievements and its international goals are evident. Where others were mired in social immobility, Sweden had created a prosperous, classless society. Where others were captive to destructive ideologies, Sweden had implemented a rational and functionalist approach. It had done nothing short of 'secularizing' its politics, turning domestic political strife into a question of efficient administration.

Internationally, this meant that Sweden brought to the table an agenda it clearly felt to be superior to others. Though Dörfer (1997, 15) dismisses Sweden's international ambitions as wishful thinking and naiveté, it would be wrong to do so. The issue is not only whether Sweden has been successful, but how Sweden interprets its international role and the linkage between identity and political choice. Indeed, as Ruth (1984, 71) suggests, 'equality at home and justice abroad have come to be regarded as complementary and mutually supporting values'.

Sweden's voice would only be heard if it was not beholden to any institution or organization that had the power to limit Sweden's independence. To act as mediator, bridge-builder, conciliator, Sweden's motives must be based on the high principles of international welfare, not beholden to the preferences of any power, camp, or institution. Sweden's goals are not political in the usual sense of maximizing utility for self-serving ends. Nor is Sweden intent on projecting power. Its goals take their cues from the deeply entrenched belief that rationality and social progress are superior to and can prevail over the pursuit of self-serving interests and discriminating hierarchy.

Seen in this light, the end of the Cold War did not affect Sweden's belief in its international mission. Being neutral during the Cold War was not about an alternative security strategy but a rejection of ideological competition as the organizational framework of international order (Wahlbäck 1986). The belief that Sweden must remain independent in order to be internationally effective is deeply embedded (Bjurner 2003, 43; Huldt 2003, 47; Sundelius 1989, 1-13; Åstrom 1989, 15-33). It also explains Sweden's reluctance towards European integration, overcome only by economic crisis in the early 1990s which paved the way towards serious pursuit of EU membership (Malmborg 2001, 38-59). But, as Malmborg argues, given the choice between abandoning its historic neutrality and modifying what European integration meant, Sweden modified both. This allowed Sweden to highlight the EU's economic dimension, emphasize the political connectedness, and turn neutrality into military non-alignment (Malmborg 2000, 39-43).

In a jointly published article in the daily *Aftonbladet* (November 20, 1999), Foreign Minister Anna Lindh and Defence Minister Björn von Sydow bluntly stated that

> ... non-alignment is a strength, not a burden. This means that we can actively work for peace and in addition have the trust of different conflict parties. Non-alignment has made

it possible for Swedes such as Dag Hammarskjöld, Olof Palme and Carl Bildt to undertake important international peace missions under the authority of the UN.

(One might add to this list Rolf Ekeus, who served as chairman of UNSCOM in Iraq, and Hans Blix, former director of the IAEA and head of the UN weapons inspection team in Iraq.)

Continuity in foreign policy features prominently in major foreign policy speeches that emphasize Sweden's global commitment, the freedom of action and the credibility of its disarmament policy afforded by military non-alignment. Yet in order to reflect Sweden's changing institutional environment, important interpretative adjustments to the concepts of non-alignment and integration continue to be made. It is important to note, however, that these adjustments have been made to *preserve* what is seen to be the essence of Swedish identity, namely its commitment to strengthening international norms, reducing international strife and bringing about a more equitable international society.

Quite clearly, as EU member, Sweden was no longer *politically* neutral (Miles 1997, 179-220). In 1992, in preparation for EU accession in 1995, the conservative government of Carl Bildt reformulated its security policy and focused it more narrowly on non-participation in military alliances in peacetime with the possibility of remaining neutral in conflicts. In a seminal speech in November 1991, Bildt declared military non-alignment rather than neutrality as the core of Swedish foreign policy (cited in Malmborg, 41).

Though this reform amounts to a significant reorientation, it is important to note that even a step as consequential as membership in the European Union did not dislodge Sweden's basic security preference (Winnerstig 2001, 89). Indeed, as Huldt suggests, more than security preferences are at stake. Swedes look to non-alignment as protecting themselves from the federalist pressures in the EU. Non-alignment '... is thus a repository for that old-time neutrality. Again, "identity" plays a role', (2003, 48).

That the relationship between integration and non-alignment was strained by Sweden's accession to the EU cannot be denied. The Maastricht Treaty on European Union was accepted in its entirety, including its integration goals in the security and defence sector.

Further definitional refinement was introduced in 2002 based on consensus among the major left and centre-right parties (Regeringskansliet 2002a). The government now states that military non-alignment 'has served us well' (Regeringskansliet 2002b). Leaders firmly reject the notion that full participation in CFSP and ESDP contradicts military non-alignment (Regeringskansliet 2004).

The fact that Sweden has been carefully balancing military non-alignment with engagement in the security dimension of the EU is clearly evident. Hallenberg (2000, 25) argues that the government has '... a clear tendency to portray the agreements in the EU on the future of the CFSP ... as having fewer ramifications for the future of the Swedish strategy of non-alignment ...' than might be warranted. In order to minimize contradictions between Swedish preferences and commitments arising from EU membership, Sweden has emphasized crisis management as the backbone of EU foreign policy and as a focus Stockholm is comfortable with.

Crisis management does not conflict with military non-alignment. On the contrary, it allows Sweden to make credible connections between what the Union does in the security field and what Sweden itself sees as legitimate foreign policy goals, namely conflict abatement, respect for human rights, restoration of functioning states, and furthering the norms of a just international society. Indeed, Swedish leaders actively pursue strengthening the EU's spectrum of crisis management capabilities in both pre- and post-conflict situations, spanning a range of civilian and military capabilities.

Evaluating Sweden's approach to security cooperation with the EU, the success of Swedish policy is undeniable. Throughout the decade of EU membership, Stockholm has combined involvement in developing CFSP and ESDP with reservations about the ultimate goals of security integration. A clear line has been drawn between crisis management and collective defence. The belief that mutual defence obligations are incompatible with military non-alignment is firmly established. Though some scholars argue that the current meaning of non-alignment is hollow (Ojanen, 2002; Vaahtoranta, 2000) and some even suggest that it is a political artefact (Dahl, 1999), the point here is a different one. Viewing non-alignment in purely realist security terms, it lacks the credibility of a robust, interest-based policy. As we have seen, however, a focus on realism ignores the synergistic link between identity and non-alignment. Sweden is as much motivated by preserving its idea of self as it is compelled to operate within a policy-shaping environment. Those same policy choices ultimately determine how identity can best be preserved. Hollow or not, balancing security integration and national identity enjoys wide public support.

Among the major political parties, only the centre-right Liberal Party and Moderate Party are strongly in favour of a NATO option yet only the Moderate Party can claim to also have a majority of its supporters in favour of alliance membership. The other two centre-right parties, the Centre Party and the Christian Democrats, are firmly opposed to Sweden joining NATO. The governing Social Democratic Party has traditionally opposed military alignment and sees itself as the guardian of Swedish values at home and abroad. Passionately opposed to membership in either the EU or NATO are the Left Party and the Greens on whose support in parliament the Social Democrats rely.

With the Left solidly against and the Right split on alliance membership, it is unlikely that a future centre-right government is going to make NATO a top priority. It may not even be likely for NATO to be prominent in an election campaign since the Right cannot make it a winning issue and, were it to try, would enhance the chances for a Left coalition. Popular rejection of NATO reflects the difficulties political parties have in effecting an alternative to military non-alignment at the national level. Opinion polls consistently show less than 25 percent support for NATO membership (Bjereld 2005). A large majority of Swedes believe NATO would compromise the independent Swedish voice in international affairs and reduce the effectiveness of the Swedish example.

The history of Sweden's international activism and commitment to human rights, justice and disarmament does not speak of policy choices based on realist conceptions of power. Sweden does not seek power in its traditional sense. Rather, Sweden seeks recognition of its normative model of international order. The connections Sweden has made between the domestic model of a just society and its international mission show that its foreign policy is a constitutive part of national identity. Military non-alignment is thus an expression of Swedish identity. It defines the normative thrust of Sweden's approach to international relations and enables the pursuit of normative policies.

At the same time, normative internationalism is recognizably consequential. In its choices of security integration, Sweden clearly identifies the preservation of non-alignment as a primary national interest and carefully weighs the cost and benefits of security integration. Sweden therefore views security integration as both necessary and desirable where it serves to enhance existing normative preferences.

The Conditionality of Security Integration: Permissive and Non-Permissive Institutional Environments

The security situation in Northern Europe offers security integration incentives and disincentives (Krohn 1996; Knudsen 1998; 1999: 3-19). The end of the Cold War opened up new security choices for countries in the region. With membership in the EU and NATO, Estonia, Latvia and Lithuania exercised these choices through full institutional integration. It was important to them to multilateralize their relations with Russia. They responded unequivocally to the break-up of the Soviet Union. The structural context that determined their security choices was the geopolitical reality of Russia as their neighbour and embeddedness in Euro-Atlantic institutions.

Finland and Sweden have made different choices. Their response to the structural changes at the end of the Cold War was to join the European Union but not NATO. Their goal was to maintain their militarily non-aligned status. What made this choice possible? What might undo it? And, what might be the implications for Finnish and Swedish identity and security?

The evidence shows that the answers are to be found in the state and shape of European and transatlantic security institutions. The more loosely defined institutional structures are, the more successful Sweden and Finland are in harmonizing the dual demands of institutionalizing their security and preserving national identity. Tightly defined institutions, where demands on members are clearly articulated and mechanisms exist to show that members indeed play their assigned parts effectively, leave states with little flexibility. Meeting their responsibilities, conforming to institutional goals, and avoiding second-rate status become primary national objectives. More loosely defined institutions, where state responsibilities can be interpreted, processes are sluggish, rules are vague, and end-states undetermined provide members with a relatively permissive environment.

Cooperation with such institutions offers states flexibility and opportunity. Flexibility creates room for states to interpret the meaning of the institution, hence its relevance to state interests and normative concerns. States can choose how to cooperate, where to get engaged and at what level. They can limit their involvement to suit a diversity of interests as well as deepen their cooperation when it appears suitable. In short, states are able to keep options open, or they can make the case that multiple interpretations about institutional purposes and goals can be accommodated. None of this suggests that the state-institution relationship is weak or marginal. On the contrary, institutional linkages can be very important to states precisely because they do not define the exact nature of the relationship. Indeed, cooperation is attractive in the first place because it offers states considerable room to manage commitments.

Loosely defined institutions allow states to take advantage of the opportunities of institutional development. Where institutional structures, rules and norms are vague or, at least, only partially defined, new initiatives can be brought in and their subsequent shape influenced. If such conditions prevail, even small states can effectively contribute, present ideas and champion causes.

The cases of Sweden and Finland show that a permissive institutional environment is more conducive to policies aimed at equitable responses to external adaptation and identity preservation. Though we have noted significant differences between Finnish and Swedish motivations regarding non-alignment, both countries have viewed the European Union as offering greater opportunity to adapt and preserve than NATO. The EU's institutional development in the defence and security field has only slowly taken shape, thereby enabling Sweden and Finland to anticipate its further evolution. Equally important is that slow institutional development has opened up opportunities for supporting the development of the EU security identity in areas that match identity preferences.

Key to Sweden's and Finland's engagement with an emerging EU security capacity has been their emphasis on crisis management capabilities. Indeed, it was a joint Finnish-Swedish initiative in 1996 that led to the inclusion of crisis management, in the shape of the Petersberg Tasks, in the 1997 Amsterdam Treaty (Vaahtoranta and Forsberg 2000, 14). This initiative, early on in their European Union membership, identified both as active players in an area that needed definition and leadership. For Sweden and Finland, crisis management as an EU task was, of course, an almost ideal opening into the European security arena. In the post-Dayton environment, the Union needed to strengthen its credibility and enhance its visibility in security affairs. Sweden and Finland seized upon this opportunity for institutional development by steering it into a direction that they could wholeheartedly support without questioning their non-aligned status. They were able to align the emerging institutional identity with their national identity and, in turn, were able to achieve compatibility between non-alignment and engagement.

Second, both have consistently resisted proposals to move to majority decision-making in CFSP, especially when emphasis seemed to shift towards the *hard security* portion of ESDP. Their insistence on unanimity in this area assures an intergovernmental approach where governments are in charge and can ultimately block undesirable developments, such as the emergence of collective defence responsibilities. Neither country would, however, regard the exercise of its veto power as a policy success. On the contrary, policy success is a function of their ability to avoid developments in the EU's security role that expose their preferences for crisis management alone as the agreed EU security arena.

Third, neither has supported calls for deeper integration in security and defence allowing some countries to move at a faster pace and streamline their defence activities more than other EU members. The danger of the EU turning into a two-tier or two-class institution is clearly understood in Stockholm and Helsinki. It would expose differences in national security policies and set Sweden and Finland apart from the rest. Indeed, Swedish and Finnish policy has been to avoid developments that would compromise their full and active participation in CFSP and ESDP and, when they were unable to do so, to insist on wording that keeps open the option of participating in deeper defence integration (Toumioja 2003; Ojanen 2004, 31-36).

Fourth, Sweden and Finland have unequivocally supported the establishment of an EU military capability and advocate close cooperation between the EU and NATO. Again, the key caveat to support has been the successful direction of EU security activities into areas that are safe for the preservation of national identity. Thus they have been opposed to the creation of a European army and maintain a fine dividing line between EU crisis management tasks and NATO collective defence responsibilities.

An equally fine line is drawn between the solidarity among EU member states and associated commitments. The EU constitution's *Solidarity Clause* commits member states to mutual assistance in case of a terrorist attack or if they are the victims of a natural or man-made disaster. If a member state is the victim of an armed aggression, '... the other member states shall have towards it an obligation of aid and assistance by all the means in their power, in accordance with Article 51 of the United Nation's Charter' (European Union 2004). Both countries emphasize that the nature and extent of assistance rests with national governments. Here again we see evidence of Stockholm and Helsinki shaping their actual obligations to avoid the impression of predetermined commitments.

Fifth, both countries have successfully introduced wording into the EU constitution that assures that obligation of mutual assistance '... do not prejudice the specific character of the security and defence policy of certain member states'. In addition, Sweden and Finland welcome the constitutional affirmation that for its members, NATO '.... remains the primary foundation of their collective defence and the forum for its implementation'.[4] Once again we see the balancing of Finnish and Swedish objectives: commitment to solidarity, but not to the extent that non-alignment and commitments become incompatible. A clear distinction is being made between NATO and EU responsibilities.

These examples of Swedish and Finnish EU policy provide convincing evidence of balance being sought between adaptation to changing external structures and

---

4 Quotations from current policy declarations.

national identity. The emphasis on crisis management has focused the EU defence and security dimension on the kinds of *common* security activities that do not threaten non-alignment in its identity function. An additional benefit is that crisis management resonates with the more traditional international engagement through the United Nations where both countries already have considerable experience. Enthusiastic support of EU crisis management is an attempt to define *how* the European Union understands its security role and *where* it brings its military capabilities to bear. In Finnish and Swedish eyes, Europe must do everything it can to equip itself with the requisite crisis management tools but must not impinge on NATO's collective defence role. Leaders of both countries make the case that NATO takes care of the collective defence needs of its members, hence the Union neither needs to acquire such a capability nor should it aim to in the future.

The preferred crisis management focus of the EU explains Finnish and Swedish support for a strong NATO, too. Though at first glance counterintuitive, in that the desire for a strong alliance should logically lead to their own membership, Sweden and Finland fear that a decline of NATO might lead to EU collective military capabilities. Such a development would inevitably threaten their non-aligned status. By the same logic, Sweden and Finland are comfortable with a close EU-NATO relationship, because it solidifies an EU crisis management profile and keeps collective defence in NATO.

From a Swedish-Finnish perspective, the permissive institutional environment of the EU has avoided marginalization and invited the possibility of institutional definition complementary to national preferences. EU membership has not demanded the abandonment of non-alignment, nor has it muffled foreign policy. On the contrary, it opened up new opportunities to actively assist in the evolution of the very dimension of the EU that holds the biggest threat to continued non-alignment, namely the Union's security role. At the same time, active participation in crisis management demonstrates that non-alignment does not mean being pacifist or free-riding.

As both countries have successfully defined their contribution to the EU's security dimension, two sets of questions have emerged. There is an obvious critical threshold beyond which security integration and non-alignment cannot go together. The goal for Sweden and Finland has traditionally been to avoid collective defence gaining ground within the EU. The Union's security dimension has focused on crisis management because it was the one security area *all* members could agree on. If this consensus were to shift, institutional focus on crisis management would erode and make it more difficult, if not impossible, for Helsinki and Stockholm to avoid the inherent contradiction between non-alignment and collective defence.

The second set of questions revolves around the future of NATO. The alliance has been engaged in large-scale transformations with efforts increasingly on crisis management, leading to convergence, if not competition with the EU. What separates the two organizations is no longer NATO's collective defence commitment but the division of crisis management tasks between Europe and the United States.

Together, these trends have produced the curious situations where commitments to the EU are potentially more costly in terms of maintaining a credible non-alignment policy than membership in NATO would exact. It is not possible for NATO to abandon Article 5 and officially declare that the alliance is no longer responsible for the security of its members. What NATO has done, however, is to evolve from a primarily Article 5 alliance during the Cold War into a global crisis management institution. The rationale for similar EU capabilities rests on the assumption that problems and crises exist in international relations where the United States is less affected than Europe. Under the Berlin Plus agreement between the EU and NATO, the Union can draw upon NATO's military capabilities to conduct its own crisis management operations. Through these arrangements, Finland and Sweden have come closer to NATO than ever before. Both countries welcome these developments since they still permit the distinction between the EU and NATO necessary for non-alignment. The real problem, however, lies elsewhere.

To increase its rapid reaction capabilities, the EU agreed in May 2004 to create rapid reaction battle groups, each consisting of 1,500 troops, deployable within ten days. Sweden and Finland have pledged their participation and are forming a joint battle group. For these battle groups to have the desired rapid deployability, they need to be readily available. Though Helsinki and Stockholm maintain that it is governments who decide when, where and how to respond militarily, the requirements of effective missions are more likely to determine how much of a pre-commitment states have to make. Thus the much treasured independence in decision-making is severely compromised. To insist that the principle of independence has been maintained is increasingly untenable.

Other developments in EU security and defence also impact upon military non-alignment. Europe's new constitution clearly shows the unprecedented progress made in this area over the past few years. As already mentioned, it contains a 'solidarity' clause and provisions for 'permanent structured cooperation' open to members who have made more binding commitments to one another. The former commits members to come to the aid of another suffering a terrorist attack. The latter permits members to make mutual defence commitments. Again, Sweden and Finland emphasize the need for the EU as a whole to develop its defence capabilities rather than for a few to set the pace. They also emphasize that members themselves can decide how to contribute to intensified defence cooperation as well as how to assist each other.

Developments in the European Union point to the inescapable conclusion that military non-alignment policies can no longer rely on the permissive institutional environment that had previously made association possible and credible. Though the EU is not about to turn into a military alliance, the requirements of crisis management impose institutional clarity (Andersson 2006). As NATO has evolved into a crisis management organization relying on coalitions of the willing, it has devolved into a much more permissive institution (Rynning 2006). The European Union, on the other hand, in its pursuit of crisis management capabilities, has had to tighten its erstwhile vague and lose provisions.

It is the changes within the European Union, not in NATO, that pose the biggest threat to non-alignment. Crisis management in the EU is imposing its own rules of commitment. The willingness of some members to think in terms of deeper defence integration exposes the fragility of Finnish and Swedish positions.

Though the rejection of the EU constitutional treaty by referenda in France in May and in the Netherlands in June 2005 has brought the European project to a grinding halt, its impact on security integration remains to be determined. No doubt, adoption of the constitution by all EU members would have locked in place a shared approach to foreign and security policy. It would have further defined the Union as an actor in the security field and strengthened an institutional approach to security integration. At the end of the day, however, the death of the constitution may not derail security integration as such since the momentum towards foreign policy and security cohesion is not driven by constitutional processes alone. Through Berlin Plus, the EU has already begun to define its relationship with NATO and its concept of rapidly deployable battle groups is not endangered by constitutional failure. What is lost with the deadlock over the constitution is a certain orderliness regarding process, transparency of how security integration is to proceed and the precise national commitments.

Neither Sweden nor Finland can credibly resist the dynamics of security integration, whether it takes place as part of a European-wide constitution or in a more ad-hoc fashion. Resistance would highlight the previously well-hidden compromises between active participation in developing crisis management capabilities and military non-alignment. Perhaps worse, resistance would not stop defence integration but weaken their voice within the EU generally. Institutional and national identity, so carefully matched heretofore, might then drift apart. It is still the case, as both countries argue, that security and defence issues will be decided by governments. Nevertheless, it has to be recognized that what other governments are now willing to do differs fundamentally from the kind of loosely defined security and defence policies military non-alignment relies on.

The critical issue for the credibility of military non-alignment is the purpose an autonomous military capability is to serve (Smith 2004, 209-264). One of the major forces driving security integration arises from the momentum towards completing the European Union. After the European Single Act in the 1980s and the introduction of a common currency in the 1990s, security has emerged as the next critical integration domain. Without integration in the security sector, Europe will not become a coherent international actor in its own right. Without security integration, Europe will perpetuate a dependence on the United States that contradicts its independent role in other sectors of public life. To avoid such lopsidedness, Europe needs to decide how much security integration it needs for the credibility of integration as a whole (Howorth 2000; Howorth and Keeler 2003, 3-21; Gnesotto 2004). With the failure of the constitution these issues have become more, not less important.

The second issue driving security integration concerns the international environment. Europe has global interests and is globally engaged in an environment that can challenge its interests. Though not threatened in its immediate vicinity,

Europe needs to be able to advance and, if necessary, protect and defend its interests wherever they may be threatened. Since Europe has relied on the United States to provide security throughout the Cold War, uncertainties in the transatlantic relationship have reinforced a growing sense among Europeans that crises in far-away places impact upon economic growth and stability back home.

Oscillating between what is necessary in support of a coherent integration process and what is desirable to safeguard EU interests around the globe, European leaders have only cautiously embarked upon defining what the Union should ultimately be capable of. Questions about the future relationship between Europe and the United States and the final shape of the EU are part and parcel of debates on what military capabilities to acquire for what missions (Daalder 2003, 147-166; Steinberg 2003, 113-146; Pond 2004).

It is therefore not surprising that security integration remains at the intergovernmental level. EU member governments are decidedly rationalist when evaluating the degree to which security integration is necessary for the EU to be a credible actor and the degree to which security integration is demanded by an evolving threat environment. Though a common security strategy was approved in December 2003, decisions on the use of force remain a national prerogative.

How the issues of managing international security are resolved between the European Union and NATO is of direct relevance to pursuing a military non-alignment strategy. The practicalities of crisis management suggest that NATO and the EU will be compelled to work together ever more closely. As Dobbins (2005) argues,

> it is possible to envisage military contingencies in which the European Union might be involved, but not NATO. It is not possible to conceive of the reverse. In any NATO-led military mission, all essential civil functions will inevitably have to be devolved to the European Union...

Thus even if the essential division between crisis management and collective defence remains institutionally separate, the very necessities of effective crisis management draw civilian and military capabilities ever more closely together. Consequently, the issue is no longer how to keep collective defence in NATO and out of the EU, but how to merge institutional capabilities in areas in which both Finland and Sweden are committed to sharing responsibility. The critical question is whether the bargain struck – i.e., the compromise between military non-alignment in its identity and security dimensions and security integration – can be maintained under conditions that compel Finland and Sweden to work ever more closely with NATO without becoming members themselves.

As we have seen, leaders in Helsinki and Stockholm managed their immediate post-Cold War environment well. They were successful in balancing identity and institutionalizing security. Finnishness and Swedishness could be successfully extended to embrace membership in the European Union. Indeed, "Europe" has successfully made it into the foreign policy and security discourse of both countries. The opportunity to embrace an entity larger than the national had presented itself with the underdevelopment of the EU's security dimension in the mid-1990s. This allowed Finland to move to connect with Europe without changing the regional balance, and allowed Sweden to pursue its international activism.

In the wake of the terrorist attacks in the United States, however, a new security era was ushered in. This is well recognized but has failed to lead to the kinds of adaptations the early post-Cold War years witnessed. Not surprisingly, questions have been asked in both countries about the ultimate goals of Finnish and Swedish security policies. In Finland, the government's position has been not to raise the issue of future EU security integration. According to Prime Minister Vanhanen, were Finland to indicate outright interest, it might suggest that the country suffered from a security deficit, an impression Finnish governments have traditionally wanted to avoid (Helsingin Sanomat, 12 September, 2005). Were the Finnish debate to shift to the security dimension proper – and the stalled EU constitution might have that effect – it would be difficult for Finland not to speak out.

Having associated EU membership with security, a dysfunctional Union has obvious security implications for Finland. Yet it appears that these implications do not compel Helsinki into greater activism. Hence, the government prefers the ambivalence of a defunct constitution to the recognition that a weakened Union might already have produced a security deficit for Finland. In addition, a less capable EU necessarily increases the role of NATO in European security. To speak under these conditions of a security deficit would return Finland to a debate about NATO membership the government has no desire to lead. To talk seriously about NATO membership would signal a departure from military non-alignment and a renewed debate about how security and identity choices are linked. As the presidential election campaign has shown, however, the NATO question has remained politically potent.

Opting for the EU as the preferable because less demanding security institution, Finland hoped to benefit from the general rather than the specific security role of the EU. Membership made Finland part of a Western institution without appearing to threaten Russia. The EU thus was Finland's *safe* security option. At the same time, NATO membership was not ruled out should conditions change. NATO thus was Finland's *fallback* security option. To keep the first option safe and avoid having to choose the second, Finland settled for crisis management as best assuring military non-alignment.

Now that the previous permissiveness of the European Union has turned into indeterminate crisis management, Finland finds itself committed to crisis management without having found a solution to its own national security. As Ries (1999) has pointed out, Finland's integration into Europe and its open door stance towards NATO are viable only as long as Finland's strategic environment tolerates postponing decisive alignment. Were Russia to take a non-democratic turn, Finland would find itself without meaningful security anchoring. The adjustments made by Finland over the course of the Cold War towards its eastern neighbour have thus left their mark on Finnish identity and inhibit the emergence of a national security debate. Gauging the potential impact of alignment with NATO on Russia has created a habit of thinking about security that precludes Finland from joining the most important forum where Russia's place in Europe is discussed.

In Sweden, the debate is less about security and more about contesting the government's assertion that Sweden has no military alignment needs. Though largely confined to sections of the military, academia, and centre-right political parties, the thrust of the critique of government policy is that even by its own measuring rod, government policy has failed. In other words, even if Sweden faces no threats to its national security, it cannot continue to justify military non-alignment in terms of cooperation and influence. Participation in PfP and EAPC creates opportunities for Stockholm to be active but, contrary to government assertion, they do not substitute for the kind of influence that comes through alliance membership.

As most EU members are now also members of NATO and, as the constitutional debacle has weakened the EU and made NATO more prominent, Sweden faces marginalization in the discussion on the future shape of Europe's security and international commitments. Already in 1998, former conservative Prime Minister Bildt warned that Sweden was moving from *alliansfrihet* to *allianslöshet* where the previous benefits of non-alliance might cast Sweden adrift. It is one thing to be free of alliance obligations and another to be without alliances. He argued that in the past Sweden made good choices, shedding neutrality for integration in the EU and cooperating actively with NATO. These decisions gave Sweden a role compatible with military non-alignment and its identity as an autonomous actor. More recently, however, the ground has begun to shift and the former freedom of action has turned into flexibility without purpose, where activism can neither be explained in terms of increased security nor in terms of influence. Independence without influence is limiting, not empowering (Bildt, 1998; 2003).

Hence Andersson asks why Sweden is so actively engaged in the development of ESDP and whether Sweden has an alternative should ESDP take an undesirable turn (Andersson 2005, 17). The country's former Chief of Defence Staff claims that non-membership in NATO increasingly excludes Sweden from Europe's inner circle of security decision-making which consists of states that are members of both the EU and NATO (Dagens Nyheter, December 17, 2003). What these critics share is a mounting sense of tension in official security policy. The longstanding government claim that Sweden can cooperate in all non-Article-5 NATO business hides the fact that only full members of the alliance take part in planning and decision-making. Sweden may not have a security deficit but a rising information and influence deficit.

With the rising prominence of NATO in international crisis management and the dynamic of close cooperation between NATO and the EU, one can identify logical next steps for the development of Finnish and Swedish security policy. In the sense that we have seen both countries moving from neutrality to military non-alignment and membership in the EU as well as extensive cooperation with NATO, a definite change in security orientation and a broadening of national identity has taken place. It was possible because institutional and national identity were moving in the *same* direction. Security integration posed no threat to national identity. Both evolved and complemented one another.

To continue this complementarity, leaders in Helsinki and Stockholm have to renegotiate what it is to be Finnish and Swedish within the context of greater security integration, including possible future membership in NATO. The political challenge is to craft a new discourse of how the alliance and national identity can be harmonized. However, with public support for NATO membership low, and NATO friendly political parties in formal or informal coalition with parties hostile to military alignment, taking the lead in such a discourse may be politically costly. Instead of bold steps, we might see a steady transformation of how the alliance is described. Whether defined as an increasingly *European* institution, as suggested by Niinistö during the presidential campaign in Finland, or as a functionally rather than territorially determined security organization as referred to in Swedish renditions, we can observe attempts to once again create a match between identity and security alignment (Swedish Government 2004:5).

Conclusion: Theorizing Security Integration

The cases of Finland and Sweden reveal that choices in the security realm can have a critical normative component, especially when the notion of alignment is seen to depend on the compatibility of institutional and national identities. In turn, we have seen that the preservation of identity can be the basis of self-interested, instrumental policies. After the Cold War, how far these two countries have institutionalized their security has been conditioned by opportunities to share institutional norms that demanded the least adjustment of national identity.

Finnish and Swedish security integration choices reveal that both ideational and rationalist motives guided policies. Both states, for different reasons, are concerned about the impact security integration has on their identity. They are also concerned about the quality of security relations in the region. History and geography have shaped identities and security perspectives. Military non-alignment, because it combines security and identity in a complementary, non-conflictual way, has expressed the conditionality they impose on security integration.

We have seen that Sweden and Finland have been able to shape institutional developments that have made it possible to maintain an existing identity – as in the case of Sweden – and postpone resolution of ambiguous identity – as in the case of Finland. More recently, we have seen that the bargain struck between security institutionalization and identity is turning increasingly tenuous. Developments within their institution of choice and increasing demands for closer cooperation between the EU and NATO have begun to demand identity adjustments neither country is prepared to face. Were either or both countries to come to the conclusion that the normative pull of further integration, including NATO membership, could no longer be resisted or, if their security environment deteriorated to the extend that further institutionalization of national security became imperative, we should expect to see changes in both alignment *and* identity.

Already, both countries are participating in EU and NATO crisis management operations and are transforming their military to have the capacities and capabilities for interoperability with NATO. To be Finnish and Swedish has increasingly meant to share in the responsibility of international engagement both civilian and military. It has not meant alliance membership. For this to happen new discourses are needed that explain Finnishness and Swedishness in terms of an evolving alliance that accommodates national identity – and in terms of an evolving sense of self that embraces the institutionalizing of security.

In light of low popular support for joining the alliance, governments would need to explain why this step should be taken and how it corresponds to the previously propagated vision of national self. Undoubtedly, they would find it difficult to make a compelling case on the basis of influencing NATO decision making alone, especially in a domestic context that prefers the status quo. Bar a dramatic deterioration in their security environment, neither country should be expected to rush to a membership decision.

Finally, these two cases of security integration offer important observations for theory. They provide examples of how normative and rationalist choices interact in the security arena and how appropriate and consequential behaviour reflects careful calibration of self-interest and normative compliance. Theoretically parsimonious approaches fail to capture the rich combination of what states regard as obligation and self-interest. States' attentiveness to both argues in favour of problem driven approaches that allow for more nuanced theorizing.

Chapter 5

Power Disparity and Epistemic Communities: The Paldiski Case

Michael Karlsson

Introduction[1]

According to Peter M. Haas, epistemic-like communities are 'network(s) of professionals with recognized expertise and competence in a particular domain and an authoritative claim to policy-relevant knowledge within that domain or issue-area' (Haas 1992b, 3). An overview of previous studies led Haas to conclude in 1992 that 'the extent to which state behavior reflects the preferences of these networks remains strongly conditioned by the distribution of power internationally' (Haas 1992b, 7). In other words, epistemic communities were assumed to be influential only as long as their proposals did not jeopardize the power distribution between states. If one state was expected to make relative gains from expert proposals on international cooperation, then the prospects of influence were inevitably reduced.

The general view in the literature at the time was somewhat nuanced in the special issue of *International Organization* in 1992 (Haas 1992a, also published in book form), which was devoted to the epistemic communities approach. Power distribution was here described in terms of a necessary but not sufficient explanation. In other words, variations in the distribution of power could not alone help to explain variations in the impact of epistemic communities.

Instead it was suggested that the answer should be found somewhere in the interplay between the international distribution of power, certain attributes of the main actors (uncertainty among policy-makers, consensus among scientists and experts), and the institutionalization of scientific advice (Haas 1992b, 3-7).

Exactly how this relationship works is rather unexplored. Part of the reason for this is that scholars have tended to be particularly interested in cases marked by a symmetric distribution of power. For example, there are several case studies of expert influence on US – Soviet/Russian relations in the 1980s and early 1990s (see for instance: Adler 1992; Checkel 1998; Evangelista 1995 and 1999; Nye 1987; Risse-Kappen 1994; Sigal 2000). These studies indicate that power symmetry leaves

---

1 The author is grateful to Regina Karp and Olav F. Knudsen for their constructive comments on an earlier draft of this chapter. He would also like to thank Karin Aggestam, Magdalena Bexell, Johan Eriksson, Jakob Gustavsson, Christopher Jones, Christer Jönsson, Erik Noreen, and Stephen G. Walker for their advice.

room for variation and that networks of experts, by influencing the way governments think about security, help to create a favourable climate for subsequent security cooperation and arms-control agreements.

But what happens if we shift our focus to cases of power disparity? Does power disparity take away the effect of the other factors emphasized by Haas? Or, is the significance of power disparity only secondary in explaining the role of epistemic communities?

The purpose of this chapter is to explore the role of power disparity in such a context by conducting a case study of an epistemic community on nuclear and radiation safety in the Baltic Sea region. The epistemic community consists of twelve experts[2] and was established in 1992 to focus mainly on risks arising from the management of nuclear power plants that had been part of the nuclear programme of the former Soviet Union.

During the first year of activity, the experts experienced a clear resistance from Russia to cooperation. This led to a number of conflicts, most notably on the definition of the Baltic Sea region, distribution of necessary information, and access to nuclear facilities. One of the first issues of conflict concerned the former Soviet Nuclear Submarine Training Centre at Paldiski in northern Estonia. The Paldiski base was a result of the 1939 non-aggression pact between Nazi-Germany and the Soviet Union, by which Germany consented to the Soviets' establishing six military bases within the territory of Estonia (Putnik 2003, 39).

In the early 1960's, the Soviet Navy built a training centre some 4 kilometres outside Paldiski for the crews of Soviet nuclear submarines (Estonia Today 1995; Putnik 2003, 40-41).[3] The aim of the centre was to educate crews in the operation of strategic ballistic missile submarines, including operation of submarine reactors and use of missiles and torpedoes. The two reactors were operational from April 1968 to December 1989, and February 1983 to December 1989, respectively. The Russian Navy continued the training programme at Paldiski until 1993, but without practical training in reactor operations (see also Fredén 2006).

After the Estonian declaration of independence in August 1991, and the subsequent dissolution of the Soviet Union a few months later, the status of the Paldiski base became the subject of several years of intense negotiations between Estonia and Russia (Putnik 2003, 42-43, Fredén 2006, 334-339, 363-386). In January 1992, the Estonian Prime Minister Edgar Savisaar received a letter from Admiral Chernavin at the Russian Navy Headquarters informing him that the Paldiski reactors had been

---

2   The experts come from the nine littoral states of the Baltic Sea, Norway, Iceland, and the Commission of the European Union.

3   There is no available information that clearly indicates that the military units on the Paldiski peninsula had been equipped with nuclear weapons (Putnik 2003, 39). However, the navy units might have been armed with nuclear warheads at certain periods of time. The reason for this suggestion is that the Soviet Baltic fleet had a common security system that meant that not every naval base was all the time equipped with nuclear weapons. A secret rotation programme was in operation whereby nuclear warheads were moved between several base locations in the area.

shut down and was in a safe condition. The Admiral did not, however, present a timetable for the Russian withdrawal from the base, but only stated that preparations had been made for dismantling and removing the training units. Eventually, the Russian Navy started to move submarine training away from Paldiski to the Obninsk Training Centre in Russia, but from the time of Chernavin's letter it took another three and a half years before the withdrawal was completed.

Following an agreement between the two countries in July 1994, the Paldiski training centre was finally transferred to the Estonian authorities on 30 September 1995. This chain of events made Riivo Sinijärv, then Minister of Foreign Affairs of Estonia, refer to the Paldiski case as 'an excellent example of international cooperation in the Baltic Sea area' (Sinijärv 1995).[4] As regards the role of the epistemic community, the Estonian Minister emphasized,

> In particular I would highlight the work of the Nuclear and Radiation Safety Working Group, which has devoted considerable attention to our problem child, Paldiski. During the last year, we have managed to reduce significantly the potential environmental dangers that emanate from this site (Sinijärv 1995).

At a more concrete level, the importance of this epistemic community was, according to the Estonian Ministry of Foreign Affairs, first of all in collecting technical data for the Paldiski nuclear facilities and in breaking the wall of secrecy surrounding the base (Estonia Today 1995). Together, this suggests that the perception at the time was that the experts actually had made a difference on this case. In retrospect however, it seems reasonable to conclude that the difference had less to do with the transfer of the site as such (it would have been transferred anyhow) and more to do with the timetable of the transfer and the safety standards of the facilities. Against this background, I intend to address the question of how the role of the epistemic community can be linked to power disparity.

The chapter is divided into two parts. The first part is devoted to the analysis of the Paldiski case and the alleged positive role played by the nuclear experts. The second part of the chapter introduces a theoretical framework for analyzing how power disparity may affect the role of epistemic communities. In this part, I first clarify what is meant by power disparity, how nuclear power resources are distributed in the Baltic Sea region, and present three views on how it may affect the role of experts. The three views are then confronted with the findings of the case study in order to see if power disparity was a favourable context or not.

---

4   At the meeting of the Council of the Baltic Sea States (CBSS) in Gdansk on 19 May 1995. Actually, it could be argued that the significance of the Paldiski case was even greater, as it was one of the first tests of the foreign policy intentions of the Russian Federation.

Case Study[5]

Here I will give further details about the working group on nuclear and radiation safety and discuss its status as an epistemic community.

The Establishment of an Expert Group on Nuclear and Radiation Safety

Even though the Baltic Sea region has been nuclear dense for a long time, it was only in April 1992 that it became possible to establish a regional network of nuclear safety experts. Before this date, there were many contacts between experts from the free and democratic states on the western and northern rims of the Baltic Sea. These contacts, which typically occurred on a bilateral basis or within the framework of international organizations such as the IAEA, were occasionally quite frequent, not least in connection with dramatic events such as the accidents in Three Mile Island in 1979 and in Chernobyl in 1986. Some contacts were more frequent than others, and gave rise to multilateral networks. One such example is the Nordic Society for Radiation Protection, which was established in 1964. However, contacts across the east-west divide were still very rare. A major reason for this was that the Communist Party of the Soviet Union did not allow transnational contacts to flow freely during its time in power (see for instance: Evangelista 1995, 157-158).

As the Cold War finally came to an end, it was an intergovernmental initiative that brought regional experts on nuclear safety together. On 5-6 March 1992, the Ministers for Foreign Affairs of the Baltic Sea states and a representative of the European Commission met in Copenhagen to establish the Council of the Baltic Sea States (CBSS). In the founding document (the Copenhagen Declaration), the Ministers among other things 'stressed the need for the strengthening of national nuclear safety institutions and expressed support for more exchange within the Baltic Sea region of know-how and information on these issues' (CBSS 1992a).[6]

Even though no specific countries were pointed out at this stage, it should be clear that the post-Cold War agenda of the Baltic Sea region has been very much preoccupied with the safety of nuclear facilities in the Eastern European countries.[7]

---

5 The empirical evidence is based on documents and secondary sources. The documents originate from the epistemic community (expert group) and from the Council of the Baltic Sea States, and include among other things minutes, expert mission reports, and annual reports. A valuable secondary source is Henno Putnik (2003), who is deputy director of ALARA (the Estonian Radioactive Waste Management Agency), which was organized by the Estonian Government to receive the Paldiski Nuclear Facility in 1995 and organize the future decommissioning work.

6 The term 'nuclear safety' is often used as an umbrella term to refer to all activities aimed at dealing effectively with risks associated with nuclear fuel, radiation, and radioactive waste (Fischer 1997, 183). This chapter focuses mainly on risks arising from the management of nuclear power plants, the supply of nuclear fuel, and the disposal of radioactive waste.

7 This is not to say that there are no concerns about the safety standards of nuclear power plants in other countries. A good case in point is the two nuclear reactors at Barsebäck, located

The reason for this is fact that many of the existing nuclear power plants in Eastern Europe were built by the former Soviet Union. Even though the USSR brought the world's first nuclear reactor into commercial operation as early as 1954, there was always deep international concern about the safety standards of its nuclear programme. Not least the Chernobyl accident in 1986 raised awareness about the shortcomings. After the dissolution of the USSR in 1991, there were, in the case of the Baltic Sea region, remains of the Soviet nuclear programme in Estonia, Latvia, Lithuania, Poland, and the Russian Federation.[8] The safety of these remains immediately became a prioritized issue for the CBSS, not least because at this point in time there were hardly any nuclear authorities in the concerned states that could deal with the problem.

The call in March 1992 for regional cooperation to enhance nuclear safety was soon followed by a joint initiative by the Foreign Ministers of Finland and Sweden, Paavo Väyrynen and Margaretha af Ugglas, to get the concrete work started (CBSS-CSO 1993). Väyrynen presented the joint initiative at the constitutive meeting of the CBSS Committee of Senior Officials (CSO), which was held in Helsinki on 27 April 1992. The immediate effect of the call was a decision by the CSO '... to undertake a study on both the civilian and the military aspects of nuclear and radiation safety in the Baltic Sea region' (CBSS-CSO 1993, item 6). For this purpose, an *ad hoc* working group of nuclear experts was established, which became formally known as the Working Group on Nuclear and Radiation Safety (WGNRS). The specific considerations behind the decision of the Committee of Senior Officials are found in the terms of reference of the working group, which is the document that formally regulates the work of the group and was adopted by the CSO at its meeting on 7-8 September 1992 (WGNRS 1993a, item 2, and annex I, § 1):

> Nuclear and radiation safety, i.e. technical safety of installations, radiation protection and radioactive waste management, both civil and military, have been widely identified as an immediate concern for the Baltic Sea region. The countries of the Baltic Sea region, therefore, are vitally interested in exchanging the necessary information about and rapidly improving the nuclear and radiation safety in the Baltic Sea region. Coordination and planning of cooperation projects in the field of nuclear and radiation safety is needed so that funding priorities can be more clearly identified. The countries agree to help each other to solve imminent problems on the subject of nuclear and radiation safety. To this end, the Committee of Senior Officials of the Council of the Baltic Sea States has decided to establish a Working Group.

The possibility of setting up working groups with a specific mandate is provided by the terms of reference of the CBSS (CBSS 1992b, item 19). The range of

---

on the south coast of Sweden only some 20 kilometers from the Danish Capital Copenhagen, which for many years have been a source of anxiety for peoples on both sides of the straits.

8   At the time of writing, there are no nuclear power reactors in operation in Estonia, Latvia, and Poland. However, former Soviet military as well as non-military practices have left a considerable amount of radioactive waste throughout the three countries (European Commission 1999b).

these mandates is rather limited, as the working groups '... may be charged with the elaboration of recommendations for approval by the Council at a subsequent session, or, in urgent matters, by silent procedure'.[9] The task of putting forward recommendations applies to the case of the nuclear safety experts as well. The working group was initially given four concrete tasks, gradually leading up to the goal of offering recommendations (WGNRS 1993a, annex I, § 4). Thus, the expert group should:

- Collect information about nuclear facilities and nuclear waste storages in the Baltic Sea region.
- Identify among the nuclear installations and nuclear facilities those that require immediate concerted action to reduce the risks to the general public and to the environment.
- Take stock of and monitor various projects – national, bilateral, regional and multilateral – aimed at enhancing nuclear and radiation safety in the Baltic Sea region.
- Suggest and develop initiatives and make recommendations towards the enhancing of nuclear and radiation safety in the Baltic Sea region.

In 1992, when the expert group was set up, there was a rising concern about the safety of nuclear installations in East European countries, and also concern among western governments about possible overlaps between international efforts. This unease was also reflected in the decision by the Baltic Sea states to create a regional expert group. The governments accordingly agreed that

> With regard to the extensive international cooperation that has been established in the area of nuclear power plant safety the Working Group shall pay particular attention to *other* installations and activities, both civil and military, with potential nuclear and radiation risk [my emphasis] (WGNRS 1993a, annex I, § 3).

Moreover, the working group was instructed to focus on sources of radioactivity '... which impose a potential risk for dangerous trans-boundary effects or major environmental effects *locally* in the Baltic Sea region' [my emphasis] (WGNRS 1993a, annex I, § 3). Taken together, these specifications reflect the intention among the Baltic Sea states to establish a more definite international division of labour.

An Epistemic Community?

The Working Group on Nuclear and Radiation Safety has a limited membership. According to the terms of reference, all CBSS member states and the European

---

9 It should be noted that decisions of the CBSS Council, which consists of the Ministers for Foreign Affairs of the Baltic Sea states and a representative of the European Commission, are taken by consensus. The same decision rule also applies to subsidiary bodies such as the Committee of Senior Officials.

Commission '... have the right to nominate two experts to the Working Group' (WGNRS 1993a, annex I, § 5). In practice, the CBSS members have for the most part been content with nominating one expert each and thereby limiting the membership to an exclusive group of twelve experts. The composition of this group has been rather stable since it started in 1992. The turnover of experts has during this time for most countries not exceeded 2-3 individuals, which has given the work a great deal of continuity.

The working group meets the criteria of an epistemic community quite well. Following the definition given in the introduction – a 'network of professionals with recognized expertise and competence in a particular domain and an authoritative claim to policy-relevant knowledge within that domain or issue-area' (Haas 1992b, 3) – I shall argue that the working group is knowledge-based, a network, and policy-oriented. First, it is knowledge-based in the sense that the members of the working group are all scientists or other kinds of highly qualified experts on nuclear and radiation safety. At least seven of the twelve members in 2003 have a doctor's degree in physics or in related sciences. The group has at times included one or two professors as well. Not least in the early years, the group benefited much from the expertise of Professor Antti Vuorinen. The Finnish Professor, who at the time was Director General of the Finnish Centre for Radiation and Nuclear Safety, was the first chairman of the working group (1992-1997). From Table 5.1 it is also clear that the members of the group are employed at highly specialized agencies and institutes (corresponding) within the domain of nuclear and radiation safety.

The experts appear in most cases to have a more or less independent status in relation to their home governments. However, in the case of Russia and Lithuania, we find that the governments have nominated persons employed at the concerned ministry. This fact suggests that there is an element of 'trans-governmental relations' in this epistemic community; that is, employees at government departments interacting directly across state borders with opposite numbers in other governments or with non-state actors (Keohane and Nye 1974). The exception of Russia and Lithuania is interesting and one might ask if it is only a coincidence that the main concern today about nuclear safety in the Baltic Sea region is linked to facilities in precisely these two countries.

Regardless of the reason we should be aware of the pros and cons of an epistemic community having high-level ministry representation in the group. On the pro side is the access argument. That is, the experts are provided with a channel for receiving and diffusing information. On the other hand, to have this type of composition of a working group obviously carries a risk of making the process already at this stage 'politically contaminated'.

Table 5.1 Members of the Working Group on Nuclear and Radiation Safety

Country	Name	Affiliation
Denmark	Bjørn Thorlaksen	Danish Emergency Management Agency
Estonia	Raivo Rajamäe	Estonian Radiation Protection Center
Finland	Raimo Mustonen	Finnish Radiation and Nuclear Safety Authority
Germany	Erich Wirth	Federal Office for Radiation Protection
Iceland	Sigurður Emil Pálsson	Icelandic Radiation Protection Institute
Latvia	Andrejs Salminš	Radiation Safety Center
Lithuania	Stasys Motiejunas	Ministry of the Environment
Norway	Finn Ugletveit	Norwegian Radiation Protection Authority
Poland	Andrzej Merta	National Atomic Energy Agency
Russia	Valery Ryzhov	Ministry for Atomic Energy of the Russian Federation
Sweden	Åke Persson	Swedish Radiation Protection Authority
European Commission	Vesa Tanner	Directorate-General Energy and Transport

Source: CBSS (2003).

In relation to the first criterion (knowledge-based), it should also be noted that the real size of the epistemic community might very well be said to be much greater than only twelve persons. Knowledge about nuclear and radiation safety is not in any way restricted to this group of experts, but is in fact shared by a much larger group of people. From this point of view, it therefore seems more correct to say that the working group is embedded in a larger international network of experts that has been formed, not least, around the International Atomic Energy Agency (IAEA).

The epistemic community on nuclear safety in the Baltic Sea region can be described as a transnational network with a certain degree of institutionalization. The experts come from eleven different countries, which all except Iceland and Norway are directly bordering the Baltic Sea, and one member is employed at the Commission of the European Union. The group does not constitute a formal organization, but is upheld mainly by regular interactions between the members. Since the start in 1992, the group has met 2-5 times each year. The frequency of the interactions has declined somewhat over the years. In the beginning the experts met about five times a year, but from the mid-1990s on they have confined themselves to a practice of biannual meetings (WGNRS 2000).

There are no provisions for how the working group should be organized, other than that a representative of the country holding the CBSS chairmanship should chair it (WGNRS 1993a, annex I, § 5). This routine has, however, apart from the first year, not been put into practice (WGNRS 2000). The member states of the CBSS assume the presidency of the Council on a rotational one-year basis. The nuclear safety experts on their part have concluded that a one-year period for the chairmanship of the working group is too short. As the mandate of the first chairman of the group, professor Antti Vuorinen, was extended by one year at a time, the experts eventually in 1997 decided that the chairmanship should change in three-year periods '... in order to ensure the continuity and to enable sufficient circulation' (WGNRS 2000).

Even though the network on nuclear safety is quite small, it is possible to discern certain sub-patterns of interactions among the members. Judging from the annual reports of the working group, there are at least two rather apparent sub-patterns.

First, the interactions between the chairman and the members constitute somewhat of a core of the network. It is true that the chairmanship has not been a full-time duty, but it has required considerable effort to lead and to coordinate the activities of the group. Apart from the regular meetings, it has therefore often been necessary for the chairman to have more frequent interactions with the members. For example, in the year 2001 the chairman had two additional meetings with selected members of the network to finalize an updated version of the Terms of Reference and a draft Agreement on exchange of radiation monitoring data (WGNRS 2001).

Second, the interactions have up to now had a slight West European preponderance. Even though all experts are full members of the group, it has been noted that some of them '... have had financial problems to participate even in two meetings per year' (WGNRS 2000). This problem applies first of all to members from countries on the eastern rim of the Baltic Sea. One consequence of this can be seen in the selection of the chairmen, who so far all have come from West European countries.[10]

The interactions between the nuclear safety experts are to a certain degree institutionally embedded. The original institution included the terms of reference and the chairmanship arrangement. The former, which was adopted in 1992 and renewed in 2001, provides a set of rules and norms, while the latter ensures coordination of the practical work. Additional institutions have been established gradually as the working group has been engaged in concrete projects. Among these is the routine of establishing special task groups for the implementation of common tasks. Moreover, to help and support the working group the Baltic Sea states in 1999 decided to introduce a contact person at the CBSS Secretariat in Stockholm. This reform was intended to strengthen the group '... by providing secretarial services and improving communication between the WG (Working Group) and other acting bodies of the CBSS' (WGNRS 1999, item 2). Taken together, these arrangements make up an institutional context for the experts on nuclear safety. But even though this context

---

10 Up to the time of writing, the working group has had four chairmen. The first two – Antti Vuorinen (1992-1997) and Raimo Mustonen (1997-2000) – came from Finland and were both employed at the Finnish Radiation and Nuclear Safety Authority. Åke Persson of the Swedish Radiation Protection Authority assumed the chairmanship between 2000-2003. The current chairman, Erich Wirth of the Federal Office for Radiation Protection in Germany, was appointed in 2003.

has become more institutionalized over the years, the epistemic community is still best described as a network.

In order to qualify as an epistemic community, a knowledge-based network should also be policy-oriented. This applies, with some modifications, to the case of the epistemic community on nuclear safety as well.[11] Certainly there should be no doubt that these experts can make authoritative claims to policy-relevant knowledge within their particular field of interest. On the other hand, in this case we must also pay attention to the fact that policy-orientation is in a way a part of the assignment itself. The mandate of the working group gives the experts a role in the initiating and preparatory phases of the policy process. More specifically the experts are expected to come up with initiatives and to give recommendations on how to enhance nuclear and radiation safety in the Baltic Sea region. By giving the network a policy-oriented role, the governments of the Baltic Sea states have opened a door for expert influence.

From a critical point of view we must, however, ask what would have happened had this door not been opened. Had the experts still been actively seeking to get access to the intergovernmental arena in order to bring about a better policy on nuclear safety? Or would they have been content with the more passive role of merely responding to the requests of decision-makers if and when they occur? It is true that we do not know the answer to this question, but by paying attention to the actions of the network we will be able to elaborate upon it in somewhat greater detail. For example, if the experts criticize individual governments or if they seek to expand the mandate of the working group, then this may suggest the existence of an independent policy-orientation. As will be clear from the following section, the experts on nuclear safety have been active in both of these respects.

Confronting the Secrecy at Paldiski

The epistemic community on nuclear and radiation safety in the Baltic Sea region had a troublesome start. At the request of the CBSS Committee of Senior Officials, the first assignment of the expert group was to carry out a study on the civilian and the military aspects of nuclear and radiation safety in the region (CSO 1993, item 6). For this purpose, the group agreed to start by collecting relevant information provided by each CBSS member state (WGNRS 1993a, item 5). On the basis of these data, the experts were then to identify potential radiation risks to the general public and to the environment, and to give recommendations on how to enhance safety at critical nuclear installations.

The expert group experienced two difficulties as it took up this task. These concerned the definition of the Baltic Sea region and the distribution of relevant

---

11 As regards the third criterion, it should be remembered that the expert group was not an independently existing scientific community before 1992. The group was established on an intergovernmental initiative. For studies of expert groups that do not fully constitute epistemic communities from the beginning, see for example Kapstein (1992) and Ikenberry (1992).

information. A common feature for the two difficulties was that they revealed a conflict between Russia and the other Baltic Sea states.

First, the definition of the Baltic Sea region proved initially to be a matter of controversy. It is true that the Council of the Baltic Sea States has eleven member-states with a given territory, but not all of this space is directly or even indirectly linked to the Baltic Sea. Because of this, there soon arose a debate within the expert group on exactly which nuclear installations should be included in the mission (WGNRS 1993a, item 5).

On the one hand, Russia adopted a minimalist position, implying that the expert group should focus only on nuclear and radiation risks emanating from nuclear installations located in the immediate vicinity of the Baltic Sea. On the other hand, most of the other Baltic Sea states argued for a wider definition of the Baltic Sea region. This position was defended by the argument that there are no obvious geographical limits when it comes to the effects of nuclear accidents. The Chernobyl crisis in 1986 is an illustrative example of this circumstance, as the Baltic Sea area then very soon was affected by fallout. However, even though the peoples of the Baltic Sea states have real experiences of the poor safety standards of Russian nuclear installations, the Russian government has so far prevented the expert group from seriously dealing with nuclear and radiological risks originating outside the adjacent areas of the Baltic Sea. The outcome of this definitional clash has favoured the minimalist position. This should come as no surprise, since the working group operates in a typical intergovernmental context where cooperation basically reflects the lowest common denominator. That is, if the group cannot find a mutually agreed definition of the Baltic Sea region, then it is the member with the strongest reservations who in practice settles the issue.

In practical terms, the expert group has therefore only been able to focus on nuclear facilities in the immediate vicinity of the Baltic Sea. In the case of Russia these include first of all the Leningrad Nuclear Power Plant. The plant, which is located in the city of Sosnovy Bor about 80 kilometres west of St. Petersburg, has four nuclear reactors. In addition, there are also two research reactors in the Leningrad region, which are located in Gatchina and in St. Petersburg. Apart from the reactors in the Leningrad region, there are a number of other nuclear related issues in Russia that have raised safety concerns within the working group. Among these are the disposal of radioactive waste in the naval base area of Kaliningrad, and lighthouses along the Russian coast driven by radioactive energy supplies. Concerns about Russian nuclear safety have occasionally also been raised by rumours about, for example, nuclear trafficking[12] and deployment of tactical nuclear weapons in Kaliningrad.[13]

As regards nuclear weapons, it should be noted that a nuclear umbrella protects the Russian Federation, but that the official policy is to keep the Baltic Sea region nuclear-free. The Baltic Fleet, which has its headquarters at Kaliningrad, has been without a nuclear weapons capability since former Soviet President Mikhail Gorbachev withdrew nuclear submarines from the Baltic Sea in 1989. Russian officials have also repeatedly referred to a verbal commitment in 1991 not to deploy tactical weapons in the Baltic region.

Besides disagreement on how to define the Baltic Sea region, the epistemic community to begin with also experienced difficulties in receiving relevant information from Russian authorities. The non-cooperative stance of the Russian authorities was particularly evident in 1992-93, and applied to installations in Russia (the Leningrad and Kaliningrad areas) as well as to facilities still under Russian control in the newly independent Baltic states (Estonia, Latvia, and Lithuania). In no case was the resistance of Russia clearer than in the case of Paldiski.

At Paldiski the Soviet Navy had a training centre in which they operated two nuclear power reactors from 1968 to 1989. After the dissolution of the Soviet Union in 1991, the site became a serious source of irritation between Estonia and Russia, because it remained under Russian control until 1995, and because Russia left behind a lot of radioactively infected waste when they finally withdraw. The spent fuel from the two reactors was transferred to Russia in 1994, but the reactor vessels, the radioactive waste, and the contaminated auxiliary facilities were left in place.

As the working group took up the first task of assessing nuclear and radiation safety in the Baltic Sea region, it immediately faced difficulties – as previously related – in obtaining information about the Paldiski base.[14] The difficulties are described in detail by the expert group in its first report to the Council of the Baltic Sea States on the 26 February 1993 (WGNRS 1993a, item 9):

> The Working Group has noted that not enough information has been made available to evaluate the safety status of the naval training reactors and waste storage's at the Russian naval base in Paldiski on the Pakri peninsula in Estonia.

---

12 The term nuclear trafficking refers to the theft and smuggling of nuclear material (Fischer 1997, 120-122). For an overview of reports about nuclear trafficking in the Newly Independent States, see the NIS Nuclear Trafficking Abstracts Database (http://www.nti.org/db/nistraff/index.html), which is operated by researchers at the Centre for Nonproliferation Studies at the Monterey Institute of International Studies in California.

13 In January 2001, some newspapers reported that Russia had moved tactical nuclear weapons to a military base in Kaliningrad. Russian officials categorically denied this rumor.

14 As regards the Paldiski base and the role of the working group, it should also be noted that the Estonian government, due to a lack of domestic nuclear expertise, actively sought to mobilize international assistance for the decommissioning of the two nuclear reactors (Putnik 2003, 43; Fredén 2006, esp. 334-39 and 381-82).

The Working Group has also noted that several Baltic Sea States and the Commission of the European Communities have expressed their readiness to assist in solving the problems related to the decommissioning and cleaning up of the Paldiski site. The Working Group encourages further cooperation between the relevant parties.

The representative of the Russian Federation in the Working Group has stated that the reactors and waste storages at Paldiski do not represent a risk to the general public or the environment and they do not require immediate concerted action initiated or supported by the Council of the Baltic Sea States. But in view of the concerns on the Paldiski site expressed by a number of Representatives in the Working Group and the absence of adequate information on its safety status the rest of the Working Group agreed that Paldiski should be presently considered a special concern requiring concerted action.

The conflicting views revolved round whether or not the Paldiski Nuclear Submarine Training Centre constituted a nuclear risk. The official Russian position was that the site did not represent a risk. This conclusion could also help explain why there was a shortage of information at the time. That is, from the Russian horizon there were no nuclear risks to inform about. The same position also appeared in Russia's official communication with Estonia. In a letter to the Estonian Government on the 13 January 1992, Admiral Chernavin at the General Headquarters of the Russian Navy declared that the two reactors had been shut down and were in a safe condition (Putnik 2003, 42).

From the point of view of the expert group however, the situation presented two problems. One was that, on the basis of available information, it could not rule out nuclear risks. The unclear safety status of Paldiski therefore presented an immediate concern. A second problem was how the shortage of information from the Russian side might affect the willingness of the other Baltic Sea states to further participate in nuclear safety cooperation (WGNRS 1993a, item 10). The intention of the working group was to establish a routine of regular exchange of information on nuclear reactors, on transport of nuclear materials, and on radiation pollution. However, echoing the classical cooperation dilemma in international politics, in a situation of uncertainty and incomplete information the likelihood of cooperation becomes quite small. In other words, if Russia proves unwilling to lift some of the secrecy surrounding the Paldiski site, then there would be a real risk that the other Baltic Sea states would defect from nuclear safety cooperation in general. The Paldiski case therefore became a critical test for such cooperation.

Following the report of the working group to the CBSS Council, Russia provided some additional technical information about the nuclear facilities at Paldiski (WGNRS 1993a, footnote). Judging from the reactions of the expert group, however, this was too little, too late. Confronted with the Russian resistance to reveal information, the working group instead developed a two-tier strategy. The essence of this strategy was to establish contacts with Russian authorities at all relevant levels. In practice, this meant that the experts approached the supreme military commanders at the General Headquarters of the Russian Navy in Moscow as well as safety personnel at the Paldiski site.

The first part of the working group strategy can be described in terms of a power approach, which in the literature on transnational relations usually refers to situations when non-state actors target top decision makers to exert influence (see for instance Moon 1988; Mingst 1995, 238; Karlsson 2004a, 131, and 2004b, 95). The high-level target in the Paldiski case was found within the leadership of the Russian Navy. This may at first seem somewhat puzzling, considering that the Ministry for Atomic Energy usually handles issues related to nuclear energy, a fact that is also supported by the observation that the Russian representative of the working group comes from this Ministry. The two reactors at Paldiski, however, were a different case. In practice, they were both part of the Soviet Navy's nuclear training centre at Paldiski, which stood under a centralized command. That is, even though the centre was located within the territory of supervision of the Baltic Fleet of the former Soviet Union, it was in fact under the direct control of the General Headquarters of the Soviet Navy in Moscow (Putnik 2003, 40). As the Soviet Union was dissolved in 1991, the command of the Paldiski site was simply transferred to the Headquarters of the Russian Navy.

The working group managed quite soon to establish contact with Russian Navy Headquarters, which resulted in an invitation to visit Moscow in mid-April 1993 (WGNRS 1993b). The high point of the visit was a meeting with the concerned military commanders that not only came down to an exchange of information, but also offered a possibility for the working group to raise questions that it wanted the Navy to look closer into. Vice-Admiral Lyashenko, Deputy Head of the General Military Navy Headquarters, then answered the questions in writing on 20 April 1993 (Lyashenko 1993). The results of this high-level communication appear to have been quite positive. After the meeting, the working group gave the following report (WGNRS 1993b, item 2 and 3):

> The WG [the Working Group, author's note] understood that the defuelling process of the two reactors is making good progress. No specific problems in defuelling are anticipated. The WG expects that the spent nuclear fuel from both reactors will be removed to the Russian Federation by the end of summer 1994.
>
> The WG was informed of the serious future challenges faced nationwide by the Russian Federation in improving nuclear and radiological waste management and arranging decontamination work. The WG was, however, informed by the representatives of the Russian Federation, that questions relating to the decommissioning of the Paldiski facilities can be dealt with separately and do not envisage constraints for the decommissioning works and successful dismantlement of the Paldiski reactors, especially if supporting international financing can be organized.

The report gives the impression of an increasing level of confidence at least at a general level. That is, on the basis of the oral information given by the Russian representatives, the experts appear to have been convinced that one important part of the dismantling process (dealing effectively with the risks associated with nuclear fuel) was making good progress. The level of confidence most likely increased further when the working group received and read the written reply by Vice-Admiral

Lyashenko (1993). His report consisted for the most part of a list of specific data on the reactors and the nuclear waste storages at the Paldiski site, which enabled the experts to make a more detailed evaluation of the potential risk sources and the security measures. In the report, it is furthermore stated that the Russian authorities have taken the necessary measures to move the risk of transition of the two reactors beyond the critical stage, but – as we shall soon see – this remained a matter of some dispute.

Apart from the technical information in the report, the Vice-Admiral also touched upon the need for joint regional efforts to deal with some of the problems associated with the dismantling process:

> According to the RF [the Russian Federation, author's note] Department of Defence the joint effort should be concentrated on economic assistance at the stage of equipment and nuclear wastes transportation as well as the rehabilitation of the territory (Lyashenko 1993).

In other words, the message that was delivered in the letter as well as at the meeting in Moscow a couple of days earlier was that the decommissioning work proceeded safely, but there was a risk that it would be drawn out in time unless international financial support could be arranged.

The second part of the working group strategy focused on the operational level, or to be precise, on gaining access to the Paldiski Nuclear Submarine Training Centre itself. This was seen as a very important step. Considering the poor cooperative experience in connection with the Chernobyl accident in 1986 and the fact that the working group had a troublesome start, access was deemed essential in order to establish some trust between the parties.

However, the door to the Paldiski base proved difficult to open. It took until 9 September 1993 before the experts were allowed a visit, which could not, however, be described as an unconditional general inspection. Instead, it was limited to 'a detailed visit to one of the two training reactors' (WGNRS 1993c). The visit therefore produced mixed results as far as nuclear safety judgments were concerned. On the one hand, the experts obtained additional information concerning the safety of the reactor shutdown process. This information seemed to have cooled down the fear of safety risks (WGNRS 1993c):

> The examination of the upper part of the reactor confirmed information previously received that the movement of control rods is prevented by electrical and mechanical means. The visit to the control room confirmed that key safety parameters (such as fuel and water temperature, boron concentration, water chemistry control, etc.) are properly recorded and their values correspond to safe shut-down conditions. On this basis, and assuming that similar conditions are also kept in the second reactor, the group concluded that the reactors do not represent at present any significant safety risk.

On the other hand, apart from the fact that the experts were not allowed to examine the second reactor, there remained some other safety questions to which the Paldiski visit could not bring satisfactory answers. These questions were mainly related to the facilities and the process for storing nuclear waste (WGNRS 1993c):

> The working group was given the opportunity to view from the outside the buildings used to treat and store liquid waste and store solid waste. Because of the limited information available and the uncertainties concerning the quality of the storage facilities, the activity of the waste, the quality of the storage tanks, the arrangements inside the storage facilities, etc. the Working Group was unable to make a technical evaluation of the waste storage facilities. Until the Working Group is able to examine the radioactive waste storage facilities in more detail it cannot make a comprehensive statement concerning the storage arrangements.

There is no doubt that the visits to Moscow and Estonia in 1993 gave the working group a more solid foundation for evaluating the safety status of the nuclear facilities at the Paldiski site. At the time, the experts themselves reported 'notable progress' in its contacts with the Russian authorities (WGNRS 1994b, item 6). Certainly, one noted a change in Russia's will to dispel some of the secrecy surrounding the Paldiski Training Centre.

On the other hand, even though the safety picture undoubtedly had become much clearer than it was in February 1993, there still remained some objects on the Paldiski Peninsula that the experts did not get access to and were therefore unable to evaluate in more detail. For example, Estonian reports of leakage of furnace oil at the boiler house of the nuclear reactors could not be verified because access was not granted by the Russian military officials (Estonian Ministry of Environment 1995, 4).

In sum, where the Paldiski case is concerned, the Working Group on Nuclear and Radiation Safety played an especially important role during the critical years in 1992 and 1993. Two circumstances in particular contributed to this. One was the fact that at this time there was still no agreement between Estonia and Russia on what would happen with the Paldiski site. It took almost two and half years of intense negotiations between Estonia and Russia before it was finally decided to shut down the Naval Training Centre (Fredén 2006, 379-83). The Paldiski agreement, which was signed on 30 July 1994, stipulated that:

> The site with two sealed reactor compartments and radioactive waste storages shall, after decommissioning, be transferred to the Republic of Estonia by September 30, 1995 together with the completion of all relevant documentation (Estonia Today 1995).

The second circumstance that impacted on the role of the Baltic Sea experts in 1992-93 was the fact that there hardly yet existed a fully developed nuclear safety framework (including for example legislation and authorities) in Estonia. It should be noted that this fact continued to be of some concern at a later stage because, when it signed the Paldiski agreement in 1994, Estonia agreed to take full custody of the site as well as future decommissioning of the reactors and the waste facilities. The need for continued international expertise support was accordingly recognized in the agreement (WGNRS 1994a). In order to support the Estonian authorities during and after the transfer of the site, a separate reference group of experts had been set up on 11 May 1994. The group, known as the Paldiski International Expert Reference Group (PIERG), was explicitly mentioned in the 30 July agreement (Fredén 2006, 383). PIERG acts independently of the CBSS framework, but has kept a close contact with the Working Group on Nuclear and Radiation Safety (see for example: WGNRS 1995).

The transfer of the Paldiski Nuclear Submarine Training Centre progressed fully in accordance with the 1994 agreement. As of 26 September 1995, both nuclear reactors had been dismantled and, together with the radioactive fuel, transported to Russia. Four days later, on 30 September 1995, the control of the former Soviet submarine training centre was successfully transferred from Russia to Estonian officials.

Power Disparity and the Role of Epistemic Communities

The case study suggested that the nuclear experts played a constructive role, most notably by breaking some of the secrecy surrounding the Paldiski site and by accelerating the timetable for the final transfer. We will now proceed with the analysis to see if this role was somehow affected by the power disparity context. In order to do this, we will first clarify what is meant by power disparity and discuss how this may affect the role of epistemic communities.

Power Disparity

Following the definition given in this book, power disparity is experienced by parties in a relationship that perceive themselves to be in one way or another disadvantaged vis-à-vis their opponents. From a general point of view, it seems possible to think of different notions of power in the Paldiski case. If power is conceived in general terms, then most actors in the Baltic Sea region will today probably perceive themselves to be small states or middle powers in relation to Russia and Germany (see for instance: Knudsen 1999).

If power is conceived as a property of the issue area in question (nuclear power), then there is reason to perceive Russia as a rather superior great power in the Baltic Sea region. Russia is the only state in the area that has nuclear weapons and it has more nuclear power reactors by far than other states do (see below).

Finally, if power is conceived in terms of control of territory and information, then all actors have reason to perceive themselves to be in a disadvantaged position vis-à-vis Russia. Transnational actors, including epistemic communities, should experience the last notion of power as well (see Krasner 1995).

Obviously, the last conception of power is important in any study of the role of non-state actors in an international system of sovereign states. However, apart from this, this case study focuses on power disparity in a regional context (the Baltic Sea region) and within a specific issue-area (nuclear power). This usage of the term is less common, as scholars have tended to associate power with a single overall international power structure. However, because such a narrow interpretation of the term raises interesting new research questions, we are inclined to agree with Baldwin (2002, 188) that 'scholars need to focus on power distribution within specified issue-areas and perhaps within specified regions.'[15]

The Baltic Sea region is characterized by an uneven distribution of nuclear power. At the end of 2002, there were 441 nuclear power reactors in operation in the world (IAEA 2003a). Of 30 countries currently using nuclear energy, five are found in the Baltic Sea region – Russia, Germany, Sweden, Finland, and Lithuania. In all, there are 66 nuclear power plants operating in these five countries, which represent some 15 per cent of all reactors in the world. In terms of the number of reactors, Russia and Germany place fifth and sixth among the nuclear energy powers in the world (IAEA 2003b). Sweden ends up in eleventh place, while Finland and Lithuania are found in nineteenth and twenty-third place, respectively. The remaining Baltic Sea countries have no nuclear power plants, nor do they have plans to build any.

In terms of power distribution, we thus have a situation of asymmetry. Considering that Sweden and Germany have adopted or announced a nuclear phase-out policy, the tendency is that the gap in nuclear power resources will change in Russia's favour. In other words, Russia, although otherwise often perceived as a declining great power, in this specific regional context is rather consolidating its position or even becoming more powerful.[16]

It is important to note that the mere existence of power disparity does not have to imply that a state has power over other states. The power aspect arises only when there is a risk that the superiority of power resources somehow might be used to affect the policies of other states. In the case of Russian nuclear power, such a risk can hypothetically take at least three forms. It can imply use of nuclear weapons, nuclear blackmail, or interruption of nuclear electricity export. In practice, however, it is only the latter two that have any practical bearing on post-Cold War relations. By occasionally playing on Western fears of a new Chernobyl catastrophe, Russian leaders have fuelled talk about nuclear blackmail as a way to force other countries to cooperate (Darst 2001, 176-183).[17] As regards Russian energy exports, there is a concern among some that projects such as the Baltic Ring Electricity Cooperation, which aims at creating one common electricity market in the Baltic Sea region, will

---

15 For a theoretically founded empirical analysis of issue-areas and inter-state power relations, see Knudsen (1979).

16 Russia has some 30 nuclear reactors in operation (1999). All except four are based in the western part of the country, reflecting the major population densities (European Commission 1999a, 5-6, 9-13). The reactors are located at eight nuclear power plants. Of these, the Leningrad Nuclear Power Plant is in the immediate vicinity to the Baltic Sea.

17 On the 26 April 1986, Unit 4 of the four power reactors at Chernobyl in Ukraine exploded (see for example: Fischer 1997, 108-109, 194-201). The Baltic Sea region was soon after affected by fallout as the radioactive cloud spread over northern and central Europe.

make Western Europe vulnerable to politically motivated interruptions in the supply of Russian electricity.[18]

Three Views on Power Disparity and Epistemic Communities

Having established that there exists a nuclear power disparity in the Baltic Sea region, we should now ask how this affects the role of the epistemic community on nuclear and radiation safety. Does power disparity make an insurmountable barrier for expert influence? Or is the significance of power disparity only secondary, upgrading the importance of the capacity of the epistemic community itself? For analytical purposes, we will make a distinction between three views on how power disparity might affect the role of epistemic communities (Table 5.2).

The views have been labelled power disparity as a favourable condition, power disparity as a restraining condition, and power disparity as a secondary condition. It should be emphasized that the views cannot be directly linked to a particular theory of epistemic communities or of transnational relations in general. However, each view can easily be associated with insights from well-established theories of international politics in which power is given a prominent role. We therefore prefer to talk about them as theoretical sources of inspiration.

Table 5.2 Three Views on How Power Disparity Affects the Role of Epistemic Communities

	Power disparity as a favorable condition	Power disparity as a restraining condition	Power disparity as a secondary condition
Entity-environment relationship	Epistemic communities have significant freedom of choice	Epistemic communities are constrained by the environment	Epistemic communities have significant freedom of choice
External effect of power disparity	Strongly positive	Strongly negative	Weak
Hypotheses	If a dominant state is able and willing to assume a leadership role, then there is a window of opportunity for epistemic communities to play a role	If a dominant state seeks to maximize its own power at the expense of other states, then there is no room for epistemic communities to play a role	If an epistemic community has actor capacity and possesses bargaining chips, then it will most likely play a positive role
Theoretical source of inspiration	Hegemonic stability theory	Relative gains theory	Realist bargaining theory

---

18 On vulnerability, see for example: Keohane and Nye 1977, 11-19; on the concrete issue in question see Larsson 2006.

The first view sees power disparity as a favourable condition. This view is inspired by a modest version of the theory of hegemonic stability, which assumes that hegemony can facilitate international cooperation (Keohane 1984, 31; see also Keohane and Nye 1977, 44-45; Haas 1990, 41-42). The theory bears upon cases when a hegemonic state is willing to invest some of its preponderance of material resources to establish and maintain interstate cooperation, but without any intention of conquering or exploiting other states. If the dominant state merely intends to protect its favoured position, then other states may benefit from cooperation as well. Such a condition is relevant to this study because the success of epistemic communities in achieving their goals has sometimes proved to depend on whether or not there are governmental actors to align with (see for example: Risse-Kappen 1995b, 13). The presence of a benevolent hegemonic leader should therefore open a window of opportunity for epistemic communities to play a role.

In the case of the Baltic Sea region, Russia seems to be the main candidate for hegemonic leadership with respect to nuclear power, especially since the other possible candidate Germany has adopted a nuclear phase-out policy. If Russia is willing to promote and coordinate regional efforts for nuclear safety, then this could give one insight to why the epistemic community managed to play the role it did.

The second view (power disparity as a restraining condition) is quite the opposite of the first one. The theoretical inspiration is relative gains theory; that is, the realist argument that state concerns about relative achievements of gains is a major obstacle to cooperation (Grieco 1988, 486-487; see also Waltz 1979, 106). The argument suggests that international politics is viewed very much as a zero-sum game in which the acquisition of power and wealth may only occur at the expense of someone else (Haas 1990, 42). Relative gains concerns therefore reflect a fear that the adversary will get more out of the cooperation. From this we may conclude that cooperation in a context of power disparity hardly can exist without some compelling behaviour of the hegemonic state. In other words, the smaller states must have been forced into the cooperation by a system of sanctions or rewards. This type of behaviour is sometimes referred to as the dark side of hegemony (Haas 1990, 42).

The second view has two implications for the case study. First, it suggests that nuclear power safety cooperation in the Baltic Sea region primarily reflects Russia's interests. From the Russian point of view, the advantages of this type of cooperation should follow from the prospects of getting financial support and transfer of know-how to improve safety standards. According to this view, on the other hand, the other countries should be more or less forced to cooperate to avoid the risk of, for instance, a new Chernobyl scenario (see also the previous discussion about nuclear blackmail). Second, any interference by an epistemic community will be interpreted in terms of relative gains. If experts aspire to a role, they must make sure that their proposals do not jeopardize the position of the hegemonic state, or that the asymmetries of gains are very small.

Finally, the third view (power disparity as a secondary condition) is inspired by realist bargaining theory, which focuses on how power is used in negotiations among states with conflicting preferences (Risse-Kappen 1995a, 20-24). The reasoning is that if a great power places high value on preserving good neighbourly relations, then small states can increase their bargaining power if they hold more intense preferences, if they threaten to defect from cooperation, if they pool resources, or if they control some issue-specific resources needed by the great power. An analogy of this reasoning can be found in the literature on transnational relations. The implication is that if a non-state actor has actor capacity (for example consensus, resources) and possesses bargaining chips (for example representativity, knowledge, or power in implementation), then this will increase the prospects of influencing governments (Greenwood 1997, 16; see also Karlsson 2004a, 119-120).

The focus of the third view is on actor-related variables rather than on the structural context (for example power disparity). From this we may hypothesize that the role of epistemic communities depends mainly on whether or not it has actor capacity and possesses bargaining chips.

Confronting the Empirical Evidence

Having presented the three views on how power disparity might affect the role of epistemic communities, it is now time to confront these with the empirical evidence. The assumption of the first view (power disparity as a favourable condition) was that the presence of a benevolent hegemonic leader should present a favourable context within which epistemic communities could work. If the hegemonic state is willing to invest some of its power in promoting a positive-sum type of regional cooperation, then experts should find it easier to establish contact with relevant decision makers and to build effective coalitions for specific policies and standpoints.

This view does not, however, seem to give an accurate picture of the Paldiski case. There is very little to indicate that Russia, which should be the main candidate for hegemonic leadership on nuclear power safety, has been prepared to assume such a role. On the contrary, there are a number of circumstantial indications suggesting that some of the small states have been the real instigators of the nuclear safety cooperation. In this case we are not primarily thinking of Estonia, which obviously had the strongest interest of all in promoting regional cooperation. Instead, we have certain other circumstances in mind. First, the decision in 1992 to move forward on this issue and establish a working group was basically the result of a joint initiative of Finland and Sweden. The commitment of the two states is also reflected in the selection of chairman of the working group. That is, between 1992 and 2003 the group had three chairmen who came either from Finland or Sweden. The first, professor Vuorinen, very much appeared to have been the driving force behind the working group during the first critical years.

Another circumstance that speaks against the first view is the fact that Russia repeatedly asked for international economic assistance in the Paldiski case. This suggests that Russia has been neither willing nor able to adopt the role of a regional paymaster. Considering these circumstances, we are therefore inclined to conclude that the epistemic community managed to play a role despite the absence of a benevolent hegemonic leader.

The second view (power disparity as a restraining condition) looks upon international politics as a zero-sum game in which states are anxiously concerned about relative gains. From this angle, it becomes difficult to establish regional cooperation because states will always fear that the cooperation takes place at their expense. This will also affect the role of epistemic communities, as states will evaluate their proposals in terms of relative gains. That is, the support for the expert proposals will depend on who wins and who loses on them. In the Paldiski case we find that power disparity can only partly be described as a restraining condition. On the one hand, we can exclude that the nuclear safety cooperation as such is a result of a compelling behaviour on the part of Russia, which according to this view should be the only situation in which cooperation can be established. On the other hand, the case study reveals some moments when Russia tried to use its power position to gain advantage and even to put certain limits on the safety cooperation. This was seen when Russia argued for a narrow definition of the Baltic Sea region, when it provided limited information about the Paldiski site, and when it indicated that the dismantling process depended on international financial support. The latter type of behaviour is sometimes described as nuclear blackmail. That is, the other countries are more or less forced to cooperate unless they want to take the risk of facing a new Chernobyl catastrophe.

It is true in this case that Russian officials maintained that dismantling the reactor facility in Paldiski would take time. However, as emphasized by Robert Darst (2001, 176-183), even though Russian leaders occasionally have played on Western fears of nuclear contamination, it would probably be wrong to simply suppose that nuclear safety is not a matter of concern in Russia.

Considering these circumstances, we arrive at a mixed conclusion about the second view. The power disparity context was enough to restrain the role of the expert group in certain respects (such as the geographical scope, or the immediate access to necessary information), but it was not enough to stop the experts from eventually breaking most of the secrecy surrounding the Paldiski site.

The third view (power disparity as a secondary condition) sheds light on the epistemic community itself. Although the situation in the Baltic Sea region may be characterized by an uneven distribution of power, this is assumed to be of secondary importance if we want to understand the role of experts. In other words, the role of epistemic communities depends entirely on actor-related variables. The answer to why the experts in this case managed to play a role should therefore be expressed in terms of capacity (such as consensus and resources) and bargaining chips (for example representativity, knowledge, or power in implementation).

The third view seems to bring some insight to the Paldiski case, but once again the results are mixed. The expert group had obviously not enough actor capacity and bargaining chips to initially overcome the resistance of Russia, but in the long run it proved persistent enough to make a difference. On the one hand, the working group was favoured by a high degree of consensus (the Russian representative was too isolated to be able to change the agenda of the working group), representativity (the members of the working group came from all Baltic Sea states and the European

Union), knowledge (the members were all in one way or another experts on nuclear and radiation safety), and power in implementation (at least to the extent that it could give concrete advice on the decommissioning process).

On the other hand, the working group has operated with very limited resources and in practice been dependent upon the resources of the individual members. The terms of reference state that the host country of the CBSS should bear the costs of the meetings, but that participants will have to carry the expenses relating to their travel and stay (WGNRS 1993a, item 6). Less surprisingly, even though all experts are full members of the working group, it has been noted that some of them – as previously mentioned – 'have had difficulty financing even travel to two meetings per year'. This problem applies first of all to members from the Baltic states and Russia. As regards the role of the epistemic community, we can therefore conclude that the experts have been forced to proceed at a somewhat slower pace than otherwise would have been possible.

Conclusions

Statements by Estonian officials in the mid-1990s suggested that the intervention by a regional expert group on nuclear and radiation safety made a difference on the dismantling and the transfer of the former Soviet Nuclear Submarine Training Centre at Paldiski. Following previous research on epistemic communities, the question arose whether or not this role could be explained by reference to the power disparity context. For this purpose, we developed three different views on how the role of epistemic communities might be linked to power disparity.

Interestingly, when the three views then were confronted with the empirical evidence, it was found that both the second view (power disparity as a restraining condition) and the third view (power disparity as a secondary condition) gave some understanding of the outcome in the Paldiski case. Russia's control of information and territory obviously set certain limits for the expert group. In this sense power disparity was as a restraining condition. On the other hand, the disparity with respect to nuclear power safety was not large enough to stop the experts from eventually reaching some important goals (most notably breaking some of the secrecy surrounding the Paldiski site and accelerating the timetable for the final transfer). By having actor capacity and by possessing bargaining chips, the group was therefore able to challenge Russia and eventually also break some of the resistance.

It would however go too far to conclude that power disparity because of this should be regarded as a secondary condition. Considering the combined support for the second and the third views, it seems more reasonable to conclude that power disparity represents an open structure. It sets certain limits for governments and transnational actors, but at the same time it is also developed by the activities of these actors.

Chapter 6

Threat Images and Socialization: Estonia and Russia in the New Millennium[1]

Erik Noreen

A Power Disparity Dilemma

In their roles as midget and giant of the Baltic Sea Region, Estonia and Russia certainly differ on a number of factors such as population, territorial area and resources. This relational circumstance has a built-in power disparity dilemma, which might be accentuated by the historical record of a half-century of Soviet/Russian annexation of the Baltic states. Thus, we have a case of an interstate relationship of unequal power, which historically has also been characterized by exploitation, that is, territorial annexation, military occupation, and political and cultural repression.

When studying relations between Estonia and Russia, we might therefore take a step further from the realist puzzle, that is, rather than enquiring whether power disparity *in itself* influences the relations in question, we should ask instead how and to what extent identities mediate power disparity. In other words, we must also consider how the above-mentioned historical record, probably deeply engraved in the minds of the people of the Baltic states, contributes to shaping their contemporary political expression.

There are various identity puzzles related to power disparity and historical experience. The people within the Baltic Sea area might identify themselves as citizens of a small state, as in the case of Estonia, or as a great power, as in the case of Russia. This puzzle brings about a number of questions. For instance, how does this kind of role identity affect the policy-makers' view of the neighbouring states in terms of threat? How do they moreover socially identify themselves in terms of belonging to, for example, Europe or the Western world? Who is the 'other', and how could this other be characterized?

---

1   An Appendix to this chapter is available at http://www.pcr.uu.se/personal/anstallda/noreen.htm. I wish to thank my colleagues at the projects *Power Disparity, Identity and Cooperative Security* and *Threat Politics*, and in particular Roxanna Sjöstedt and Stephen G. Walker, for their highly useful comments. Anjelika Mamytova has been a great help in collecting Russian data.

From an Estonian point of view, the process of leaving the tyrannous Soviet Union for the democracy of Europe should be interpreted within the context of finding a new post-Cold War identity, in addition to regaining their inter-war identity as an independent European state. How, then, is Russia assessed within the process of forming a collective Estonian 'self'? To what extent do Estonians assess Russia as a threat?

After almost a decade of peaceful relations with Russia, a majority of Estonian citizens still assessed the former occupying power as a threat to their state. According to opinion polls on threat perceptions, 60 to 78 percent of the Estonian people perceived the Russian state as an ominous force in relation to Estonia, figures that had not significantly changed since the 1990s (Rose 1997, 54; Rose 2000, 36-37). Nonetheless, more recent polls indicate another trend. Between the years 2000 and 2004 the percentage of Estonians who believed in the probability of being attacked by another state steadily decreased from 33 to 12 percent (Estonian Ministry of Foreign Affairs 2005b; Eesti Varbariigi Kaitseministeerium 2003). Even though Russia is not directly mentioned in these surveys, it is – due to Estonia's historical record – fairly obvious which state one has in mind as a possible threatening actor. Still, the point stressed here is that this (at least from a traditional International Relations perspective on small state – great power relations) self evident threat image has gradually become secondary to the average Estonian in the 21st century. Instead, out of the 'main factors of security instability' listed in a press release concerning a survey carried out in February 2004, international terrorism and organized crime ranked highly (Estonian Ministry of Foreign Affairs 2004).

In Russia too, other issues than military threats from foreign nations seem to worry ordinary citizens. For example, drug addiction, crime, terrorism, the situation in Chechnya and economic problems have been highly ranked on the list of items that people find 'most dangerous and worrisome for the nation' (Public Opinion Foundation 2003). Similar lists could be found back in the mid-1990s (Wagnsson 2000, 92). As regards NATO, the statistics paint a somewhat different picture. When the public was *explicitly* asked whether it assessed NATO or the NATO-enlargement as a *threat*, a large part of the population (47-65%) during the last decade always answered in the affirmative (Petrova 2004; Public Opinion Foundation 2002; Wagnsson 2000; Zimmerman 2002). On the other hand, the figures also indicate that the Russians 'dislike NATO, but agree to collaborate' (Petrova 2001); and on other occasions a majority of the Russian population wants to develop collaboration with NATO (Public Opinion Foundation 2004).

Turning to the political elites of Estonia and Russia, we find that the public threat perception can largely be regarded as a reflection of the framing of these elites. In Estonia, the latter, however, appears to have been much quicker than the public in modifying any previous assessments of Russia as posing a severe threat to Estonian security. In the political elite discourse, the threat stemming from Russia was downplayed in relation to other issues in general, and to other threats in particular, even before the turn of the millennium (Aalto 2003; Noreen 2001; Noreen and Sjöstedt 2004).

Trying to mirror the above findings and then discern a corresponding trend concerning Russian policy-makers may at first glance seem absurd. In what respect should they have ever considered the Baltic states as military threats? This question becomes less peculiar when one looks at these states in the context of being NATO members. There are reasons to believe that the policy-makers in Moscow have made such assessments, at least since the middle of the 1990s when the Baltic states started to express their wishes to join NATO. However, what actually happened in the new Millennium might have been considered as quite unexpected. Although Russian policy-makers, from time to time, expressed their fear of a 'Cold-War NATO', they nevertheless accepted the fact of the NATO-enlargement – including the Baltic states. The softened critique in Moscow against Baltic NATO-membership harmonized fairly well with the softer threat framing in Tallinn.

In this chapter I will analyze the threat images presented by the respective Estonian and Russian governments after the Cold War era, with particular emphasis on the first years of the new Millennium. The aim is to investigate and compare how different theoretical approaches attempt to provide viable explanations for the way in which threats are presented within Estonian and Russian political discourses, placing particular emphasis on the formations of identities which are, in turn, linked to processes of socialization. I will attempt to demonstrate how this approach can present an alternative explanation to more traditional approaches in International Relations literature, particularly regarding the transformation of threat images among Estonian and Russian policy-makers.

Methodological Considerations

Although an investigation of a popular discourse would be relevant in illustrating and comparing any discursive gap between a public and an elite discourse, such a gap is not the focal point here. One could also argue that the elite discourse as such is a system of statements and practices stemming from a great number of divergent elite actors besides those who make up the government – i.e. the political opposition, civil servants of governmental agencies, judicial representatives, etc. – and that all these elites do not necessarily construct and/or reflect the same discourse. These considerations aside, I have decided to focus on the official governmental discourse in Moscow and Tallinn, respectively.

This choice is based on the logic of centrality and appropriateness, meaning that among all different entities of the assemblage called the political elite, ministries such as the Ministry of Foreign Affairs, the Ministry of Defence, the Presidential office, or in the case of Russia, the Security Council, are selected, since these are assumed to be the most central actors in formulating each respective security policy line after the Cold War.

However, it is worth mentioning here that discourses are inextricably interwoven with practices. As has been suggested by discourse analysts 'practices are discursive, both in the sense that some practices involve speech acts…and in the sense that practice cannot be thought outside of discourse' (Neumann 2002, 628). This implies that we not only focus on the content of texts, or the language as such, but also how these texts are put in practice. Because policy-makers normally have a mandate to act (make policy) it is thus reasonable to study the context within which they act, as well as the acts per se.

The problem here is to determine how these practices could be delimited for my research purposes. It might be reasonable to connect the concept of practices to some form of 'socially recognized ... activities' (Neumann 2002, 630-631). It might furthermore, be fairly recognized that there is a multitude of activities going on in, for example, the Russian government, that may in turn be – more or less explicitly – connected to threat images. This can be exemplified by such activities as taking decisions on the withdrawal of troops from the Baltic area to publishing certain documents on official websites, that is, a range of activities from a higher to a lower level of security policy importance.

Nonetheless, the point of departure of discourse studies might be on the framing of language: how policy-makers' reasoning and views are expressed in official texts. There are two reasons for choosing this kind of approach. Firstly, official statements are assumed to be credible in that they essentially correspond with practice, which I also find evidence for. Secondly, I assume that authoritative statements contribute in shaping the political and societal discourse, both domestically and internationally (cf. Buzan, Waever, and Wilde 1998, 177-178; Milliken 1999).

Threat Images Held by the Midget

Let me begin with President Meri's pointed interpretation of the Estonian experience:

> In Russia's case most of the European politicians tend to forget the time factor. The Americans – and the French – believed in 1989-1990 that the almighty power of the Bolshevist party had been undone, and that the USSR had overnight, just like in a fairy tale, become a stable democratic regime. This will take a little more time! In Estonia, we were still struggling to restore our pre-war state in 1991... Our relations with Russia were very strained, and many public servants in Europe could not understand this. Estonia knows the Russian history much better than an average European. We have no doubt that some day, Russia will be a democracy. It is only a question of time. We have never thought that the change would be quick. And the actual developments have proved us right from the beginning. In some sense, we are more realistic than you are, and this realistic attitude gives us more certainty (President Lennart Meri 2000).

The post-Cold War history of Estonia can be divided into three phases: the *proto-independence* mobilization under the last years of Soviet occupation, the first years of *formal independence*, and the *state building phase*. The first phase of proto-independence started at the end of 1988, when popular movements openly began to manifest demands for a politically independent Estonia. Already in this period a language law was initiated, which established the 'status of Estonian as the sole official language of national and local government' (Smith 2003, 14). An essential foundation for Estonian national identity had thereby been laid. The period ended in August 1991, when the provisional Estonian government declared its country's *de jure* independence.

The second phase of independence was then initiated and was completed in August 1994, when the Russian government, after drawn-out negotiations, withdrew all its troops from Estonian territory. Like the other Baltic countries, Estonia was now *de facto* independent. During this period, Estonia had become a member of several international organizations. It was also associated with the Western European Union. Furthermore, the Estonian government declared that it also wanted to join NATO and the EU.

The period was characterized by tension between, on the one hand, the Estonian government, and on the other, organizations that tried to mobilize the Russian speaking-minority (approx. one third of the Estonian population in the beginning of the 1990s) and Kremlin policy-makers. The tension was fuelled by the Citizenship Law of 1992, which excluded the Russian settlers from having any immediate influence on important political instances in Estonia.

Moscow's view could be exemplified by President Yeltsin's New Year speech in 1994, where he referred to the Russian minority in the Baltic states in terms of '[y]ou are inseparable from us and we are inseparable from you ... we defend and will defend you and our common interest ... we will do this with greater energy and greater resoluteness' (Kauppila 1999). In addition, Estonian policy-makers were greatly affected by Russian statements in line with the so-called *Near Abroad* doctrine, meaning that post-Soviet territories belonged to the Russian sphere of immediate security interest (Noreen 2001, 88).

The last completed phase could be characterized as a *state-building* phase, that is, a phase of economical, societal, and political consolidation. This period extended over almost a decade and ended in 2004 when Estonia became a member of NATO and the EU. A turning point occurred already at the end of 2002:

> With the invitation to accession (to NATO) negotiations given in November 21, 2002, Estonia is on the threshold of an historic breakthrough, leaving behind the unprivileged status of a transition status of a transition state and joining the family of western countries who share and defend common values (Berg 2003).

The years that preceded the historic events were characterized by the Baltic states' attempts to prove themselves as ideal nation-states, not only in terms of economic progress, but also in the way they handled certain political and societal problems. A problem of the latter kind was obviously the Russian-speaking minority issue. The way the Estonian government handled this issue was carefully scrutinized not only by organizations such as the EU and the CSCE/OSCE, but also, as we have seen, by the Russian government.

The Russian minority problem directly affected the relations between Tallinn and Moscow in various respects. We can identify a number of contradictory landmarks that were related to this issue. They included, on the one hand, a series of Estonian amendments and laws up to 1997 that 'witnessed further "nationalizing" measures intended to further undermine the position of the Russian-speaking minority within society' (Smith 2003, 24), and, on the other, hand the outcome of the negotiations on a border agreement in the end of the 1990s, eventually signed by the respective foreign ministers in Moscow in May 2005, but still, as of June 2006, not ratified by the *Duma* (RIA Novosti 2006). The issues of contestation concern, above all else, contrasting views on how the relationship between Estonia and Russia should be categorized during the period from World War II to the end of the Cold War. Whereas Tallinn has thus far characterized it as a Soviet occupation, Moscow is eager to stress that this interpretation, referring to '"aggression by the Soviet Union against Estonia" in 1940 and "occupation," and the "illegal" incorporation of Estonia into the Soviet Union' could lead to a series of claims on Russian territory (Gryaznevich 2005; St. Petersburg Times 2005).

These examples involve, on the one hand, a fairly nationalistic, anti-Russian gesture, at least as judged by the Russian government. On the other hand, Estonia demonstrated a complaisant and flexible attitude vis-à-vis Russia, as the Estonian government, in contrast to the Russian interpretation referred to above, gave up its demand of some 2,000 square kilometers of territory held by Russia since 1944 (Haab 1998, 119).

In the latter half of the state-building phase we can, moreover, discern a shift in the Estonian attitude to the minority issue. There was a clear tendency to acknowledge that Estonia after the occupation really had become a multicultural and multiethnic society. In March 2000 the government approved a *State Integration Program*. A cornerstone in this policy was to obtain '… a significant reduction in the number of persons without undetermined citizenship, a substantial breakthrough in teaching the Estonian language and full participation of non-Estonians in Estonian society at all levels' (State Programme. Approved by the Government of Estonia 2000).

In addition, a more liberal language policy led to action the following year, as the Parliament abolished the requirement it had adopted several years before, implying that members of Parliament and the local councils no longer had to prove their command of Estonian (*Estonian Review* 23.11, 2001). It might not be far-fetched to conclude that the integration policy of the Estonian government alleviated any possibly tense relations between the former occupied state and its occupant. This policy also found fertile ground in Washington and Brussels, as it eased the way to both EU and NATO membership (Asmus 2002, 228-238).

Nevertheless, a vast majority of the Estonian public opinion, seen in opinion polls as late as 2000, assessed Russia as a threat against the Estonian state. The question then becomes, how did the Estonian policy-makers frame the threats with reference to Russia? What else, if anything, did they refer to in terms of being a threat to Estonian national security?

The image of Russia that was given in interview sessions in Tallinn in May 2003 was not straightforward. On the one hand there were expressions of worries concerning an unpredictable development in Russia. On the other hand, it was stressed that 'our relations with Russia are improving', as well as, 'we don't want to consider any country, at the moment, as a military threat.' The somewhat mixed feeling about Russia was well summarized by an Estonian representative: 'We don't see Russia as a threat, but we are neighbours and we are following what's going on there.' Several policy-makers accordingly underscored that they were now on speaking terms with their counterparts in Moscow. As long as the Putin administration was staying in office it was fairly sure that the Estonian-Russian relations were on the right track. In fact, these relations had never been better, and the more relaxed attitude to Baltic NATO-membership in Moscow supported this assessment. But, as exemplified above, there were at the same time severe concerns in respect to the domestic streams of public opinion within Russia.[2]

An account of the Estonian political elite's threat images after the Cold War based on quantitative and qualitative text analyses has been given elsewhere (Noreen 2001; Noreen and Sjöstedt 2004). It is worth mentioning here that in these studies a paradox was found: The military threat from a former occupant – although this is being assessed from a historical point of view rather than current conditions – creates Estonia's interest in NATO membership. The prospect of this membership, in turn, contributes to the precedence of soft threats rather than hard ones on the Estonian security policy agenda, that is, a focus on non-military, unconventional threats rather than military, conventional ones.

If we look somewhat closer at the development of policy-makers' presentation of threat images over time, it is fairly obvious that soft security language increased immediately after the Russian troop withdrawals in 1994, almost concurrent with more direct statements on the necessity of Estonian NATO membership. Moreover, references to any immediate military threats directed towards Estonia have become increasingly rare after 1994. The tendency of prioritizing softer at the expense of harder threats, and of emphasizing structural rather than actor (read Russian) based threats, seems to somewhat correspond with the expressed prospects of becoming a member of the Western alliance.

References to terrorism were, not surprisingly, very frequent in speeches and statements after the 9/11 events. Literally speaking, there was an explosion of allusions to terrorism in comparison to the period that preceded these events. In the regularly held Guideline-speech addressed to the Estonian Parliament in October 2001, terrorism was mentioned forty nine times (Ilves 2001). In the corresponding speech held in the autumn of the previous year, nothing was said about terrorism (Ilves 2000). This tendency to stress terrorism every time threat issues were brought up also continued for some period of time.

The closer the crucial decision as to whether the new group of Central and Eastern European countries would join NATO became, the more prevalent inclusive views

---

2   Interviews with A. Laneman, (Colonel, Chief of the General Staff of the Estonian Defence Forces), 23 May, 2003; M. Mikhelson, 23.05 2003 (Estonian Parliament, Foreign Affairs Committee); S. Mikser, 21.05 2003 (Estonian Parliament, Defense Committee); R. Mälk, 21.05 2003 (Estonian Ministry of Foreign Affairs); S. Sakkov, 22.05 2003 (Estonian Ministry of Defense).

vis-à-vis Russia were in Estonian statements. Thus, it was pointed out, for both international and domestic audiences, that cooperation with Russia was necessary within the framework of the security policy architecture in which Estonia would become a natural building block. It was emphasized that 'in order for NATO to be an effective and successful security and defense organization, intensive co-operation is essential between the United States, Europe, and third countries, including Russia' (Ojuland 2002; also Berg 2003).

Previous research (e.g. Kuus 2002a; Kuus 2002b; Mouritzen 1998) has been all too quick to assume that the Russian Other is the only determinant in understanding both Estonian images and its actions. A study of the Estonian political discourse, as it has developed during the post-Cold War era, which explores how the elite categorize themselves, their state, and the world surrounding them, reveals on the contrary that the *dynamics* of collective identity formations provide a feasible explanation of the dynamics of threat framing (Noreen and Sjöstedt 2004). Since the construction of collective identity is such a dynamic phenomenon, yesterday's antagonistic Other could become tomorrow's ally.

From this perspective, the Estonian wish to join the EU and NATO is not solely guided by a perceived Russian threat, but rather is driven by a desire to re-establish bonds with the western political culture. It is also stressed in the Estonian discourse – predicating Estonia as industrious and modern – that Estonia intends to join international organizations to have a say in various international issues, rather than only using them as a means of protection. There is naturally no question as to whether the Estonian elite discourse to a large extent resents the idea of belonging to an eastern collective identity formation. However, the issue here concerns whether Estonian policy-makers are framing the Russian state or its own Russian minority in terms of threat – militarily, culturally, or otherwise.

The assumption concerning Estonia's ongoing antagonistic relationship with Russia, or its Russian minority, is something which I call into question. Much has happened since; for example, the Estonian foreign minister in 1994 drew a parallel between the Russian governments' relations to the Russian minority in Estonia, and Hitler's program of protecting the so-called *Volksdeutsche* living outside the boundaries that then constituted Germany (Luik 1994). Although this is an example of rhetoric, this kind of verbal politics gives a sense of how relations between states develop, as well as how the domestic contexts within a state evolve. The integration policy initiated by the end of the 1990s indicates the introduction of an alternate Estonian discourse. This may have contributed in turn to a better climate between Estonia and Russia, thereby decreasing Russian objections against Baltic NATO-membership (Asmus 2002, 235-237).[3]

---

3 See also the discussion of Estonian elite images of Russia in Knudsen 2004, and the discussion in Ch. 9 of this volume.

Threat Images Held by the Giant

Again I turn to the interpretation of the President of the country concerned, this time Vladimir Putin:

> Indeed, NATO was established to counterbalance the Soviet Union and the Eastern bloc that was created by the Soviet Union. Today there is no Eastern bloc. In fact, even the Soviet Union is no more. In other words, the reasons that brought NATO to life are no longer there. Yet NATO exists. It not only exists, but it is expanding, moreover, towards our borders. As you know, some time ago, several months ago one of your colleagues, your American colleagues, asked me: 'Do you allow for a possibility of Russia joining NATO?' I replied: 'Yes. Why not?' And very soon we got an answer – true, an unofficial one, but it sounded at a sufficiently high level – that nobody in NATO was expecting Russia. But if nobody is expecting us there why should we rejoice at the expansion of NATO and NATO's approach to our borders? (President Vladimir Putin 2000)

NATO could certainly be considered as one of the traditional threats from the point of view of the Russian policy-makers. The alliance was, after all, once created as a response to the presumably aggressive union within which Russia was the principal actor. That is, the remembered experience of Cold War relations between NATO and the Soviet Union, rather than the current intentions of this organization, fuel the image of a threatening alliance. Consequently, during the latter half of the 1990s Russian policy-makers became exceedingly hostile to any enlargement of NATO eastward (Wagnsson 2000, 133). Some 60 percent of the Russian elite perceived the 'spread of NATO in Eastern Europe as a security threat.' And even more alarming; between 1993 and 1999 the share of the elite that perceives the U.S. as a 'threat to the Russian security', increased from 27 to 62 percent (Zimmerman 2002, 91-92).[4]

Turning to the policy-makers' statements, the picture becomes much more multifarious than the result from the opinion polls.[5] Although the politicians' negative views vis-à-vis NATO expansion have been fairly manifest throughout the post-Cold War era, we can certainly discern nuances. The rather complex and somewhat contradictory presentation of the NATO problem was well captured in the above

---

4 One population poll reveals that, in spite of the 9/11 incidents, which might have bridged any gap between the former superpowers, 57 percent considered NATO expansion as a threat to Russia in late September 2001. The share had significantly increased since 1997 (47%) (Public Opinion Foundation 2001).

5 A principal difference between the polls and texts examined in this study is that a majority of the survey participants, when asked if they consider NATO to be a threat, answered in the affirmative: none of this is apparent in the documents from the Ministry of Foreign Affairs. Rather, the policy-makers prefer to talk about other issues such as international terrorism and Islamic fundamentalism in *terms* of threats. However, the survey also indicates that when participants are free to choose between several potentially threatening issues, it was not 'military threats from other nations' that worried them, but drug addiction, crime, terrorism, low living standards, corruption, the situation in Chechnya etc. (Public Opinion Foundation 2003).

cited interview with President Putin in October 2000. The skepticism against NATO was clearly voiced, and there was a tendency to depict the organization as an outdated Cold War phenomenon. However, there were also incentives among the policy-makers to strengthen cooperation between Russia and NATO. A chain of cooperative steps since the 1990s rather points towards a pro-NATO view (Wagnsson 2000, 81-82). Putin's 'Yes. Why not?' to a Russian NATO-membership might at least indicate that the alliance was not perceived by him as a threat to Russia (Putin 2000a).

Notable here is that the Russian Government's attitude towards NATO during the 1990s was not always entirely negative. In the literature there has so far been a few attempts to describe the Russian foreign policy discourse vis-á-vis NATO, which reveals a far from clear pattern of distinguished waves (e.g. Ambrosio 2003; Trenin and Lo 2005). To briefly summarize, one could claim that from 1994, when NATO's intentions on an eastward expansion became more or less established, to the spring of 2004 when seven new members joined NATO, Russian decision-makers have watched the process from outside, expressing their concerns to varying extents (Alexeev 2004).

However, looking at the discourse of 1994, one could at first argue that a form of consensus existed between Russia and NATO, at least regarding cooperative efforts between the two of promoting peace and security. In line with this discourse, Yeltsin's Foreign Minister Andrei Kozyrev stressed the importance of establishing good relations with the West, arguing that '[b]oth Russia and the NATO members are like-minded nations. We belong to one and the same democratic community of nations' (Kozyrev 1994b, 1). Due to these shared democratic ideals, Kozyrev also denounced the idea that the West would pose any form of threat remotely similar to the ones of the Cold War.

Nevertheless, this situation would turn out to be somewhat more complicated than what appeared initially. Russia faced difficulties in balancing the role of simultaneously being a great power – maintaining geopolitical influence – and being an open, democratic, and modern society. This resulted in a somewhat distrustful Western view on Russia, and served as an obstacle to one of the central aspects of the NATO-Russian relationship; the one of an equal partnership. Kozyrev claimed that since the development of Russian internal and external affairs did not 'fit the usual Western criteria and stereotypes, [s]ome analysts cannot accept the idea of a strong Russia'. This, in turn, led to a form of 'lagging partnership' between the two camps and '[w]hile elements of cooperation exist on some concrete issues, a mature strategic partnership has yet to emerge' (Kozyrev 1994a, 60).[6] Kozyrev did not, however, abandon his pro-West stance altogether, and his somewhat mixed message and inconsistent policies eventually led to his forced resignation.

Kozyrev's replacement, Yevgenii Primakov, advocated a somewhat different approach. While claiming to want to maintain good relations with the West, he

---

6 These claims turned into discursive practice in November 1994, when Kozyrev chose a tougher stance towards the West and refused to sign previously agreed-upon Partnership for Peace documents with NATO (Sakwa 1996, 280).

clearly voiced the idea of Russia being a great power, and aimed to make Russia 'one of the influential centers of a multipolar world' (Primakov 1997 in Lo 2002, 59). As regards NATO, Primakov was less amiable than his predecessor, stating that it was '"absolutely inadmissible" to Russia to have any of the ex-Soviet republics, including the Baltic States, join the Alliance' (Primakov 1998 in Matz 2001, 252). These anti-expansionist sentiments increased around the time of the Kosovo crisis in 1999, where, in particular, the Russian military leadership stressed an increased threat from NATO, something that 'was facilitated by the fact that NATO's action in the Balkans was widely perceived across Russia's political spectrum as an act of aggression' (Jackson 2002, 391).

The anti-NATO language following the Kosovo crisis within Russian military circles was also an indication of harsher tones against NATO among civil policy-makers. For instance, in the *National Security Concept* of 2000 some aspects of NATO policy were recognized as being threatening to Russia, specifically, 'the strengthening of military-political blocks and alliances, above all NATO's eastward expansion' (Russian National Security Concept 2000, 2). However, this policy document, which to a large extent was a product of the Yeltsin administration (albeit published under Putin) above all else served to emphasize another threat which was to become the main threat image of the international security discourse in the coming years. It was thus stated that: 'Terrorism represents a serious threat to the national security of the Russian federation. International terrorism is waging an open campaign to destabilize Russia' (Russian National Security Concept 2000, 2).

This focus on international terrorism as a threat represents a fundamental shift in Russian security policy, especially when considering the previous corresponding policy document from 1997. This document did indeed address international terrorism as a threat, but rather as one among other international problems, such as transnational crime and ethno-national interests (Rossiiskaya Gazeta 1997, 4-5).

Previous research has been eager to stress that the external shock of 11 September 2001 caused a fundamental shift in Russian security policy, particularly in relation to the U.S. and the West. It is reasonable that the Russian government took advantage of this 'window of opportunity' to convince particularly the U.S. to 'join forces to confront together the dangerous threats and challenges that humanity will face in the twenty-first century' (quoted in Ambrosio 2003, 7).

Moreover, the tragedy of 9/11 might have helped Putin to convince his domestic audience that 'his pro-Western shift' was necessary (Shevtsova 2005, 103). However, the attempts to make this shift dependent on the effects of 9/11 is somewhat exaggerated by the literature, especially when it is stated, with reference to 'Russian strategic thinking', that '(a)fter 11 September ... a new outgroup emerged: international terrorism' (Ambrosio 2003, 7-8). In this context it might be worth noticing that the Russian government had warned the West against this outgroup already, in early 1999, in connection to the Kosovo-crisis:

> Can European people take advantage of the emergence of a center of Islamic extremism on the continent? Why don't Americans understand that backing extremist Muslims

in Kosovo amounts to helping a new Bin Laden to emerge? ... Does Europe need the constitution of a centre of Islamic extremism, a centre of weapons and drug trafficking? (quoted in Guillaume 2004, 25)

When browsing through the hundreds of references to the term 'threat' in the year 2000, stored at Russian government's websites, it is obvious that the policy-makers much more frequently refer to terrorism rather than conventional threats, such as missiles, nuclear weapons and NATO (see appendix, footnote 1). When explicitly mentioning threat, it is obvious that the Russian Government prefers to highlight other issues than for example NATO.

This is apparent, for example, in references dated ten days before 9/11. When the Russian president is asked why he has difficulties in accepting the Baltic states joining NATO, he replies in a fairly prophetic manner:

What problems is NATO solving? Protecting from whom? For the real threat today is terrorism, the spread of narcotics, organized crime, the traffic in arms. That is what really can threaten us today (Putin 2001a).

The skepticism against NATO per se has obviously been toned down at the turn of the new millennium. Moreover, the 9/11 events have convinced the greatest of powers of something that Moscow continually has asked for; namely, a strengthened cooperation aimed at combating international terrorism – the threat of all threats.

Comparing texts before and after al Quaida's attacks on the United States is rather interesting, because the focus on *international* terrorism was also common before 9/11. For example, the Russian President stated, in connection with one of the many outrages against civilians in Moscow, 'I should note that terrorism, unfortunately, is not our national disease, it's a disease of international prevalence' (Putin 2000b). In addition, the developments in Afghanistan were closely followed, and various speakers warned against the effects of the Taliban rule. The Russian discourse stressed time after time the danger of 'religious extremism and international terrorism', and references are made to 'Afghanistan, where the internal conflict is acquiring an ever more dangerous international dimension' (Losyukov 2001; also S. Ivanov 2000; Ministry of Foreign Affairs of the Russian Federation 2001; Chhikvishvili 2003; Chizhov 2004; Rogozin 2002).

The emphasis on an international aspect is obvious: militant extremism is expanding beyond the Asian region; the Usama bin Ladin-led network is '*terrorist internationale*'; and this group is a globally destructive force, which threatens international peace and general values. It is occasionally stressed that 'Russia in population composition, spirit, culture and prevalent religions is a European country', although it is also emphasized that Russia is 'the natural bridge between Europe and Asia' (Ivanov 2001).

To characterize Russia as primarily European places the country in the same in-group as the other states in the European/North Atlantic region. They are presupposed to be subject to the same threats, above all else international terrorism. Because of its strategic location, the Russian discourse portrays Russia as an especially important and responsible actor within the Western in-group:

> Terrorism is a worldwide pain, and an analogy involuntarily suggests itself that Russia, which is now on the frontline of the struggle against international terrorism in Chechnya and Central Asia, is saving the civilized world from the terrorist plague just as it saved Europe from a Tatar-Mongol invasion in the 13th century through its own suffering and deprivations (Ivanov 2001).

Due to this framing of terrorism as an international matter, it is no surprise when scrutinizing texts after 9/11 that these texts in essence contain the same message as previously, albeit with more emphasis (Ministry of Foreign Affairs of Russia 2001a). In addition, the 'Chechnya-problem' has, particularly during the second Chechen war, been framed as being a part of a larger threat of international terrorism (e.g. Ministry of Foreign Affairs of Russia 2001b). It was, for example, emphasized that the centuries-old Chechnya problem above all else should be characterized as a fundamentalist invasion (Putin 2001c). With regard to the threat posed by religious fundamentalists, there is a clear sense of 'we' against 'them' in the discourse and Russia is perceived as belonging to the European/Western ingroup, vis-à-vis the Muslim outgroup (Putin 2001b; also Ivanov 2003a; Matviyenko 2001; Safonov 2001).

Threat Image Trends

The threat image trends in Estonia and Russia in the first half-decade of the new millennium are summarized in the diagram below. References to threat in the documents (e.g. speeches by, and interviews with Presidents and Ministers of Foreign Affairs), stored at the governments' websites in Russia and Estonia, respectively, have been categorized according to two main typologies. These are *terrorism* and *non-military threats*. The various sub categories within each main typology are presented in tables in the appendix (footnote 1). However, some points should be made here in connection to the typologies. Terrorism is, in the case of both Estonia and Russia, mentioned to such an extent that it deserves a typology of its own. Before the 9/11 events it was sometimes referred to as a 'soft' security threat, but as it has been officially stated in, for example, Estonia, 'these acts of terror changed the whole paradigm of security risks' raising terrorism 'to the level of hard security' (Tiido 2002). Moreover, non-military threats represent a broad category, and one may consider it to be too broad.

However, the common denominator of the sub-types presented here is that they fall into the political, economical, societal, and ecological sectors, and thereby demand primarily non-military means to be prevented (Buzan et al. 1998).

The value on the Y-axis of Figure 6.1 constitutes a so-called salience rate based on the relation between the absolute frequency of references to threats during a specific year divided by the referred type of threat, e.g. terrorism. (If 50 of 100 references to threat in a particular year referred to terrorism, the salience rate of terrorism that year is 0.5.)

From the graph we can draw the following conclusions. The framing of terrorism turned out to be 'the threat of all threats' in 2001 and 2002, due to the 9/11 effect, but with a slightly decreasing trend already in 2003, whereas the Beslan tragedy increased the salience rate another year in Russia (but not in Estonia since most of the references to terrorism were identified before that event). The distinct trend in Estonia and Russia, that is, an exceptional focus on terrorism after 9/11 but less so on conventional Cold-War threats, is hardly unexpected.

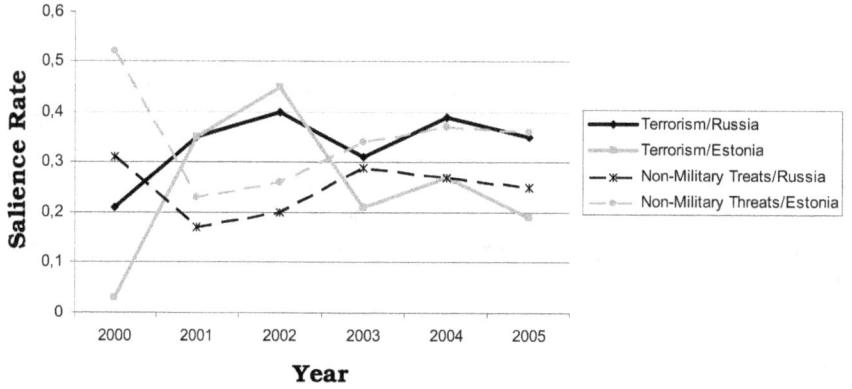

Figure 6.1 Threat Image Trends

What is more remarkable and perhaps even surprising is that the trends for each category to a great extent converge. The framing of threat images with respect to this categorization exhibits a high degree of co-variation between the otherwise – in many respects – dissimilar neighbouring states.

To sum up the threat image pattern more in detail, the tendencies to downplay any threats from NATO in general and NATO-enlargement in particular are discernable in Russia in the new millennium, whereas Estonian policy-makers have toned down any threat from Russia since the 1990s. Moreover, both states have broadened their threat image agendas since the mid-1990s in line with the security policy language of the western world. In other words, they have begun to focus on non-military threats such as organized crime, drug trafficking and environmental threats, as well as – of course – terrorism. The focus on the latter threat is particularly apparent in Russia at the turn of the millennium, before the 9/11 events, due to a series of terror incidents initiated as a consequence of the first Chechen war.

Hence, the threat image on terrorism, which Russian leaders prefer to frame with international overtones, is nevertheless based, first and foremost, on domestic experiences. The same cannot be said about the threat framing in Estonia. Before 9/11, terrorism is considered to be *one* of several threats on the broadened security agenda, but after the terrible incidents in the U.S. there is an explosion of allusions to terrorism, a trend which substantially has declined since 2003 (Noreen and Sjöstedt 2004).

As shown in speeches by and interviews with Estonian policy-makers in the new millennium, Estonian policy-makers are not particularly concerned about Russia *in terms of being a threat*, which is remarkable against the historical background that Estonia was annexed by Russia over the course of a half-century. NATO is rarely brought up by the Russian policy-makers in the context of a threat. Instead, in both countries international terrorism, organized crime, drug trafficking, etc., are framed as severe threats.

Thus, there seem to be interesting similarities in the way the language of threat has developed in Russia and Estonia. One may wonder whether there are any ambitions among policy-makers in Moscow and Tallinn to develop a common understanding of not only what is threatening but also what is threatened in terms of values and identities. Would it be possible to develop cooperative security, in terms of a security community, between an extreme relationship such as the one between Russia and Estonia? Or for that matter, is it even possible to develop a security community in the Baltic Sea area?

In trying to answer this, we have to consider that the development of a security community, that is, developing mutual interaction, which in turn creates 'dependable expectations of peaceful change', often is a fairly slow progression of social learning (cf. Adler and Barnett 1998).

Explaining the Pattern

In this section I shall first consider traditional approaches, then approaches that emphasize identity formations and international socialization.

Traditional Approaches

There is a rich flora of approaches to choose from, on different levels of analysis, when it comes to explaining the development of threat images in Estonia and Russia. On a structural level we find explanations that either constrain or permit policy-makers' opportunities to act (cf. Carlsnaes 2002).

Great changes in *the international system*, in particular the much debated question whether we are moving from a bipolar Cold War order towards a multipolar or a unipolar order, belongs to this category of explanations connected to realism. The Baltic states' choices regarding a Westernized security policy profile must thus be interpreted within this structural context. Power disparity matters, meaning that small states' policies are dependent on the balance of power between great powers in general, as well as the more regional or the 'salient environment' balancing conditions, be that in terms of 'bandwagoning' or some kind of 'balanced co-operative security' (more on this in Noreen and Sjöstedt 2004, 741-742; also, Hansen and Heurlin 1998; Mouritzen 1998).

When it comes to Russia, this power's relatively weak interest in the Baltic Sea region – as far as Russia lacks any particular Northern European security doctrine – has been explained in realist and geopolitical terms. Moscow's tendency since the 1990s to play down the strategic importance of the Baltic Sea area could thus simply be understood in the light of Russia's decreasing possibilities of dominating the region in military terms. The Kremlin policy-makers are far more concerned with the risk of losing territories in the South or East than with any NATO enlargement in the West (Sergounin 1998, 16-18; Spruds 2002, 350-351; Wagnsson 2000, 121).

Realism may well explain why international terrorism has been moved high up on the agenda of Russian policy-makers. The political elite perceives their state as one of the most important great powers of the world (e.g. I. Ivanov 2000; Ivanov 2003b; Ministry of Foreign Affairs of Russia 2000; Putin 2002; Putin 2003b). To simply give in to the demands from Chechen 'terrorists' would create a domino effect and thereby threaten Russia's status as a great power.

However, it seems that realism explains too much, that is, all possible outcomes of the dependent variable. On the one hand, it may explain why it has been important to overlook the threat from NATO for the tactical purpose of pooling resources with the Western alliance to combat the more dangerous threat, international terrorism. On the other hand one could, according to realism, equally have expected that Russia might have highlighted the threat from NATO. The reason for this is that since the 1990s the alliance has continuously expanded closer to the Russian heartland, thereby constantly challenging Russia's status as a great power. It is thus difficult to see any clear causal links between this kind of structural factor and the variance of threat framing.

Similar objections can be raised when scrutinizing other structural explanations such as the development of *domestic conditions*, which may trigger rivalry between various political camps in each of the respective Baltic Sea states. The domestic explanations can be of various kinds. What brings this fairly disparate group of explanations together is that they do not, in contrast to realism, treat the state as a unitary actor. Hence, it has been argued, that 'contrary to the realist assumption states are not unitary actors with a single purpose. Unless we know how different interests are reconciled into a single decision, we cannot know what particular policy will result' (Russett, Starr, and Kinsella 2000, 120).

Applied to the Russian context, domestic sources, such as various interest groups in the political life and the society at large, have been scrutinized as explanatory factors of the foreign policy directions of the Yeltsin as well as the Putin administrations. On the one hand, the shift in Russian foreign policy in the mid 1990s towards abandoning the relatively explicit pro-Western position has been explained as Yeltsin's domestic strategy 'to close the rhetorical gap with the communists, so there is no longer a serious difference between government and opposition on the issue (of NATO enlargement)' (Williams and Neumann 2000, 381; Hopf 1999, 7).

On the other hand, Putin's more Westernized foreign policy profile in the new millennium could at least partly be explained by the outcome of a struggle between various interest groups in Russian society, where we find, for example, the security services and the oil and gas lobby in the 'winning coalition' (Bukkvoll 2003, 225; Jonsson 2004, 175-176).[7]

Nevertheless, it is in general difficult to understand how domestic factors, such as various actors in the society with contrasting interests, can directly explain the variance of threat framing in Russia or Estonia. These factors are rather to be considered as background conditions, which may constrain or enable actors in their ambitions to pursue a certain policy. There seems to be a lack of middle range theories that transform the domestic level into causal mechanisms, which in their turn explain how threats are framed (cf. George and Bennett 2005; Hudson 2005).

Another plausible framework that may help us to understand the dynamics of how threats have been framed involves process explanations. *Cognitive factors* such as stereotypes or schemas could be seen as process phenomena, since these factors concern our mindsets, which are under constant, albeit slow, change (see e.g. Stein 2002, 303). Translated to the Baltic context, it has been argued that fear and stereotyped images of Russia among Baltic policy-makers are the driving forces behind their security policy choices. In one study it is simply stated that the 'Estonian image of Russia is often colored with personal love-hate reminiscences' (Park 1995, 30). The memory of the half-century Soviet occupation is lurking in the dark, implying that the policy-makers' wish to join NATO is based on lessons learned from history (Haab 1998, 119; Mouritzen 1998, 8-9).

This approach would thus lead us to assume that Baltic policy-makers in the 1990s would accept NATO as the one and only solution to their respective state's security problems, referring to history rather than current military threats. According to cognitive schema theory, decision makers often use past events as guidelines to help them in finding the right policy direction. They may, for instance, draw analogies to events from earlier periods, determining a course of action based on the imperative: 'never again will we make the same mistake' (Reiter 1996).

Cognitive schema theory seems to be a powerful explanation when it comes to understanding why, on the one hand, a majority of the Estonian public opinions, at the turn of the millennium, still perceives Russia as a threat, while on the other hand, a large part of the Russian public opinion fears any NATO enlargement, as been revealed in several polls in the 21st century.

In this respect, the public's cognitive resistance may have a stabilizing effect on the political elite in Tallinn and Moscow, respectively (cf. conceptualization on cognitive and political 'stabilizers' in Goldmann 1988). In other words, public opinion serves as a stabilizer for policy-makers' desires to go far beyond the attempts that have been reached so far in cooperation between Russia and NATO. In this sense, the stabilizing process outlined here is counterproductive to the process that I will turn to below, namely the socialization process.

Events are an additional group of explanatory factors that may have more of an immediate effect on the framing of threat images. Dramatic events, interpreted as

---

7   For a study on the Baltic states' security policies in the light of domestic contexts, see Heinemann-Grüder 2002.

crises or external shocks, often imply that central values are perceived to be at stake; that time is short, and that extraordinary measures are justified (Hermann 1990, 12, cf Ch. 3 in this volume).

There is no doubt that the 9/11 attacks immediately moved international terrorism to the top of the agenda around the world. Terrorism has long been viewed as a grave problem that several authorities in countries such as the U.S. have had the specific mission of counteracting. A great deal of research and many policy suggestions have circulated among experts for a number of years without making an impact in the form of decisions about the allocation of resources and new programs (cf. Parker and Stern 2002).

In Russia the situation was different due to, above all else, the second Chechen war. Russia was, as we have seen, already in the 1990s a forerunner when it came to warning the rest of the world about terrorist attacks from religious extremists. However, the unprecedented scope of violence, drama and symbolism around the attacks of September 11th undoubtedly meant that a window of opportunity was opened for terrorism as a threat image, and for different proposals on how to tackle the problem by an anti-terror coalition.

Identity Formations and International Socialization

With few exceptions, Baltic security studies during the 1990s rarely scrutinized threat images *per se* (for an early descriptive study, see Petersen 1992). The image of threats from Russia was, as stated above, almost self-evident. However, at the end of the 1990s there were observations concerning Baltic leaders' appreciation of 'softer' security threat images (Archer and Jones 1999, 171). In the latter half of this decade policy-makers in, for example, Tallinn began to frame threats differently. Apparently there were other things than Russia to be concerned about, even in a security policy context. In addition, the concept of *identity* began to show up fairly frequently in various studies on Baltic security (see index in Knudsen 1999; also e.g. Aalto 2003; Kuus 2002c; Kuus 2002b; Kuus 2002a; Made 2003; Noreen 2001). Concurrently an interest in the notion of identity could be discerned in studies on Russian security policy (e.g. Wagnsson 2000, cf. also Ch. 1 in this volume; Morozov 2003; Hopf 2002; Kassianova 2001; 2004; Williams and Neumann 2000).

Linking identity to security, i.e. using the notion of a collective identity as an explanatory variable to show *how* or *why* agents act the way they do in a security context, has become a fairly well researched area (e.g. Aalto 2003; Kuus 2002c; Kuus 2002b; Noreen 2001; Noreen and Sjöstedt 2004; Risse-Kappen 1996; Wæver, Buzan, Kelstrup, and Pierre Lemaitre 1993; Wagnsson 2000).

Identity exists on several different levels of analysis – from the individual level to the systemic one. The most important category in terms of affecting national security, and thus the one discussed here, is collective or *social identity*. The creation of this kind of identity occurs within a defined social sphere, and is mainly sensed when contrasted to other external identities. The constellation of an identity – the *in-group* – as well as its relations to external groups, is, however, neither static nor constant, but must instead be regarded as a highly dynamic process. For instance, who is included in a certain group and the basis for this inclusion/exclusion can change greatly over time. The same can be said about the in-group's relation to any external group, *the out-group*. What is important to note, however, is that although the relation between the in- and out-group is often characterized by difference, this difference does not necessarily imply conflict. It is not the existence of two contrasting groups *per se* that creates negative assessments of each other. Instead, as the so-called *social identity theory* implies, it is the constitution of the groups themselves that bring about conflict (Wendt 1999, 241-242, also; 2002; Schafer 1999; Theiler 2003).

Two contrasting assumptions can be derived from this theory. On the one hand, it has been suggested that in a group attempting to strengthen its sense of collective identity, the more strongly members identify with each other, the more negative their attitudes vis-à-vis external groups. In other words, the in-group, under these circumstances, is more apt to depict the out-group as a threat, and in extreme cases this antagonism may lead to conflict.

On the other hand, it is assumed that a strong feeling of identity is necessary and healthy for individuals. Units with a well-developed sense of social identity, in terms of who they are ('we are Russians"; "we are Estonians", etc.) are more apt to invite and include external entities into their collective identity formation ("we are Europeans"). According to this assumption, states can 'learn additional "social" ... identities above and beyond the state, creating "concentric circles" of group identification.' (Wendt 1999, 241) Whereas the former identity construction is often determined by the way the in-group distances itself from the out-group, often defined in terms of 'we are *not* as the other', the latter identity construction concerns what 'we admire and strive to become' (Flockhart 2006).

Empirically, both assumptions fit sequentially in the process of nation state building. In the 1990s the Estonian government was, for example, eager to stress what it didn't belong to anymore, that is, anything like the Eastern hemisphere centred around Moscow. Russia was consequently depicted as a threat against Estonia. As identity strengthened among Estonians, and the self-esteem of this national entity increased, there were no longer any reasons to emphasize a Russian threat based primarily on historical experience. Estonians were rather socialized into the European context; they adopted a focus on other threats, for example terrorism and environmental pollution, perhaps even in collaboration with the former occupying power.

By analogy with the security community approach we may suggest that if the we-feelings, i.e. mutual sympathy and loyalty, among the population of a state have matured to a certain extent, the prospects of developing dependable expectations of "peaceful change" with other states are better than if the we-feelings were poorly developed in the state in question (Deutsch 1957).

In line with the assumptions of social identity theory, I propose that the more developed the sense of collective identity between citizens of a state, the more inclined they are to become socialized into larger social identity formations, such as being 'Europeans'. It may not be too far-fetched to conclude that state identity is more developed in Estonia than in Russia, although the existence of some 165.000 so-called stateless persons in Estonia somewhat contradicts this argument (Agence Europe 2004b).

However, Russia is probably not less problematic, in the sense that this extremely vast country makes up 'an agglomeration of different cultures: European, Mediterranean, and Near Eastern Christian culture along with Near and Middle Eastern Islamic, Buddhist-Mongolian, Chinese cultures, and more' (Hopf 1999, 6). The process of developing a negative identification, that is, to specify who 'we' are in relation to an inferior 'other', as well as a positive identification, which occurs 'when a collective perceives of positive models in the surrounding world', might be far more complicated and time-consuming for the multi-ethnic Russia than the relatively homogenous Estonia (cf. Hopf 1999, 8; also Wagnsson 2000, 40-42).

Although identity discourses may be considered to be social structural phenomena, they consist of more malleable and flexible elements than the relatively stable and predictable elements of the realist approach. It is true, also according to Realism, that any international system can change, but the power disparity problem between small states and great powers remains in all essentials. Hence, I see the dynamics of various social identity constructions – in terms of whom we belong to; who are the others – related to a process of *international socialization*. The concept of international socialization – an object of debate for decades – has been defined in terms of *internalization*, 'the adoption of social identity, values and norms into the actor's repertoire of cognition and behavior' (Schimmelfennig 2003, 73; also Flockhart 2006; Thies 2003).

A recent study proposes a fairly broad view on internalization based on two kinds of processes. Firstly, 'an agent learns new roles, acquiring the knowledge to act upon them', that is, a 'role playing socialization.' Secondly – and this type might manifest itself at a later stage of the socialization process – an agent may 'accept …community or organizational norms as "the right thing to do." … conscious instrumental calculation has now been replaced by taken for grantedness' (Checkel 2005, 804).

Rather than engaging myself in the 'conceptual minefield' of elaborating on definitions of international socialization (cf. Thies 2003), I suggest, in line with previous research, that this contested concept can tentatively be divided into various components concerning actors' modes of learning a new language. I thus agree with scholars who claim that the process of socialization is to some extent similar to a teaching and learning relationship. The West teaches post-communist countries social norms and practices, and the latter need incentives to learn (e.g. Archer and Jones 1999; Schimmelfennig 2000).

According to rationalist assumptions, the socialized states thus might have something to gain, in terms of security or welfare for instance, which is assessed at a higher value than the cost of adaptation. In this respect, the learning process can be considered instrumental, which is not the same as saying that the objects of this process do not believe in what they learn, or that the identity formations they give expression to are necessarily 'manipulated' (Schimmelfennig 2000, 131).

My point of departure is that actors do learn from other actors, something that may lead to a shift of identity. I argue that initial evidence of the occurrence of this shift is found in the language-use by policy-makers; how they present issues to audiences, i.e. the *framing* of language. The next step in the socialization process is to *formalize* the new language in, for example, 'law, bureaucracy, official policy, or international agreements' (Howard 2004, 10). The type of socialization I refer to here is a pre-stage to a more far-reaching socialization. It might thus be related to the first of the above-mentioned types according to Checkel, i.e. 'role playing socialization.' The intention of this study is not to prove that the language in use has been cognitively internalized by individual policy-makers. I believe that by looking at language and the political outcome of this language, we are able to avoid the methodological problems of assessing changes within individual cognition, or the even more complicated notion of aggregated cognition.

The language in use, in this case the language of threat, which also indicates the values that are threatened, and the formalization of this language in terms of an official policy, could thus be considered an indication of how relations develop between states in an area such as the Baltic, within the framework of a socialization process.

The described threat image trends reveal obvious similarities between Estonia and Russia. However, there are also statements that indicate what is threatened in terms of values and identities. When the Russian Foreign Minister emphasizes 'that Russia belongs to Europe not only geographically, but also by the very nature of its culture and civilization', and continues to talk about '[t]hreats or challenges [that] currently face Europe', he has managed to articulate that not only 'we as Europeans' are facing the same threat, but also that 'our values' are threatened by 'them', that is, Islamic fundamentalism (Ivanov 2003a, also; Federal News Service 2006; Lavrov 2005; Lavrov 2006; Putin 2003a). This is one example of Russian tendencies to frame post-Soviet Russia as a *European* power, which implies increased interaction with the EU (including Estonia). Still, the question is how language is put into practice. Are there any correspondences between talking and acting?

This is not the place to provide a detailed description of the 'complex and comprehensive partnership covering almost all policy areas and issues' that has developed between Russia and the EU during the last fifteen years, since this has been thoroughly done elsewhere. (Kux 2005, 170) The enormous potentialities of this very dynamic relationship is thus highlighted, and the first mentioned scenario 'assumes that Russia will eventually join the European Union and actually make use of the accession process to Europeanize its institutions' (Kux 2005, 171). Other studies point in the same direction. These are, thus, several studies that do not refute the assumption that the foundation of a security community between Russia and the EU has already been laid (Bengtsson 2004; Morozov 2004).

Still, there is the somewhat overlooked controversial issue of the Russian-speaking minority, the hottest and most frequently debated bilateral issue between Estonia and Russia since the troop withdrawals in 1994. In Moscow the authorities have not been satisfied with the Estonian way of handling this question (Yakovenko 2003).

Russia's role as a watch-dog for the Russian minorities was intensified during the spring of 2004 when the Baltic states entered both NATO and the EU. A case in point was the positive reactions in Moscow to the EU's monitoring assignments vis-à-vis Estonia's Russian minority policy, that is, to 'further promote integration of the Russian minority by, in particular, continuing to increase the speed of naturalization procedures and by taking other proactive measures to increase the rate of naturalization' (Ministry of Foreign Affairs of Russia 2003). 'We hope' – as it was expressed in an official statement from Moscow – 'that, with the active participation of the EU, it is possible, even in the coming months, to ensure some real shifts in the improvement of the situation of the Russian-speaking communities of these countries [Estonia and Latvia]' (Ministry of Foreign Affairs of Russia 2004).

What is notable here is that the Russian authorities had much more confidence in the EU than in the Baltic governments concerning the destiny of the respective minorities in the Baltic states. When Russia and the EU in April 2004, after a period of discussions, finally signed an accord extending the partnership and cooperation agreement between the two, Moscow was all in all essentially satisfied with the references, even if vague, to the protection of human and minority rights in the Baltic states (Agence Europe 2004a).

Baltic EU-membership could in this perspective be seen as a guarantee that Estonian integration policy was moving in the right direction, both from a Russian – as well as from a European – point of view. The enlargement of the EU was actually, from Moscow's point of view, considered to be beneficial as regards the Russian minority issue, or as the Chairman of the Duma Foreign Policy Committee put it:

> ... in the context of the EU enlargement, in particular the problems we have in relations with the Baltic states, Russia now gets new levers of influence. While in the past discussions related to the Russian-speaking minorities in the Baltic nations were held in a bilateral format and with organizations which could only issue recommendations on that situation – I mean the OSCE, the Council of Europe – shifting those issues to the EU level, in our opinion, gives us certain prospects, and I think Russia will energetically raise those issues in its dialogue with the EU. At least parliament members plan on doing this in the framework of the parliamentary cooperation committee formed by Russia and the European Union (Federal News Service Russia 2004).

Other statements from Russian government officials point in the same direction. The EU was a partner that Russia could cooperate with concerning the crucial and fairly complicated issue on Russian-speaking minorities' rights in the Baltic states:

> [Presenter] Does this mean that via the declaration Russia has offloaded care of the Russian-speaking minorities in the Baltics onto the EU and Brussels?
>
> [Yastrzhembskiy] We are not giving up any responsibility here, but of course the EU has much more administrative and legal resources and can demand standardization in all spheres of life in countries that have just joined the EU. The EU, obviously, is able and

simply obliged to honour its promises because otherwise the whole basis of the EU is undermined – the identical understanding of the values on which it is built. And among the most important of those values are human rights and the rights of national minorities (BBC Monitoring Former Soviet Union 2004).

Although Russia and Estonia continue to argue about the Russian-speaking minority (Volkova 2006) – and they will perhaps do so until the number of persons with non-citizenship has decreased to a certain limit – there are still signs of a continually improving neighbourly relationship. One obvious example is that high level diplomacy has become fairly routine in the 21st century, as compared to 1990s, when visits in the respective capitals at a ministerial level were almost non-existent (Estonian Ministry of Foreign Affairs 2005a). As has been suggested in a recent study, 'a security community is neither conflict-free nor power-free. Its distinctive features are that its internal conflicts are solved peacefully, and that power is expressed by means short of physical violence' (Pouliot 2006, 125).

The Explanatory Power of International Socialization

It seems that international socialization is a strong candidate to the position of becoming the causal mechanism when it comes to explaining threat image trends in Estonia and Russia. The explanatory power of international socialization might become even stronger when considering the structural and situational factors that condition this causal mechanism.

The structure of the international system, which according to Realism, determines the distribution of power and the degree of equality between states, might influence international socialization. One important circumstance in this context is the regional structure characterizing the Baltic states as typical small states, positioned next to the gigantic Russia. There are reasons to believe that an unequal distribution of power between socializing agents tends to facilitate rather than obstruct socialization, in the sense that the small states of Eastern Europe have more incentives to learn from and adapt to the West, than Russia has, due to *inter alia* the status of the latter as a great power (cf. Alderson 2001).

To take this a step further, I would suggest that the latest enlargement round of the EU in 2004, which included the Baltic states, has increased the power disparity ratio between Russia and the EU to the advantage of the latter. This might facilitate socialization between Russia and the EU rather than the other way around. It is too early to systematically test this proposition, but continuously increasing cooperation between Moscow and Brussels, and Russian confidence in the EU's intentions to keep an eye on Estonian integration policy, are both indications of an ongoing socialization of the first type described above.

The domestic context should also be considered as a conditional factor in relation to international socialization. The recurrent struggles between various political camps in Russia, be it in the name of Euro-asianists or Slavophiles vis-à-vis Atlanticists or Westernizers, might determine the limits on how far-reaching socialization processes can develop from Moscow's point of view. There seems to be a fairly established view among experts of Russian politics that the Putin administrations of the new millennium have been essentially Western-centric in outlook (e.g. Motyl, Ruble, and Sevcova 2005; Sakwa 2005; Trenin and Lo 2005).

Although Russian governments, particularly under Putin, could be characterized as being bureaucratic authoritarian, due to *inter alia* historical traditions, the main direction during the one and a half decades of the reborn Russian state has been one of democratization according to Western standards. Despite setbacks such as the restrictions on the liberty of the press in connection with the Chechen conflict, Russia could still be considered a 'student of Western democracy', albeit somewhat disobedient (Sakwa 2005, 391).

I therefore suggest that domestic factors favouring a Western-centric political leadership, pursuing a policy of continued modernization and economic liberalization of the Russian Federation, make a strong case for an increase in international socialization between Russia and the West.

A third structural factor, of a social kind which might influence socialization, involves the various identity discourses, in terms of Russian or Estonian national or state identity and of how 'we' as Russians or Estonians identify ourselves vis-à-vis Europe. These discourses are, as mentioned earlier, already 'out there', they have been formed over centuries and are constantly changing.

To be more precise, there is a reciprocal relationship between the developments of collective identities and socialization; the identity discourses influence the process of socialization, but since the change of state identity follows from this process, there is also a feedback loop from socialization to the structural identity discourses. To exemplify, there are presuppositions developed during centuries of 'who we are' as Estonians or Russians that might influence processes of international socialization. But these processes also shed new light on 'who we are' *in relation to*, for example, Europeans. The language in use, and the institutionalization of this language, has an impact on how the state's social identity is framed. The logic is that agents influence structures as well as the other way around.

Concluding Remarks

This study has demonstrated an increasingly explicit consistency in the way policy-makers in Estonia and Russia are framing social identity, in terms of belonging to Europe. Still, the language of identity within the context of a process of a Western socialization is more apparent in Tallinn than in Moscow. Whereas Russia's part in this process is more restrained, Estonians are more eager to adapt to fairly everything that is European and Western in outlook.

In line with the assumptions of social identity theory discussed earlier, I propose that the more developed the sense of collective identity is between the citizens of a state, the more inclined they are to become socialized into larger social identity formations, such as being 'Europeans'. Although I leave for future research to systematically test also this proposition, it may not be too far-fetched to conclude that a state identity is more developed in Estonia than in Russia, due to a variety of reasons that were pointed out above.

Accordingly, we have so far three conditional factors that, combined, make a strong case for an increased socialization between post-communist states and the EU: power disparity, pro-Western governments and well-developed state identities. Whereas all three conditions seem to be valid for the Estonian case, it is less certain whether this also concerns Russia. Indications of the two former conditions might, however, support the claim that an early stage of socialization has come about between Russia and the EU.

In addition to international socialization as an explanation for the framing of threat images, there are the above-mentioned cognitive factors, such as stereotypes rooted in peoples' minds based on lessons from history. Opinion polls indicate that these cognitive factors seem to have directly influenced individuals' threat images. One example is the Cold War philosophy of Estonians in the 1990s thinking about Russia as *the* enemy, which made NATO into a natural friend.

However, in the post-Cold War era we have witnessed countermeasures against this traditional thinking. First, there is the socialization process, according to which Estonian policy-makers positively identify themselves with the EU. The strategy of the EU has ever since the dissolution of the Soviet Union been to avoid topics that may jeopardize its relations with Russia. This might in the long run lead them to positively identify with one another. Second, we might take into consideration the triggering dramatic events, for instance, the terrorist attacks in Moscow, New York City, and Washington, which caused policy-makers in both Estonia and Russia to resolutely replace threat images of the Cold War with international terrorism. This language of security has often been followed by related threat images such as arms-and-drugs-trafficking and organized crime.

Still, common assessments of threat are not sufficient but may well be, in Adler and Barnett's conceptualization, a 'precipitating' condition for the development of a security community (Adler and Barnett 1998, 38). This means that when the Baltic states finally are on speaking terms with Russia concerning their crucial minority policies, including a border treaty between Estonia and Russia, they will have moved closer towards a security community in the Baltic Sea area.

Chapter 7

Power Disparity in the Digital Age

Johan Eriksson

The Problem: Hacked Power or State Resiliency?

This chapter addresses the pertinent question of the impact of the information revolution on the power of the territorial state. Two contending answers have been given in the existing literature.[1] According to the most common line of reasoning, the information revolution implies a serious challenge to state power. This would imply that traditional conceptions of great powers and small states might be turned upside down, and that a vast array of non-state actors might gain an asymmetric advantage over states that are strong in traditional military and economic terms but weak and vulnerable in terms of cybersecurity. Allegedly, national sovereignty is being eroded by the development of real-time global electronic communications, which know no territorial boundaries. The development and interconnectedness of information and communications technologies (ICTs) such as the internet, e-mail, satellite television, global positioning systems (GPS), and cellphones are diffusing globally at an impressive speed. The internet is undoubtedly the most significant symbol of this diffusion. From only a handful of websites in the early 1990s, the internet comprised several million websites at the turn of the millennium. Consequently, national security is at stake because of the increasing vulnerability that follows from depending on computerized information systems which are accessible online at all times through broadband networks. In contrast to conventional wars, the identity, motives, means, and actions of adversaries in 'information warfare' are difficult to discern. It is argued that historically small states, as well as a wide range of non-state agents (including hackers in liaison with rogue states, criminal networks, and terrorist organizations), may develop asymmetric power if they have access to advanced information technology. The information revolution is considered a new stage of globalization, resulting in an extreme form of complex interdependence (Eriksson and Giacomello 2006a, 2006b; Giacomello 2004b; Nye 2004b; Arquilla and Ronfeldt, 2001; Keohane and Nye 1998).

In contrast, most international relations theorists consider the information revolution as either irrelevant or only modestly important for state power. To the extent that such analysts pay attention to the issue – an exception rather than a rule – the general response seems to be that the information revolution has more

---

1 For reviews of the literature on 'information age security,' see Eriksson and Giacomello (2006a); Softa (2004).

impact on the economy than on security (Rosecrance 1999). This position implies a narrow view of security, focused on the military dimension of interstate conflict. In some quarters of strategic studies, however, information age security has been taken seriously. Yet the commonly held view is that the information revolution is merely adding advanced new electronic means of warfare to an arsenal already abundant with advanced weaponry, including nuclear, biological, and chemical weapons (Lonsdale 1999). It may be noted that 'electronic warfare' has been around both as a concept and a technology since the Second World War, for example, the jamming of radar and radio communication. In this perspective the information revolution implies a fundamental continuity in terms of what power is about, who the main actors are, and how international relations are to be analyzed. In this view, there are new data (the influx of new, globally connected ICTs), but there is no need for new theory.

The problem with these approaches is that they are formulated as diametrically opposed universal claims. There has been little interest in searching for conditional generalizations, that is, clarifying patterns of similarity and difference across time and space. Advocates of either perspective seem inclined to either exaggerate or downplay the challenge of the information revolution in global terms. Hence, both approaches fail to account for the complexity, variety, and simultaneity of continuity and change that arguably characterize the information revolution, and thus ignore its impact on the power and security of states. As a result of the universalistic ambitions and contentious argumentation of the dominant approaches, insights from comparative analysis, case studies, and middle-range theorizing are downplayed or simply ignored. The specific debate on power and security in the information age thus mirrors the major debates in international relations theory, especially the stalemated dispute on whether the nation-state is obsolete or obsolescent (see Goldmann 2002; Weiss 1998; Camilleri and Falk 1992; Hoffmann 1968).

Rather than asking simply whether the information revolution strengthens or weakens the power and security of the territorial state in general, this chapter asks under what circumstances the information revolution might strengthen or weaken the power and security of states. This leads to an analysis emphasizing the contextual and multidimensional character of both power and the information revolution.

Empirically, the analysis draws on case studies of Russia, the United States, Sweden, and Estonia.[2] This selection represents a variety of different types of states, specifically two states commonly perceived (and self-defined) as major powers (one great power and the only remaining superpower), and two small states. Moreover, these states show quite different political, cultural, and technological backgrounds and development. The ability to draw on and compare the experiences of countries

---

[2] The case study of Swedish power and security policy in the digital age is based on previous work by the present author (Eriksson, 2004; Eriksson, 2001a, 2001b). The analysis of the three other countries is original, however, and refers directly to primary and secondary sources.

from both sides of the former Iron Curtain presents a rich opportunity to conceptualize power disparity in the digital age.

In the following section a conceptual framework for the study of digital power is outlined. Subsequently, an analysis suggesting a few general and conditional assertions on digital power is presented, which is informed by the country-specific case studies. A concluding section pulls together arguments and observations.

Conceptual Framework

Following the general definition suggested by Knudsen in this volume, power is understood here simply as getting what you want even when facing resistance. This incorporates all 'faces of power,' including A's ability to get B to do what B would otherwise not do (Dahl and Stinebrickner 2003), controlling agendas, and influencing the minds of others (Bachrach and Baratz 1962; Lukes 1974). This broader, multi-dimensional understanding of power is also an attempt to combine insights from relational and capability-oriented approaches to power in international relations, rather than to uphold the unfruitful separation between the two (Baldwin 2002, 179; Guzzini 2000; Knudsen 1979). Moreover, objective as well as subjective aspects of power form part of our framework. The objective aspects are *scope, domain, resources,* and *means,* while the subjective aspect is *role identity*.

Scope defines the range of issues in which power is exercised. Emphasizing this dimension implies being more specific than just referring to 'overall power,' such as identifying states as 'small states' and 'great powers.' Analysis of scope may reveal that a state is quite powerful in one issue area (say, military relations), and quite weak in another (say, economic relations), and that these relations can vary considerably depending on who is the opposite actor (Baldwin 2002, 178; Baldwin 1989; Hagström 2005; Knudsen 1979). The information revolution is adding not only new technology to existing issue-areas in inter-state relations, but also a new 'world' of digital relations commonly known as 'cyberspace,' largely but not exclusively meaning the global computer network that we call the internet.[3] This development implies that the distinction and relationship between what happens 'offline' and 'online' are important new elements of analysis (Eriksson and Giacomello 2006b). Hence power analysis may give quite different results depending on whether relations are observed offline, online, or both.

Domain concerns how many states (and other agents) are affected by the actions of A, or, in other words, how many B's there are (Baldwin 2002: 178; Baldwin, 1989; Hagström 2005). The domain of a state can vary from the local to the global, and the relations concerned can be either bilateral or multilateral. The definition of a superpower is largely about the size of its domain. If the state has global reach, especially in military terms, it can be considered a superpower (Buzan and Wæver 2003, 34–35).

---

3   The term cyberspace was coined by novelist William Gibson (1984).

The information revolution has the potential to expand the domain of power. Digital attacks such as the spread of internet 'viruses' and 'worms,' defacing of web pages, e-mail spamming, and electronic break-ins can be made without concern for geographical distance, and one single attack may very rapidly affect computers and networks in countries all over the world. Virus attacks in particular have the capacity of affecting the whole world. Yet such attacks are not particularly 'smart' weapons. They function more like minefields or chemical and biological attacks, which cannot tell foes from friends. A hacker located in Amsterdam may seize control over a computer in Boston and use that one for attacking a computer network in Copenhagen. It is by no means certain, however, that even if a country has a developed network society, its government has such information warfare capability or that it will actually use it in a conflict situation.

A multidimensional concept of power implies that the analysis of power disparity (or 'asymmetric power' – a major buzzword in the contemporary international relations literature) is a lot more complex than simply ranking the 'overall' power of states, such as objectively defining some as 'small states' and others as 'great powers' (see Knudsen 1979; Frey 1985). When scope, domain, and other dimensions of power are taken into account, one can expect all kinds of disparities to appear. When using a multidimensional concept of power, the notion of asymmetry (or symmetry) can never be used generically, but only for characterizing a particular relationship at a particular time, in which the scope and domain, and preferably other dimensions of power, are identified in detail.

Yet notions of 'great powers,' 'middle powers,' and 'small states,' for example, are still important as subjective categorizations in our analysis, though they do not represent the analyst's assessment of the objective power of states. Following Knudsen (see the Introduction to this book), such conceptions are approached here as *role identities* (cf. Wendt 1999), that is, as self-perceived power positions in international relations. These identities may or may not necessarily correspond to the actual capabilities or performance of states in actual situations. This implies a possibility of subjective asymmetry (or symmetry), that is, self-identification may or may not necessarily correspond to objective aspects of power relations. For instance, a state may perceive itself as a 'small state' in conventional military terms, but define itself as a 'great power' in terms of digital power. Similarly, a state that has relatively advanced digital resources, may nevertheless perceive itself as weak and vulnerable. This makes Jervis's (1976) classic analysis of perception and misperception in international politics equally relevant for the digital age.

Critics of the relational approach to power often claim that it fails to take capabilities into account (Waltz 1979, 191–2). There is no reason, however, why capabilities, or *power resources*, cannot be included in analyses that also focus on relational dynamics. Capabilities define the power base, that is, the potential power of a state. Wealth, military resources, population, territory, and natural resources are factors commonly considered in capability-oriented analyses of power, and they are all important for understanding the potential power of a state. The mistake that power-as-resource theorists make, however, is to equate the power base with power itself (Baldwin 2002, 179; see also Knudsen's Introduction to this book). Potential power, measured in terms of military, economic, and other resources, may or may not be successfully employed in attempts at influencing the behaviour of other states.

It can be argued that technology, including information technology, is an additional power resource. Technological advancements such as the development and interconnectedness of ICTs might improve other capabilities, including the military arsenal, but they might also be seen as resources in their own right. This development is captured by the notion of the *network society* (Castells 2000; Eriksson and Giacomello 2006a, 2006b; Giacomello 2004b; Mowlana 1997). Yet the development of the network society varies considerably among countries. There is a noticeable *digital divide* that separates rich from poor societies and rich from poor individuals (Norris 2001). The general trend is clear however: the shrinking costs of ICTs are making them available on a widespread, decentralized basis, far beyond the political and economic elites of Western societies (Nye 2004a; Nye 2004b, 215–16).

In any case, a *national network society* can and will be considered an important resource of digital power. It provides technology and infrastructure, but also human resources, businesses and organizations, all of which may have an impact on governmental capability. Importantly, the network society is seen as separate from governmental capabilities and dependency on ICTs (Fountain 2001), and this follows the traditional analytical distinction between society and state. This perception is crucial because the role of the state in controlling and developing the network society varies considerably among countries (Giacomello 2004b).

Power may also be based on intangible resources such as culture, ideology, norms, and institutions. These aspects are captured by Joseph Nye's extremely influential concept of 'soft power,' which he defines as 'the ability to get what you want through attraction rather than coercion or payments. It arises from the attractiveness of a country's culture, political ideals, and policies [...] Soft power rests on the ability to shape the preferences of others' (Nye 2004a, x, 5). In my reading, soft power is about the battle for minds, based on intangible, non-military resources. The spectrum of soft power behaviour includes agenda-setting, attraction, and co-option. Nye explicitly separates this from 'hard' command power which is based on military and economic resources. Baldwin (2002, 186) criticizes this concept for confusing the dimensions of scope, power base, and means. Yet it serves a useful purpose of illuminating behaviour and sources of power, which are ignored or underestimated in approaches limited to analysis of capabilities.

Importantly, Nye argues that soft power is becoming more significant in the digital age than it has ever been before, mainly because of the evolving multiple channels of global communication which easily transcend sovereign boundaries (Nye 2004b, Ch. 7). In particular, the internet opens up multiple modes of global communication: one-to-one (such as e-mail), many-to-one (electronic broadcast), one-to-many (homepages), and many-to-many (online chat rooms and discussion forums).

Another dimension to consider is that of *means*. Though difficult to separate from power resources, means should be analytically seen as a separate category. Soldiers and tanks are military resources, but putting them to use in an attempt at seizing territory would make them a military means. Baldwin distinguishes between symbolic, military, economic, and diplomatic means of power (Baldwin 2002, 178–9). Information technology that improves the accuracy of conventional missiles and artillery, for instance by using global positioning systems, implies a boost of that kind of military means. But there is also information technology that provides means of a separate kind, such as technologies for hacking websites and computer networks. Moreover, information technology in general, and the internet in particular, has contributed a new arena and new tools for symbolic power. Defacing websites, such as replacing an official site with one that shows the enemy's slogans and symbols, is a humiliating act comparable to burning the enemy's flag. National security (in terms of physical survival of the state) is not necessarily at stake, but being a victim of hacking signals a loss of control, and thus portrays the state as weak and insecure.

Contextualizing Digital Power Disparity: Assertions and Analysis

This section reaches beyond the basic observations that the information age may expand the scope, domain, resources, and means of state power. Politics and power are not everywhere the same, but patterns may still be discerned across time and space. Technological determinism should be avoided – that is, the idea that the development and increasing reliance on information technology in itself changes power relations, regardless of how actors think and act. Likewise, assuming that the information revolution is merely adding new resources (ICT as a 'force multiplier') and that its impact on state power and interstate relations is minimal does not further our understanding of the relationship between information technology and power (Eriksson and Giacomello 2006a). The contention here is that the information revolution implies a major, multi-faceted transformation of society.

Disparities in the Digital Age

Power disparities are the rule rather than the exception in real world politics. As suggested by Garfield (2004), there can be disparities not only of military capabilities, but also of interest, will, beliefs and values, mental timelines, strategies, and types of actors. This is even truer when the focus is on cyberspace. The sheer size of the rapidly growing online world and the common utilization of encryption technology make it impossible for any single actor to dominate cyberspace. If there is one world to which the concept of anarchy[4] truly applies, it is the online world. Everyone is an underdog in cyberspace.

---

4 In the realist sense of the word: absence of central government.

Power and security in the digital age are multi-faceted and highly variable attributes. Therefore it is very difficult to make generalizations of states as weak or strong digital powers. Nevertheless, this is one challenge, among others, that I will take on in the following analysis. There are three reasons for this. Firstly, by making a clear distinction between governmental warfare capability and a national network society, a more diverse picture of power disparity in the digital age can be portrayed than is the case with standard country-based indexing. Secondly, I will argue that the governmental capability of information warfare is the single most important dimension of digital power. Its importance is most visible when contrasted with the development of national network societies, which also vary considerably among countries. Thirdly, the complexity and fluidity of disparities in the digital age make it impossible to consider all aspects and dimensions at once. Focusing on only a few, arguably important ones is necessary to make sense of power in the interconnected world.

Power disparity in cyberspace may also have a different logic than power disparity in the offline world. From a military strategic point of view, power in the digital age is often interpreted in terms of attempts to achieve dominance over an opponent. ICTs such as satellite-based communication, surveillance, and guidance of missiles play an increasingly important role in this thinking. Supposedly this technological development carries the possibility of diminishing the importance of territory, front lines, and armed soldiers, while increasing the significance of the information sphere of operation. Such ideas are expressed through influential concepts such as 'revolution in military affairs' and 'network-centric warfare' (Latham 2003; Arquilla and Ronfeldt 2001). The purpose of information warfare, as opposed to conventional armed attacks, is to achieve information superiority rather than physical control of territory.

The first of eight theoretical assertions (A1, A2, etc) on power and security in the digital age is now presented. Some of these assertions are general, while others are conditional. The assertions will be summarized in Table 7.2.

A1 *Complete information dominance is not only unlikely but also counterproductive – soft power depends on the opponent's continued ability to communicate.*

But information superiority is not like air superiority. A complete shutdown of the opponent's information and communications systems is very hard if not impossible to achieve, and may indeed cause more problems than it solves (Lonsdale 1999). Digital power disparity cannot imply complete information dominance. Indeed, it may prove counterproductive to deny an opponent all means of communication. If completely isolated, attempts at persuading an opponent to surrender through soft power means are bound to fail. This might give rise to continued resistance, even when the conflict is over, or to hostilities despite appeasement by the central leaders. This is what happened with some isolated Japanese soldiers scattered on Pacific islands after the end of the Second World War. The problem could also apply to isolated submarines equipped with intercontinental nuclear missiles, whose commanders, following the strategy of mutually assured destruction, might launch their weapons after having jumped to the conclusion that broken communications are a result of an attack on their homeland. An isolated opponent may of course put down its arms anyway, even if not because persuaded to do so through successful information operations. Commanders cannot rely on chance, however, so it is vital to let the enemy have some means of sending and receiving information.

Scarcity of Cyberwar, Abundance of Cyberplagues

Since the mid-1990s, information warfare and cyberterrorism have gained a salient position on the security policy agendas of many nations. This is especially the case in the US, but increasingly also in many other parts of the world. Several states, including the US, Russia, Canada, Britain, China, and Sweden, have developed particular strategies for information operations and cybersecurity. This is also on the agenda internationally, for example in NATO and lately also in the EU. It is hardly controversial to consider the US the leading country in the development of cybersecurity concepts and strategies, so it is useful to quote US assessments of cyberthreats:

> Not only does cyberspace provide the ability to exploit weaknesses in our critical infrastructures, but it also provides a fulcrum for leveraging physical attacks by allowing the possibility of disrupting communications, hindering U.S. defensive o offensive response, or delaying emergency responders who would be essential following a physical attack. (US Government 2003, 7)

> Terrorists may seek to cause widespread disruption and damage, including casualties, by attacking our electronic and computer networks, which are linked to other critical infrastructures such as our energy, financial, and securities network. Terrorist groups are already exploiting new information technology and the internet to plan attacks, raise funds, spread propaganda, collect information, and communicate securely. As terrorists further develop their technical capabilities and become more familiar with potential targets, cyber attacks will become an increasingly significant threat. (US Government 2002, 9)

The most cataclysmic dramatization is that of an 'electronic Pearl Harbor',[5] a metaphor that has been floating around since the mid-1990s (Bendrath, 2003; Forno 2002; Smith 1998). The story comes in many shapes, but some of the more common exemplify how phone systems could collapse, subway cars suddenly stop, and the money of thousands of people be frozen because banks and ATM machines stop functioning, or more generally how infrastructure is disrupted to the point that society and government lose the ability to function normally. This threat image has been openly reported by several representatives of the US Department of Defense (including former Deputy Defense Secretary John Hamre), other governmental bodies

---

5 The influential and fear-mongering notion of 'electronic Pearl Harbor' was coined by Winn Schwartau (1997, 49). He has even written a novel entitled *Pearl Harbor Dot Com* (2002). See also <http://www.thesecurityawarenesscompany.com/chez/winn_bio.pdf>

around the world, academics, computer experts, IT businesspeople, and journalists (Bendrath 2003). The events of September 11, 2001 reinforced the fear-mongering trend. For example, the FBI issued warnings that cyber-attacks could be directed against dams and nuclear power stations, potentially causing power breakdowns and even loss of life (Gellman 2002). This traumatic incident prompted some experts to replace the metaphor of an 'electronic Pearl Harbor' with that of an 'electronic 9/11' (Nicander and Ranstorp 2004).

These threat perceptions do not correspond to the empirical record however. The scarcity or indeed almost complete absence of incidents of cyberwar or cyberterrorism[6] makes the threat perceptions look more like fear-mongering than realistic accounts of actual dangers. This may change as the globalization, diffusion, and dependency of ICTs increase. Most experts, however, see cyberwar and cyberterrorism more as potential future scenarios than as a current possibility (Giacomello 2004a; Jackson 2002; Denning 2001; Libicki 1997).

Many terrorist groups, including al-Qaeda, use the internet and other ICTs as a means for planning, organizing, and communicating amongst themselves, and occasionally also for malicious activities such as fraud, theft, and 'denial-of-service' attacks such as spamming and web defacing (Nicander and Ranstorp 2004; O'Day 2004). But there are no reports of any physical destruction or people being killed directly as a result of digital attacks (Giacomello 2004a). Hacking and virus attacks cause humiliation and billions of dollars in damage, but so far they have hardly inflicted the physical damage or human suffering caused by ordinary bombs. In the words of Dorothy Denning, professor of computer science at Georgetown University, who has testified on this topic in the US Congress:

> Few if any [cyber-attacks] can be characterized as acts of terrorism: fraud, theft, sabotage, vandalism, and extortion – yes, but terrorism – no. Their effect, while serious and not to be taken lightly, pales in comparison to the horror we witnessed on September 11. (Denning 2001)

That cyberwar and cyberterrorism maintain their positions on the American security policy agenda might partly be explained by the intelligence service credo that the unimaginable is the most serious threat. This view seems to have gained a particular significance in the US after 9/11. Partly, however, the view can also be explained by the fair amount of fear-mongering that is visible in reports from the

---

6   Cyberwar and cyberterrorism are similar in that both have physical effects, such as shutting down electric power systems, causing havoc in air control systems, remotely controlled opening of the gates of dams to cause floods, or even causing the unauthorized launching of electronically guided missiles. (Stealing, replacing, or changing information through digital attacks is merely cybercrime – not cyberwar or cyberterrorism.) Cyberwar and cyberterrorism differ in that the former essentially is about comprehensive interstate conflict in cyberspace, while the latter may involve single incidents caused by states as well as non-state actors. See also Nicander and Ranstorp (2004, 15); O'Day (2004); Latham (2003).

defense sector and the computer security industry, which has been criticized by some experts (Libicki 1997, 37-38; Bendrath 2003).

A2 *The abstract, global, dynamic, and technologically advanced nature of cyberspace has nurtured fear-mongering, futuristic threat images, which do not correspond to the empirical record.*

Actual experience of threats is dominated by the spread of electronic viruses. These are by far the most commonly reported incidents worldwide.[7] Indeed, these incidents have now become so common that the US government's Computer Emergency Readiness Team Coordination Center (CERT/CC), which is a generally recognized center of expertise and statistics in these matters, has recently stopped reporting the number of incidents.[8] The Center claims there is no point in further reporting. The reason given is the development of automated attack tools, which are easily available on the internet (CERT/CC 2005). This type of software is not used for attacking any particular target, but scans the internet for unprotected computers and may try to install Trojan horses ('backdoors' which make unauthorized access possible), and a host of other viruses and worms.

In terms of interstate cyberconflicts – the focus of the present study – there is not much to report. The most common usage of digital means in interstate conflicts seems to be intelligence gathering, psychological operations, and denial-of-service attacks such as e-mail spamming or web defacing (Arquilla and Ronfeldt 2001; Denning 1999). Denial-of-service attacks are common in the ongoing conflicts between the Republic of China and Taiwan, and the Israeli–Palestinian conflict. Fundamentalist Islamic movements have resorted to what they call 'e-Jihad,' which implies using the internet for mobilization, propaganda, and computer-based attacks on the West in general, and Israel in particular (Barak 2004). The actual perpetrators, however, are mostly non-state actors. Whether governments support them is hard to say, although it cannot be ruled out that this happens occasionally.

Turning now to the cyber-relations between the four states in focus in this study – Russia, the United States, Sweden and Estonia – it is noteworthy how little is being said about these relations, at least in the available open sources. Russia, the US, and Sweden have all developed particular policies for information security, as

---

7 An FBI survey reported that the most common type of incident affecting US public administrations and private business was virus attack, the second being insider abuse of net access (Computer Security Institute 2004, 8).

8 The US CERT/CC reported six incidents in the US in 1988; 132 in 1989; 2,412 in 1995; 9,859 in 1999; 21,756 in 2000; and 137,529 incidents in 2003. The total number of incidents reported (1988-2003) was 319,992 (CERT/CC 2005). This may to some extent be compared with the Russian experience of cyberplagues. The Russian Ministry of Interior reported 8,739 incidents for 2004 (Ministry of Interior 2004, 5; Goroshko, 2004). These statistics do not include general virus attacks, however, but only antagonistic digital attacks against specific targets. The count includes unauthorized access, interception of information in electronic payment systems, and other direct attacks against specific information systems.

part of their overall national security strategies. In Estonia, however, there is no such strategy; very little is being said about security issues in this sphere, and then only in terms of cybercrime (Estonian Ministry of Foreign Affairs 2001).[9] Even in Russia, the US, and Sweden, relations to other states are only discussed very superficially. Threat assessments and policies are mostly discussed in very general terms, and only very rarely are adversaries or partners mentioned by name.

Cybersecurity strategies in interstate relations, however, can at least partly be discerned in other ways. It is, for example, quite obvious that Sweden has looked very carefully at the US and their cybersecurity strategies. Sweden cannot be said to jump on the US bandwagon, but is rather selectively imitating American cybersecurity policy (Eriksson 2004, 2001a, 2001b). Although cybersecurity does not have a very significant position on the Estonian agenda, the national government is very actively adapting (bandwagoning) their security policy to NATO's, both rhetorically and in action. Thus, Estonia has abandoned the earlier narrow definition of security as military security, and does not overtly talk about Russia as the main threat anymore. By contrast, Estonian policymakers have adopted a much broader security concept similar to that of NATO and the EU. This is noticeable in, for example, the Estonian *National Concept of Security* (Estonian Ministry of Foreign Affairs 2001, 2004; cf. Noreen and Sjöstedt 2004, also Ch. 6 in this volume).

The cyber-relationship of Estonia and Sweden versus Russia seems very much to be a non-issue. In policy documents, and in interviews with civil servants and decision-makers, Russia is not mentioned as a serious cyberthreat – or partner for that matter. Their perceptions of cybersecurity threats seem to be more focused on non-state agents, specifically criminal organizations and terrorist networks (Estonian Ministry of Foreign Affairs 2001, 2004; Eriksson 2004).[10]

In contrast, the cyber-relationship between the US and Russia is more complicated. Their traditional 'offline' rivalry continues also in cyberspace. At times, their respective leaders emphasize their renewed cooperation and trust in each other, especially as partners in the new global 'war on terrorism' which followed after 9/11. Nevertheless, when Russia in 1998 submitted a proposal for a global regime against cybercrime in the UN General Assembly, the US did not support it (Denning 2001, 284–285; UN 1998).

---

9   Also personal interviews with U. Kaalames, (Head of Information Department, Ministry of Internal Affairs), Tallinn, 19 May 2003; A. Laneman, (Colonel, Chief of the General Staff of the Estonian Defence Forces), 23 May, 2003; Männik, M. (Head of the Estonian Informatics Centre), Tallinn, 22 May 2003; A. Ott (Head of State Information Systems, The Ministry of Economic Affairs and Communication), 23 May, 2003; V. Praust (Senior Officer at the Estonian Data Protection Inspectorate), 22 May 2003; L. Tabur (Head of the Internal Security Police Department, Ministry of Internal Affairs), Tallinn, 22 May 2003; I. Upan (IT systems administrator at the IT Department of the Ministry of Defense), Tallinn, 22 May 2003; U. Vallner (Senior Officer at the Ministry of Economic Affairs and Communication), 20 May, 2003.

10 Also personal interviews, see note (9) above.

The US occasionally mentions Russia as one nation among others which have developed systems of offensive computer attacks.[11] A number of cyberattacks on US targets have been mounted through Russia. In some cases, it has been unclear who were the culprits – criminal groups, teenage hackers, industry, or governmental actors.

In 1999, there was a series of concerted cyberattacks through Russia on computer systems belonging to the Pentagon and nuclear weapons laboratories run by the Department of Energy. Deputy Defense Secretary John Hamre, who had overall responsibility for Pentagon computer security, called it a 'major concern' and defined it as 'an ongoing law enforcement and intelligence matter' (Starr 1999). It was unclear if the attacks were actually made by actors in Russia – whether state or non-state – or if Russian computers were simply routing attacks from other locations. Yet US officials said they would treat 'any Russian threat similarly whether it comes from the government, industry, or high-technology interests' (Starr 1999).

Another incident was the 1994 cyberattack on American Citibank, in which a large sum of money was stolen. The investigation showed that the perpetrator was Russian hacker 'Vladimir Lenin' from St Petersburg (PBS Online 2002; Freedman 2000). It should be noted however that in some instances, US and Russian police have worked together in hunting down Russian hackers, especially those involved in financial fraud and theft (Knowles 2000). Indeed, Russia in general (and St Petersburg in particular) is sometimes seen as a breeding ground for computer hackers (Saytarly 2004; 'Sostojanie prestupnosti...' 2004; Borchgrave 2000, iv–v; Polikanov, 2001, 20).

Russia has also expressed fears of an American cyberthreat. Their threat perceptions are quite different from the American perceptions of Russian threats, however. While the US fears Russian hackers and governmental cyberattacks, Russia seems less worried about direct US attacks, but is more concerned about US technological dominance and Russian 'backwardness' (*Kontseptsija informatsionnoj bezopastnosti* 2003; *Doktrina informatsionnoj bezapastnosti Rossiskoj Federatsii* 2000; Saarelainen 1999). Though the nature of their threat perceptions differ, they certainly corroborate a digital power disparity between Russia and the US, an issue that I will return to in a following section on role identity.

Domains of Digital Power

The global reach of cyberspace expands the potential domain of digital power far beyond that of neighbouring states, to the extent of making geographical distance irrelevant. Every actor in cyberspace potentially has global reach. Territory is not unimportant in cyberspace, however. Territorial disputes are played out also in cyberspace. Interstate patterns of amity and enmity (Buzan 1991) do not seem to have been affected that much by the information revolution. The Russian–American

---

11 China is clearly the most feared cyber-enemy, but Russia is also on the list (Bendrath 2003; Borchgrave 2000, i, 19; DSBTF 2001, ES-4; BBC News 1998; Nye 1998, viii).

power game, which is basically inherited from the Soviet–US Cold War conflict, continues also in the digital age. As noted earlier, there is a mutually shared wariness of Russian and American cyber-security strategies.

A3   *Access to cyberspace potentially provides actors with a global reach, and thereby broadens the domain of both the number and types of foes and friends.*

The development of cyberspace not only facilitates a global reach, but also widens the types of potential foes and friends considerably. Russia, the United States, and Sweden have very similar conceptions of cyber-culprits. Their threat images include criminal organizations, terrorists, corporate infiltrators, insiders, as well as foreign intelligence services and militaries (Eriksson 2004, 128–41; Bendrath 2003; *Kontseptsija informatsionnoj bezopastnosti...* 2003; Eriksson 2001a, 2001b; Denning 1999). In the words of the US President's Commission on Critical Infrastructure Protection:

> What is the Threat? Anyone with the capability, technology, opportunity, and intent to do harm. Potential threats can be foreign or domestic, internal or external, state-sponsored or a single rogue element. Terrorists, insiders, disgruntled employees, and hackers are included in this profile. (PCCIP, 2002; cf. *Kontseptsija informatsionnoj bezopastnosti...* 2003; *Doktrina informatsionnoj bezapastnosti Rossiskoj Federatsii* 2000)

Nevertheless, the United States, Sweden, and Estonia seem to emphasize non-state adversaries somewhat more than Russia is doing. In the case of the US, which before 9/11 talked a lot more about 'information warfare' between states, the ensuing 'war on terrorism' has made them focus considerably more on the essentially non-state international terrorist networks (Bendrath 2003). Indeed, although the terrorist attacks on 9/11 were of a physical rather than digital nature, they spurred a renewed interest in the cyber-capacity of terrorist organizations:

> While the attacks of September 11 were physical attacks, we are facing increasing threats from hostile adversaries in the realm of cyberspace as well. (The National Strategy to Secure Cyberspace 2003, 5)

Role Identity: Great Powers and Small States in Cyberspace

As argued previously, everyone is an underdog in cyberspace. This is true on a general level, as no actor can claim hegemony over the highly complex and dynamic structures and relations that compose cyberspace. All of the countries studied express fears of a general vulnerability of their globally interconnected information systems. Even the US, which certainly acknowledges its leading position in ICT development as well as in international security policy, occasionally expresses fears of increasing vulnerability. Yet when focusing on relations between particular actors, more stable patterns of power disparity can be discerned, especially if seen in terms of role identity.

A noteworthy difference in Russian and American framing of information security is that the Russian government alone considers the 'digital gap'[12] a serious security threat. It is obvious that the Russian government first and foremost considers its own relative 'backwardness' in ICT development as a serious vulnerability, and something that a more advanced enemy might take advantage of. In the words of the *Russian National Security Concept*, a document which explicitly refers to our topic:

> There is an increased threat to the national security of the Russian federation in the information sphere. A serious danger arises from the desire of a number of countries to dominate the global information domain space and to expel Russia from the external and internal information market; from the development by a number of states of 'information warfare' concepts that entail creation of ways of exerting a dangerous effect on other countries' information systems, of disrupting information and telecommunications systems and data storage systems, and of gaining unauthorized access to them. (*Russian National Security Concept* 2000)

In similar terms, the Russian *Information Security Doctrine* specifies one of the external threats as:

> [...] the desire of some countries to dominate and infringe upon the interests of Russia in the world information space and to oust it from the external and international information markets; [...] the widening of the technological lead of the main world powers and the buildup of their potential to counteract the creation of competitive Russian information technologies. (*Doktrina informatsionnoj bezapastnosti Rossiskoj Federatsii* 2000)

It does not seem far-fetched to suggest that the US is one of the countries that Russia believes are striving for domination of the global information space and which are trying to oust Russia from that space (cf. Sherstyuk 2003). The fear of the US and of US allies also permeates the explicit threat framing of (for instance) NATO's eastward expansion (Russian National Security Concept 2000). This implies not only a particular problem identification ('backwardness' as threat), but also that blame is assigned not so much to the Russians themselves for not being able to develop a stronger information society, but more to foreign powers, including the United States. In general terms, the impact of the digital divide on role identity can be formulated in the following way:

A4 *The 'digital divide' nurtures role identities of dominant and backward states, which generally correspond to offline identities.*

---

12 The digital gap refers to the uneven development of information and communications technology in different parts of the world. In practice, this means a new technological gap between the 'haves' and the 'have-nots' which basically corresponds to economic, social, political, and other well-known differences between the developed (industrialized information societies) and the less developed parts of the world. See Norris (2001).

In contrast to the Russian understanding, the digital gap is considered an advantage rather than a security threat in US documents. In some passages an ongoing arms race in cyberspace is mentioned, and that the US must ensure its leading position in this field. In the US *National Security Strategy* (2002, Ch. 8) the following is stated:

> [The United States should] take advantage of the technological opportunities and economies of scale in our defense spending to transform NATO military forces so that they dominate potential aggressors and diminish our vulnerabilities.

Thus both the US and Russia apply a power language in their framing, reminiscent of Cold War rhetoric, even though the present issue is about the new domain of digital age security. The US government is clearly aware of this and explicitly tries to downplay any resemblance to Cold War talk, and officially stresses cooperative relations with Russia. Nevertheless, the US is still framing security relations in traditional power terms, again recognizing the relative weakness of Russia. Moreover, this cooperatively oriented framing clashes with the previously cited emphasis on NATO domination, something which Russia views as a security threat.

> With Russia, we are already building a new strategic relationship based on a central reality of the twenty-first century: the United States and Russia are no longer strategic adversaries. The Moscow Treaty on Strategic Reductions is emblematic of this new reality and reflects a critical change in Russian thinking that promises to lead to productive, long-term relations with the Euro-Atlantic community and the United States. Russia's top leaders have a realistic assessment of their country's current weakness and the policies – internal and external – needed to reverse those weaknesses. They understand, increasingly, that Cold War approaches do not serve their national interests and that Russian and American strategic interests overlap in many areas. (US *National Security Strategy* 2002, Ch. 8)

In many ways, the Russians seem to consider the new power struggle in cyberspace as a continuation of the 'offline' competition between the Soviet Union and the US, and thus as a means for revitalizing its lost superpower status. In this perspective, the Russians consider information security and information warfare capability mainly as a 'force multiplier' in an ongoing power struggle, rather than as a separate cyberworld with its own rules of the game.

The Variable Scope of Digital Power

The dimension of scope, that is, what issues are concerned, can be specified in more detail than simply as 'cyberspace'. More specifically, ICT can be seen as:

i) technological means of power in its own right, such as software tools for computer hacking;
ii) force multiplier, boosting offline power (e.g. GPS guided munitions); and
iii) means of soft power, facilitating propaganda, psychological operations and real-time communication through global communications networks.

Unlike the other countries, Russia especially emphasizes the psychological dimension of information security – soft power (Thomas 1998, 1996). The internet, e-mail, cell phones/mobiles, and satellite television are means for quickly disseminating information and propaganda worldwide. It is difficult for national governments to try to filter or block these media, although it is not impossible, as shown by the harsh measures taken by the Chinese government to control internet access. Russian leaders seem to fear psychological threats much more than their American counterparts, although they have not set out to stop or filter the Russian public's access to the internet. On the contrary, the Russian government has an ambitious plan of turning the whole country into an advanced and open information society ('e-russia' 2001; 'Vistuplenie predstavitelja Rossii...' 2005). Still, the government is obviously afraid of what this development and the consequential global interconnectedness would imply for national stability. This is how some of these threats are framed:

> [D]epreciation of spiritual values, the promotion of specimens of mass culture based on the cult of violence, on spiritual and moral values that contradict the accepted values of Russian society; the lowering of the spiritual, moral and creative potential of the Russian population which would significantly complicate the preparation of labour resources for the introduction and use of the latest technologies, including information technologies; manipulation of information (disinformation, concealment or distortion of information). (*Doktrina informatsionnoj bezapastnosti Rossiskoj Federatsii* 2000)

A possible interpretation of this threat framing is that the Russian government is still struggling with the disintegrative forces of the crumbled Soviet empire, as witnessed for instance in the Chechen conflict. For this reason, the Russian government is sensitive about anything that could be interpreted as undermining the national 'spirit' and identity – that is, what are seen as the bonds that keep this vast country together. In contrast, the US government does not see any immediate or real danger in terms of secessionism or other large-scale threat to national identity and sovereignty.

The US government is a lot more worried about what it defines as critical infrastructures, a concept that is virtually nonexistent in the Russian documents. In almost every US document on information security, the main goal is stated as protecting critical infrastructure from attacks. CIP (Critical Infrastructure Protection) has become an established acronym and is also part of the name of several governmental and advisory bodies in the US, as well as in many other countries in the Western world. In other words, while the Russians frame threats as mainly affecting immaterial values – moral, psyche, spirit – the Americans frame threats as affecting material functions – transportation and physical infrastructure, information systems and telecommunications, the energy system, the financial system, etc. (*National Strategy to Secure Cyberspace* 2003; PCCIP 2002).

The US and Sweden emphasize ICTs as means in their own right, and as force multipliers (the first and second aspects), but not so much digitally improved psychological operations (the third aspect). Cybercrime, cyberterrorism and cyberwarfare are the major concerns in both of these countries, as seen in major policy documents (*US National Strategy to Secure Cyberspace*, 2003; Eriksson 2004, 2001a, 2001b). In addition, ICT as a booster of other technologies (such as aircraft and missiles) is included in the notions of 'revolution in military affairs' and 'network-centric warfare,' which have gained a strong foothold in both US and Swedish military doctrines. This implies that a particular role is given to IT-enhanced weaponry, intelligence, planning, communication, and execution of operations.

A5 *The scope of digital power depends on whether a government perceives IT as a means of online attack on critical infrastructures, as a booster of offline technologies, as a means of soft power, or as any combination of these.*

Estonia is the odd one out among these countries, as the attention the government pays to digital power and security are limited in comparison with the other countries, and also that its concern for these issues has emerged relatively late. Cybercrime was briefly mentioned as one of many threats in the first *National Security Concept of the Republic of Estonia*, written by the government and adopted by the parliament in 2001 (Estonian Ministry of Foreign Affairs 2001, 9). In the revised *National Security Concept*, adopted in 2004, information security is briefly discussed as one of many other threats, mainly in terms of cybercrime:

> The instability or breakdown of information systems could cause serious threats. The constantly increasing rate at which electronic information systems are adopted in Estonia, and their connection with and dependence upon worldwide information systems, increases the threat of computer crime as well as the vulnerability of information systems, including spheres of primary importance to national security. During the last few years, there has been an increase in the number of persons who, through their activities in the internet environment, could endanger government databases and registries. [...] To prevent computer crime and threats to internal security, which could arise from the vulnerability of IT systems, as well as to ensure the security of national data bases and registries, necessary organisational, information technology, and physical security measures are being implemented. Unless this is done, computer crime could develop into a dangerous form of organized crime on par with illegally trading in arms and narcotics. (Estonian Ministry of Foreign Affairs 2004, 8, 19)

The way this is written suggests that it is an adaptation of NATO's *Strategic Concept* (1999) and the EU's *European Security Strategy* (2003). Indeed, the importance of these documents and the Estonian NATO and EU memberships are explicitly discussed in the Estonian *National Security Concept* (2004, 3–5).

The above indicates that the Estonian government considers IT security as a growing concern, although its position on the general security policy agenda is relatively weak. This is corroborated by interviews with Estonian officials in May 2003.[13] Many of the interviewees working on ICT issues did not even mention computer hacking, information warfare, or cybercrime as security threats. Some

---

13 Praust interview; see note 9 above.

argued instead that the major threat was a lack of resources, weak legislation, or lack of educated users and administrators of ICT systems.

Network Society: A Double-Edged Sword

The literature on the information revolution convincingly shows that an increasingly developed network society implies increasing vulnerability (Eriksson and Giacomello 2006a, 2006b; Nye 2004b; Arquilla and Ronfeldt 2001; Henry and Peartree 1998). Enemies with information warfare capability can exploit this vulnerability and susceptibility to technical system failure. Societies (and states) which are largely depending on ICTs for the functioning of vital sectors (such as the financial, public administration, medical, education and research sectors) are more vulnerable to information warfare attacks than societies which are not as dependent on ICTs. Thus, information warfare would be quite ineffective against countries such as Somalia and Afghanistan, but would be more of a risk for advanced information societies such as the United States, Germany, and the Nordic countries. This is another consequence of the digital divide. Since less developed also means less vulnerable, the digital divide implies a more limited domain of power than usually suggested in the information warfare literature.

A6 *The more a country depends on ICTs for vital functions (e.g. electricity, government, communications, financial transactions), the more vulnerable it is to information warfare, and technical system failures.*

Comparative statistics on the development of national network societies show that among the 25 top-ranking countries are the Nordic countries, most other Western European countries, the United States, and Canada. Singapore and South Korea have recently climbed to the very top of these rankings. Estonia is the only Central/Eastern European country that ranks among the top 30. Russia is ranked considerably lower, usually in the same group as other 'middle access' countries, for example Brazil, Bulgaria, Lebanon, Mexico, Thailand, and Turkey. African countries, with the exception of South Africa, a 'middle access' country, stand at the very bottom of the ranking. Many African countries cannot produce even basic indicators of ICT development. The available indexes are produced with a variety of indicators, and there is no universally defined measurement. Nevertheless, the indicators used in some of the most cited indexes include internet access (in households, education, business, and government), households with computers, and broadband subscribers. Authoritative annual reports are produced by the International Telecommunication Union (ITU), the World Economic Forum (WEF), and International Data Corporation (IDC).

Table 7.1 displays network society rankings for Sweden, the United States, Estonia, and Russia. According to these rankings, Sweden and the United States seem to be more vulnerable than Estonia, while Russia appears to be the least vulnerable of these four countries. At the same time, without a developed network society, it will be harder for the government to develop its ability to withstand and conduct computer network attacks (cf. Giacomello 2004a, 2004b). A well-developed network society provides a pool of technology (software and hardware) and human competence on which a government can draw. Indeed, not only is ICT development generally driven by private business, but also the critical infrastructure is often owned and controlled by private corporations. This is particularly evident in the US, but is also significant in Estonia and Sweden. In Russia, the IT industry is to a greater degree controlled by the government.

Table 7.1 Network Society Rankings

Country	ITU Index (2003)	WEF Index (2004)	IDC Index (2003)
Sweden	1	6	2
United States	11	5	3
Estonia	28	25	n.d.
Russia	63	62	41*

Sources: ITU (2003); WEF (2004); IDC (2003).

* That Russia ranks higher in the IDC index than in the ITU and WEF indexes is merely a result of the fewer number of countries covered in the IDC index.

There is a possibility that a particular national government is fairly advanced when it comes to information technology in general and information warfare in particular, but that its national network society is weakly developed. This implies a powerful combination of state capability and low societal vulnerability. Such is largely the case with Russia and China, even though their comparatively underdeveloped national network societies are also expanding. (China typically ranks somewhat lower than Russia on the network society indexes.) Indeed, the costs of producing, using, and communicating information has constantly decreased, which has made ICTs available to an increasing number of people all over the world (Nye 2004b, 215–16). Still, it seems safe to suggest that a digital divide will continue to exist between and within states and societies.

The Crucial Power Base: Information Warfare Capability

An essential factor of state power in the digital age is whether *governmental information warfare (IW) capability* has been developed or not. Information warfare is about using ICTs for exploiting, disturbing, or destroying the ICTs of an adversary, as well as defending one's own systems against such attacks (Giacomello 2004a;

Denning 1999). For example, IW includes various means of electronically breaking into an opponent's information systems, spreading digital worms and viruses, and mounting denial-of-service attacks. IW capability also implies a technological boost for traditional psychological warfare (or soft power more generally), of which the basic elements have been practiced since the beginning of group conflicts, and which have been theorized about at least since Sun Tzu wrote his *Art of War* in the fifth century BCE.

A7   *A country's digital power base essentially depends on whether the government has developed a policy, an organizational structure, technology and competence for information warfare.*

If the government in question has developed a policy, an organizational structure, technology, and competence for information warfare, then it has expanded its power base as well as the scope of its power. Some 20 to 30 countries have invested in IW, especially the US, and increasingly also China and Russia (Giacomello 2004a; DSBTF 2001, memorandum). The US government has an advanced information warfare policy, ongoing research and development in the field, and several organizational units working with (allegedly mainly defensive) aspects of information warfare, including military information warfare battalions, as well as cyber security units within the CIA and the FBI (Bendrath 2003). Some smaller states, such as Sweden, have developed a similar capability, but on a much smaller scale than the US (Eriksson 2004; Eriksson, 2001a, 2001b).

It is thus not enough to have an advanced national network society. Such a development implies a *potential* base and scope of state power, but not an actual power boost. Estonia, for example, has a relatively advanced network society, with a high number of internet users, cell phones, an advanced internet banking system, and paperless cabinet sessions (*Principles of Estonian Information Policy*, 2003; *Information Technology in Public Administration of Estonia*, 2002).[14] Yet the government has failed to produce an overarching information warfare policy, letting each governmental unit take responsibility for its own information security. Terms such as information warfare and cyberterrorism are hardly spoken of in the Estonian capital (*National Security Concept of the Republic of Estonia* 2004).[15] This capability includes not only know-how within specially designed governmental IW units, but also constantly updated technology, and a system for monitoring, reporting, and responding to ICT incidents.

Emphasizing governmental information warfare capability also means that only those states that have the capability might pose a serious digital threat to other states. If the discussion is limited to interstate relations, it is quite easy to map out which states might potentially end up in information wars with one another. Hence there are obviously many more potential victims than there are potential bullies. There is no consensus on the ranking of the IW capabilities of individual states,

---

14 Personal interview with Männik, see note 9 above.
15 Also personal interviews, see note 9 above.

mainly because of differences in methodology and the composition of indexes. The United States ranks highest in all available studies, however, not only in terms of governmental IW capability, but also in terms of the estimated number of highly skilled hackers. In other words, most non-state actors capable of attacking the US information infrastructure are US citizens.

Of the other countries in the present study, Sweden tends to rank high, but is still not comparable to the digital superpower status of the United States. Russia is in some studies ranked on the same level as Sweden, but in other studies on a considerably lower level. Estonia is generally ranked very low in terms of IW capability. Thus, generally speaking, the United States is an uncontested superpower also in cyberspace (Giacomello 2004a, 394–395; Dunningan 2003, 372; Vatis 2001; US Department of Defense 2000).

Computer network conflicts between states are not the only digital security problem states have to worry about. Threats from non-state agents are significant, although most experts tend to argue that only (a limited number of) states have the capacity to wage fully-fledged information wars capable of shutting down the information infrastructure of an entire country (Giacomello 2004a, 395; Denning 2001). But non-state agents are not only countless but often also faceless, and are not necessarily bound by sovereignty or territorial boundaries (Rosenau 1993). In traditional conflicts, the identity, location, goals, means, and resources of an adversary are often known. In the digital age, however, there is a much greater variety of factors, and it is also harder to get information on them. When an information system breaks down, it can be hard to know if it was a technical failure or a remote attack that caused it (Libicki 1997). Even if system administrators can verify that an attack is actually taking place, it is often difficult to know whether the culprits are a hostile government, a terrorist group, insiders, teenage hackers, or any combination of the foregoing. They can be located on the other side of the globe, or in the next room. It is hard to find out whether they are doing it as part of a hostile strategy, or simply for fun. This uncertainty helps to explain the high level of fear of information security threats expressed by many governments, even though there are very few examples of real information wars, and allegedly no incidents of cyberterrorism, that is, attacks resulting in bloodshed or physical destruction. This prospect still seems to be a potential threat rather than a reality (Giacomello 2004; Nicander and Ranstorp 2004, 18; Jackson 2002; Denning 2001; Libicki 1997).

Even if the scope is limited to two states confronting each other in cyberspace, power disparities may appear in unforeseen and highly complex ways, regardless of the general capacity for digital warfare in each country. In addition to each party's IW capability, the ability to withstand a particular information warfare attack also depends on what kind of attack it is (for instance, electronic break-in, denial-of-service attack, or propaganda campaign), the intelligence available to the perpetrator, what the target is (such as a computer network of a particular public administration, or the electric power network of a country), and the defensive systems of the intended victim (including firewalls, anti-virus software, and procedures for handling incidents and sensitive information).

A8 *Power disparities in digital battles depend* inter alia *on the type of attack, the skills of the perpetrator, the type of target, and the defensive systems of the victim – all of which are variable over time, within and between polities.*

Moreover, technologies for attacking and defending information systems are constantly developing, while the application of them is very uneven, often even within the same governmental apparatus. Malicious software is easily available for everyone with access to the internet. According to some estimates, approximately 30,000 websites contain software for hacking and spreading electronic viruses (Cordesman 2002, 11). This means that someone with the will, an online connection, and some computer knowledge may at least temporarily engage in an asymmetric conflict with a digital great power such as Germany or the United States.

Weak and Strong Digital Powers

As has been emphasized in the foregoing analysis, governmental IW capability and the development of a national network society are crucial for understanding power disparity in the digital age. Only states with IW capability have a real power boost in the digital age. Otherwise, they are limited to dealing with varying degrees of vulnerability.

Taking both IW capability and network society into account, four basic types of 'digital powers' can be suggested (see Figure 7.1): (1) states with both governmental IW capability and an advanced network society (such as the US and Sweden), (2) states with IW capability and a less developed network society (such as Russia and China), (3) states with a weak IW capability and an advanced network society (such as Estonia), and (4) states with both weak IW capability and an underdeveloped network society (such as Somalia and Afghanistan). Against this background, it appears as if states of the second type (e.g. Russia and China) have an advantage over the other types of digital powers, while the states of the third type (e.g. Estonia) have an asymmetrical disadvantage in terms of increased vulnerability. It is also noteworthy that the domain of digital power mainly concerns the first three types of states. The fourth would be largely unaffected by an adversary's attempts at using IW resources. Digital attacks on Burundi would be futile – there are simply few if any targets to attack.

The analysis becomes more complex, however, if non-state agents are brought into the picture. There is every reason to do so, since digital and other means of information power are becoming increasingly accessible, mainly because of shrinking costs of producing and using ICTs. Indeed, bringing transnational actors back in implies a whole new spectrum of asymmetries. It can be argued that the most asymmetrically powerful opponent is not another state, but a non-state agent with IW capability.[16] This could, for instance, be an international terrorist organization

---

16 This implies a further development of what James Rosenau (1993) defined as sovereignty-bound as opposed to sovereignty-free actors.

with the ability to commence computer attacks. Not only is such an agent equipped with offensive capability, but it also lacks the vulnerability of a national network society, and does not have the responsibility to protect it.

		Governmental Information Warfare Capability	
		Strong	Weak
National Network Society	Strong	1. (USA, Sweden)	2. (Estonia)
	Weak	3. (Russia, China)	4. (Afghanistan, Somalia)

Figure 7.1 Types of Digital Powers

Conclusion

The digital age implies that power disparity is ubiquitous, highly dynamic, and multi-faceted. Cyberspace is too vast and complex for a single actor to seize complete control. Moreover, cyberspace provides actors with a real-time global reach, thus expanding the potential domain of power. At the same time, it is possible to discern recurrent patterns of power relations. Well-known offline conflicts and power imbalances seem to be reproduced in cyberspace. The historical Russian-American power game continues in cyberspace. Russia perceives itself as the technological underdog, and America is aware of its leading position.

In terms of role identity, the general observation made here is that established offline identities largely correspond to identities in cyberspace. The notion of a digital gap is considered a threat in itself in Russia, which is not addressed in those terms in the other countries discussed here. Sweden, however, in some respects considers itself as an emerging 'great power' in terms of digital power, especially if civilian and business-oriented aspects are taken into consideration. In contrast with Sweden, Estonia has not so far developed any concept, organization, or policy for information warfare, but the Estonian government has strong aspirations towards developing a leading network society.

The information revolution and the continuing global diffusion of ICTs harbours the possibility of changing established role identities. States generally considered to be 'small' but which invest in ICTs and IW capability may gain an asymmetrical advantage over traditional 'middle powers' and 'great powers' which do not develop the same capacity. The general trend, however, seems to be that states historically considered to be major powers are also investing a lot in the development of their network societies and their governmental IW capability. In particular, all states historically perceived as 'great powers' have developed a significant IW capability, including Russia, China, India (increasingly), and several other countries. The major difference seems to be how their national network societies are developing, which implies a greater variety in terms of vulnerability.

The analysis conducted in this chapter can be summarized as a number of theoretically oriented assertions on power and security in the digital age. Some of these assertions are general, while others are conditional (see Table 7.2).

Table 7.2 Assertions on Power Disparity in the Digital Age

General assertions:

A1 Complete information dominance is not only unlikely but also counterproductive–soft power depends on the opponent's continued ability to communicate.

A2 The abstract, global, dynamic and technologically advanced nature of cyberspace has nurtured fear-mongering futuristic threat images, which do not correspond to the empirical record.

A3 Access to cyberspace potentially provides actors with a global reach, and thereby broadens the domain of both the number and types of foes and friends.

A4 The "digital divide" nurtures role identities of dominant and backward states, which generally correspond to offline identities.

Conditional assertions:

A5 The scope of digital power depends on whether a government perceives IT as a means of online attack on critical infrastructures, as a booster of offline-technologies, as a means of soft power, or as any combination of these.

A6 The more a country depends on ICTs for vital functions (e.g. electricity, government, communications, financial transactions), the more vulnerable it is to information warfare, and technical system failures.

A7 A country's digital power base essentially depends on whether the government has developed a policy, an organizational structure, technology and competence for information warfare.

A8 Power disparities in digital battles depend inter alia on the type of attack, the skills of the perpetrator, the type of target, and the defensive systems of the victim – all of which are variable over time, within and between polities.

Nonetheless, the problems of digital power and security must not be exaggerated. To be sure, since the early 1990s, information warfare, cyberterrorism, and cybercrime have become the hottest topics in international security discourse among analysts, policymakers, businesspeople. Electronic viruses and worms, e-mail spamming, web defacing, theft of information or money, and distortion of data are truly significant security threats in today's globalized world. Yet a face-off in cyberspace between states resulting in a shutdown of essential parts of critical infrastructure is highly unlikely. If such an event is to happen (say, the immobilization of all telecommunications in a country), it would most likely be the result of conventional offline attacks. In short, while cyberattacks may destroy bits and bytes, they are still only potentially capable of achieving the bloodshed and physical destruction caused by real bombs.

Chapter 8

Generalizing About Security Strategies in the Baltic Sea Region

Stephen G. Walker

The Baltic Sea Region offers the opportunity to construct and maintain a variety of security complexes among the states bordering the Baltic Sea. Buzan and Waever (2003, 491) define a regional security complex as 'a set of units whose major processes of securitization, desecuritization, or both are so interlinked that their security problems cannot be reasonably be analyzed or resolved apart from one another.' The potential architecture for a regional security complex among neighboring states extends along a continuum of conflict and cooperation from an enduring rivalry to a security community, in which the members of the former expect and plan for conflicts between them to escalate to war while the latter neither anticipate nor plan for conflicts between them to become violent (Lake and Morgan 1997; Buzan and Waever 2003; see also Deutsch 1957; Diehl and Goertz 2000).[1]

A security strategy of cooperation employs soft power and positive sanctions to move states toward a positive peace at one end of this continuum while a security strategy of conflict utilizes hard power and negative sanctions to create a negative peace at the more violent end of this continuum of possibilities (Nye 2004; Baldwin 2002). The exercise of soft power is the use of confidence-building measures, appeasement tactics, and positive sanctions (rewards) to create an atmosphere of trust and a network of cooperative institutions that encourages interdependence between states while not ruling out the use of hard power toward third parties (Keohane and Nye 1989). The exercise of hard power is the use of threats, the deployment of military force, and negative sanctions (punishments) to instill fear and create a set of competitive institutions that fosters independence among states (Waltz 1979).

---

1   Some theorists of regional security complexes do not define the Baltic Sea Region as a regional security complex. Buzan and Waever (2003) have the most restrictive definition and would identify Latvia, Estonia, and Lithuania as 'insulator' states located outside and between a West European regional security complex and a post-Soviet regional security complex in the post-Cold War world, which together encompass the remaining states along the Baltic Sea. Lake and Morgan (1997) would be more receptive to the game theory approach to the processes of securitization and desecuritization in this chapter with their emphasis on multi-level games between actors. See Buzan and Waever (2003, 77-82) for a discussion of the construct of a regional security complex as conceptualized by different theorists.

It is possible for both kinds of arrangements to coexist within a region around the paradox that intense conflict between blocs of states may create intense cooperation within each bloc. The East-West conflict in Europe during the Cold War era is an example of this dynamic, in which the European Union's emergence among some members of the Western bloc was due partly to the competition between the military alliances led by the USA and the USSR. The failure of the Eastern bloc's members to evolve a lasting cooperative arrangement was due partly to the enduring national identities of the less powerful states in the Warsaw Treaty Organization and the Soviet Union and the use of military coercion within the alliance by the USSR to settle conflicts with such countries as East Germany and Hungary.

The exercise of power within each alliance was characterized by different institutional arrangements in which individual NATO members exercised a veto over common decisions while individual WTO members were dominated by Soviet rule in the form of puppet governments and military occupation. These institutional rules for the exercise of power resulted in a coercive strategy of hegemony within the Eastern bloc and a cooperative strategy of appeasement within the Western bloc. Nationalist divisions and various conflicts also occurred between the USA and its allies in NATO during the Cold War and did lead to the use of negative sanctions by one side or the other. The United States directed economic sanctions at Britain during the 1956 Anglo-Egyptian conflict over the Suez Canal, and France expelled US nuclear weapons from French soil in a diplomatic dispute over NATO's military strategy toward the USSR. Although these coercive tactics fell short of the actual deployment or use of military force against one another, critics of US foreign policy saw these actions by the United States as a hegemonic strategy met by Anglo-French resistance.

With the demise of the Soviet Union in the 1990s, the power vacuum in Eastern Europe and the corresponding absence of a security threat to Western Europe unleashed different local forces in each region. The European Union's institutions, created with the exercise of soft power during the Cold War, continued to flourish while nationalist sentiments initially carried the day in Eastern Europe. However, the small states of Eastern Europe have now gravitated toward membership in NATO and the European Union as a cooperative security strategy against the possibility of a future Russian hegemonic strategy *vis a vis* the new Eastern Europe.

The countries of the Baltic Sea Region share a common history and geographical proximity with Russia, the independent states of Eastern Europe, and the expanding European Union. West Germany and the Nordic states were either members of the NATO alliance (West Germany, Norway, Iceland, and Denmark) or pursued a policy of non-alignment (Sweden and Finland). Estonia, Latvia, and Lithuania were annexed by the USSR in 1940 and administered as provinces of the Soviet Union while East Germany and Poland became members of the Warsaw Treaty Organization. With NATO allies in the west, Soviet clients in the east, and non-aligned states in the middle, the Baltic Sea Region became one of the frontiers of the Cold War. However, regional tensions did not rise to the level exhibited at such central European flash points as the Berlin Wall or the border between East and West Germany.

In the aftermath of the Cold War, can the states of the Baltic Sea Region employ soft power as a cooperative security strategy to create a single security complex that resembles a security community? Or will the particular configurations of regional power disparities, nationalist identities, and the lack of a common external threat lead to more than one security strategy and the creation of a security complex based on the exercise of both soft and hard power? In order to address these possibilities in a systematic way that leads toward generalizability, I shall draw on a couple of sources for analytical assistance. One is a typology of grand strategic orientations and the other is a set of general theoretical orientations. The former suggest the kind of security complex that is likely to result from the adoption of different grand strategies. The latter specify the conditions under which different types of grand strategies are likely to be adopted.

Table 8.1 Grand Strategy Typology

		Grand Strategies	
	Positive Sanctions	Appeasement (Settlement)	Bandwagoning (Submission)
POWER			
	Negative Sanctions	Competition (Domination)	Balancing (Deadlock)

The typology in Table 8.1 characterizes each strategy in terms of the exercise of positive and negative sanctions (Baldwin 2002). Nye (2004: x, 5) defines soft power as 'the ability to get what you want through attraction rather than coercion or payments…This soft power…co-opts people rather than coerces them. Appeasement and bandwagoning are cooperative security strategies and characterized by the exercise of soft power accompanied by promises and rewards as positive sanctions. Competition and balancing are coercive security strategies characterized by the exercise of hard power in the form of resistance, threats and punishments as negative sanctions.

A more precise operational definition of each grand strategy is in terms of their ranked preferences for the political outcomes of settlement, domination, deadlock, and submission. An appeasement strategy has settlement as its highest ranking outcome while balancing has deadlock as the highest ranking outcome. Domination is the highest ranking outcome for a strategy of competition. Submission is the highest ranking outcome for a bandwagoning strategy. Although it may seem counterintuitive for any state to rank submission as its highest-ranked outcome, the logic of a bandwagoning strategy is 'aligning with the source of danger' (Walt 1987, 17, 21-2; Waltz 1979, 126) or to "give in to threats" in return for safety or profit (Schweller 1994, 251).

152   *Security Strategies, Power Disparity and Identity*

This typology of grand strategies expands in two ways below in Table 8.2. One is to differentiate variants of each grand strategy by reference to the ranking of the other political outcomes. The other is to distinguish pairs of states with identical grand strategies from pairs with different grand strategies toward each another. These moves specify the possible security constellations resulting from the intersection of grand strategies adopted by different states toward one another within a particular region. In Table 8.2 are the possible variants of each grand strategy, which can intersect to form a strategic interaction dyad between pairs of states.

Table 8.2 Families of Grand Strategies

	Four Sets of Grand Strategies	
	Appeasement Strategies	**Bandwagoning Strategies**
	Settle>Submit>Deadlock>Dominate	Submit>Settle>Deadlock>Dominate
	Settle>Submit>Dominate>Deadlock	Submit>Settle>Dominate>Deadlock
SOFT	Settle>Deadlock>Submit>Dominate	Submit>Deadlock>Settle>Dominate
	Settle>Dominate>Submit>Deadlock	Submit>Dominate>Settle>Deadlock
	Settle>Deadlock>Dominate>Submit	Submit>Deadlock>Dominate>Settle
	Settle>Dominate>Deadlock>Submit	Submit>Dominate>Deadlock>Settle
EXERCISE OF POWER		
	Competition Strategies	**Balancing Strategies**
	Dominate>Submit>Settle>Deadlock	Deadlock>Submit>Settle>Dominate
	Dominate>Submit>Deadlock>Settle	Deadlock>Submit>Dominate>Settle
HARD	Dominate>Settle>Submit>Deadlock	Deadlock>Settle>Submit>Dominate
	Dominate>Settle>Deadlock>Submit	Deadlock>Settle>Dominate>Submit
	Dominate>Deadlock>Submit>Settle	Deadlock>Dominate>Submit>Settle
	Dominate>Deadlock>Settle>Submit	Deadlock>Dominate>Settle>Submit

All of these strategies are possible selections, but some are more likely than others, depending on conditions identified by different approaches to general theories of international relations. A neorealist approach emphasizes the distribution of power between states and assumes that the self-help nature of international relations biases states toward strategies of competition or balancing that emphasize the exercise of hard power (Waltz 1979; Elman 1996; Walt 1987; Keohane 1986). A neoliberal approach emphasizes the distribution of interests between states and assumes that incentives for cooperation created by complementary or common interests biases states toward strategies of appeasement or bandwagoning characterized by the exercise of soft power (Keohane and Nye 1977; Baldwin 1993; Moravcsik 2003). A constructivist approach emphasizes the social construction of identities between states and assumes that the role identities attributed to states by others in the international system bias them either toward cooperative strategies of appeasement and bandwagoning or toward conflict strategies of competition and balancing (Katzenstein 1996; Wendt 1999).[2]

The particular concepts of power, interests, and identities within these structural approaches to international relations suggest different assumptions as points of departure for making core predictions about the grand strategies pursued between states that result in a security complex for a region. The realist school's power-oriented assumption implies the core prediction that strong states are more likely to pursue competitive strategies of hegemony while weak states are more likely to pursue balancing strategies of autonomy toward one another. The liberal school's interest-driven assumption implies the core prediction that states with shared, i.e., common or complementary, non-security interests are more likely to pursue cooperative security strategies toward one another regarding security interests than states without shared non-security interests.

The constructivist school's identity-sensitive assumption implies the core prediction that states with common or complementary role identities are more likely to pursue symmetrical security strategies of cooperation or conflict toward one another than states without such role identities. Wendt (1999) identifies three role identities, Friend, Rival, Enemy, associated with their respective Kantian, Lockean and Hobbesian cultures of friendship (unconditional cooperation), rivalry (conditional conflict), and enmity (unconditional conflict). He argues that states assume these role identities symmetrically as their respective cultures of anarchy become dominant in a geographical region or a historical era. Wendt does not directly investigate international systems of anarchy in which asymmetrical identities and strategies may be the rule,[3] however, nor does he identify a Rousseauvian culture of conditional cooperation in which defection is a cultural norm in the absence of effective binding communication or strong institutional constraints.

The possibility of a Rousseauvian culture is implied in Rousseau's famous stag hunt example when hunters band together (cooperate) in the state of nature to catch

---

2 The emphasis in this chapter is on assessing the consequences of assuming a particular identity rather than on reconstructing or deconstructing how the identity was assumed by a state. Constructivists are divided by various authors into different schools, depending on which emphasis informs their research (Ruggie 1998; Katzenstein, Keohane, and Krasner 1998, 674-82; Hopf 1998; Checkel 1998). See Checkel (1999) and Smith (2001) for applications and more discussion with European examples. Fearon and Wendt (2002) offer a thoughtful assessment of the significance of making distinctions of this sort.

3 While Wendt does not examine mixed cultures directly, he does so indirectly by investigating the processes of transition from one culture to another.

a stag to feed all of them. However, when the opportunity for one of them arises to catch a rabbit, that hunter defects from the stag hunt to feed himself at the expense of the others (Waltz 1959). The stag hunt example suggests the possibility of a culture of anarchy with a norm of conditional cooperation and a role identity of Collaborator. The analysis in this chapter expands Wendt's theoretical account by modeling formally the possible combinations of symmetrical (Friend-Friend, Collaborator-Collaborator, Rival-Rival, Enemy-Enemy) role identities and corresponding strategic interactions along with some of their asymmetrical variants under the conditions of power equality and power disparity (see also Walker 2004).

While the assumption for each of these structural approaches can simply be pitted against the others in a contest of rival predictions about particular cases, it is probably more fruitful to ask when each of the assumptions qualifies the predictions of the others. For example, holding constant the condition of non-security interests as the focus of attention between a pair of states: Does neoliberalism's core prediction hold when there is a power disparity between a pair of states? Similarly, does the core prediction of neorealism hold when there are not complementary identities between states? Does the core prediction of constructivism hold when there is an absence of shared non-security interests between states?

These questions identify only some of the possible combinations of antecedent conditions that may lead to conflicting predictions across theoretical approaches for the same pair of states. Taking turns with each assumption as a starting point in constructing a model suggests how each core prediction can be refined and qualified, depending on the presence or absence of antecedent conditions highlighted by other approaches. These possibilities are modeled below with the aid of 2 x 2 ordinal game theory, which is reviewed in the Appendix to this chapter for the reader who is unacquainted with its basic concepts (see also Rapoport, Guyer, and Gordon 1976; Stein 1990; Brams 1994).

The Generalizable Power of Game Theory

Snidal (1986) notes that game theory has been employed in three ways to generalize about the study of world politics: as a metaphor; as a conceptual framework, and as a formal model. Used as a metaphor, a game such as prisoner's dilemma can highlight similarities across different domains of behavior. Two prisoners can both choose silence by refusing to testify against each other and face a short jail sentence, or both can choose defection by agreeing to testify against each other and face a long jail sentence. Each prisoner can also choose defection while the other chooses silence, leading to freedom for the one turning state's evidence and a long sentence for the one choosing silence. A similar dilemma faces two states who can both decide to cooperate and risk one state defecting from an agreement in order to exploit the other. Or both can decide to choose conflict and create a deadlock that is a worse outcome for both states than mutual cooperation but avoids the risk of being exploited.

The rational choice for prisoners and states is to choose defection in the absence of communication or some other mechanism that would bind them to the choice of cooperation. This outcome is worse than the mutual cooperation outcome but also avoids the worst outcome (being exploited) for both prisoners and states. The metaphorical relationship is between two domains of choice by two different kinds of actors in which an understanding of the choice set in one domain has similar features to the choice set in another domain (Snidal 1986: Beer and Landescheer 2004).

A second use of game theory is as a vehicle simply to describe an empirical phenomenon. The concepts in the vocabulary of game theory – players, preferences, strategies, outcomes – are employed to give general labels to empirical phenomena associated with a domain of cases. States play games with one another in which they choose strategies in the context of identifiable preferences and alternative foreign policy choices that produce outcomes between players. However, there is little or no attempt to model the relationships among concepts so that the outcomes are a function of the available strategies that are chosen because of the distribution of interests and preferences. In short, the concepts of game theory can provide a conceptual framework to describe inductively *what* the cases are without supplying a theory that explains *why* the cases have the strategies and outcomes that they do (Snidal 1986).

A third use of game theory is to use the assumptions and propositions of game theory to specify formal models of the cases that link their various features logically to form an explanation of why players with different preferences choose different strategies that produce different outcomes. This use of game theory is to deduce what some features of a case should be, given other features as antecedent conditions and assumptions. Given the assumptions that both players in a game know the preference rankings of both players for the possible outcomes of the game and that each seeks to win the game, then the proposition is true that they will choose strategies which lead to a predictable outcome. In this combination of statements, the proposition explains the outcome by reference to the strategies. In turn, the strategies are specified by reference to the assumptions about preference rankings known to both players and their desires to win the game (Snidal 1986).

The use of game theory in this chapter to generalize about Baltic security strategies approaches the third use of game theory identified by Snidal in its formal specification of security games with different strategies and ranked outcomes attributed to players. These games predict that states with different combinations of power relationships, role identities, and distributions of secondary and vital interests known to both players will choose particular strategies that intersect and lead to particular kinds of outcomes. So these games are formal models that can link preferences, strategies, and outcomes together logically as an explanation.

However, to assess the validity of these explanations requires empirical tests of the deductions in the models as they apply to particular cases. Critics of game theory and other forms of rational choice explanations often indict game theorists for engaging in 'casual empiricism' to establish the link between their models and particular cases (Green and Shapiro 1994). Selecting too few cases (often a single case) or an otherwise unrepresentative set of cases may reflect a 'selection bias' that limits the generalizability to cases that fit the model (Geddes 1991). Observations of the variables in the model also may not be reliable or valid, creating measurement errors that undermine confidence in the empirical fit between the model and cases.

Therefore, establishing the fit between game theory models and cases in this chapter should be viewed with caution as methodological examples of adduction rather than deduction or induction. Deduction would require systematic measurement of the variables in the model from information in the case studies while induction would infer a model from systematic observations of variables in the cases. The use of adduction below simply assesses whether a case fits a pre-existing model based on evidence about the case, thereby providing an example of how the logical argument in the model works.[4]

Power Equality and Security Strategies

The symmetrical games of cooperative and coercive security strategies in Table 8.3 represent situations in which both players are equal in power but have different combinations of role identities and interests at stake, which condition them toward different variants of appeasement and competition as grand strategies. A combination of secondary interests as the stakes and mutual Friends as the role identities for players with equal power leads to an unconditional appeasement game in which cooperation (CO) is the dominant strategy for both players. That is, each one will select (CO) no matter what the other selects. When vital interests are the stakes for both players, however, the prediction is a conditional cooperation strategy between Collaborators that is contingent on each player selecting (CO). That is, if one player shifts to (CF), then the other player will, too.

Under the two-sided information assumption associated with classical game theory, each player knows the preference rankings for both players so that the outcome of both cooperative security games in Table 8.3 should be mutual cooperation (4,4) in which each player gets its highest ranked outcome. This security game has the most stable cooperative equilibrium in terms of the background conditions specified by realist, liberal, and constructivist theories of international relations. Its equilibrium is also homeostatic, i.e., 'self-righting,' even if exogenous shocks in the form of unexpected events or moves by other actors in a region cause the players to shift choices from mutual cooperation (CO,CO) to mutual conflict (CF,CF). Because the logic of sequential game theory (Brams 1994) demonstrates that the Nash equilibrium of (3,3) is Pareto-inferior to the non-myopic equilibrium of (4,4), the player with the next move at (3,3) will choose (CO) followed by a reciprocal choice of (CO) by the other player to return to (4,4).

---

4   Adduction is defined in *Webster's Third International Dictionary* (1976, 25) as 'the act or action of adducing or bringing forward,' and adduce is defined as 'to bring forward (as an example, reason or proof) for consideration in a discussion, analysis or contention' to provide some legitimacy to a hypothesis.

Table 8.3 Power Equality Games with Symmetrical Strategies

Power Equality Security Games								
Cooperation Security Games Interests				Conflict Security Games Interests				
Secondary Friend		Vital Collaborator		Secondary Rival (G57)		Vital Enemy (G32)		
	CO CF		CO CF		CO CF		CO CF	
Friend CO	<u>4,4</u>* 3,2	Collab. CO	<u>4,4</u>* 1,2	Rival CO	<u>3,3</u> <u>2,4</u>*	Enemy CO	<u>3,3</u> 1,4	
CF	2,3 1,1	CF	2,1 3,3*	CF	<u>4,2</u>* 1,1	<u>CF</u>	4,1 <u>2,2</u>*	
Unconditional Appeasement		Conditional Appeasement		Conditional Competition		Unconditional Competition		

Note: Each player's preferences are ranked 4 (Highest) to 1 (Lowest) for the outcomes of settlement (CO,CO), deadlock (CF,CF), domination (CF,CO), submission (CO,CF) for Row and settlement (CO,CO), deadlock (CF,CF), domination (CO,CF), and submission (CF,CO) for Column. Non-myopic equilibria and dominant strategies are underlined. Nash equilibria are asterisked. The G-number refers to the ID number assigned to conflict games by Brams (1994, 217-219).

The only ways to disrupt the (4,4) equilibrium of these cooperative security games beyond their homeostatic range are: (a) either allow exogenous shocks to alter the role identities and/or the distributions of power and interests between the players; or (b) relax the two-sided information assumption and allow the players to miscalculate the preference rankings for self and other and/or misperceive the distributions of identities, interests, and power between them. The effects of altering identities and interests while keeping power equal is illustrated by the conflict security games in which both players' identities shift to Rival or Enemy.

The stable outcome in Table 8.3 between Rivals, i.e., when secondary interests are the stakes, is either (4,2) or (2,4 – domination by one player and submission by the other player. The stable outcome between Enemies, i.e., when vital interests are the stakes, is (2,2) deadlock. These outcomes are the Nash equilibria predicted by classical game theory's assumption of two-sided information and simultaneous moves by both players. Even if both players initially choose (CO) in the conditional competition game in order to avoid their worst outcome (1,1), the (3,3) outcome is unstable because either one can defect to (CF) and achieve a higher-ranked preference.

Sequential game theory addresses this problem of (3,3)'s instability by relaxing the assumption of simultaneous moves and introducing the concept of a non-myopic equilibrium, which qualifies the stability associated with a Nash equilibrium. Sometimes the two equilibria overlap, but the (3,3) settlement outcome in both games of competition is only stable as a non-myopic equilibrium. Depending on the 'initial state' of the game and which player has the next move, it is possible to reach a non-myopic equilibrium of (3,3) in each conflict security game. These two games are the well-known ordinal games of Chicken and Prisoner's Dilemma analyzed extensively by game theorists (Rapoport, Guyer, and Gordon 1976; Rapoport and Chammah 1970; Brams 1994).

Brams' Theory of Moves (TOM) specifies (3,3), (4,2), and (2,4) as non-myopic equilibria for Chicken and both (2,2) and (3,3) as non-myopic equilibria for Prisoner's Dilemma. By allowing pre-play communication between players before selecting a move, it is possible for one player to move toward or stay at (3,3) by exercising a credible threat to move to a worse outcome following a failure by the other player to also move toward or stay at (3,3) mutual cooperation (Brams 1994). The basis for stable cooperation in these conflict security games rests on shared power and the willingness to exercise threat power while the stability of the cooperation security games rests on shared identities.

Table 8.4 Power Equality Games with Asymmetrical Strategies

Expanded Power Equality Security Games									
		(G37)			(G33)				
	Collaborator			Rival			Enemy		
		CO	CF		CO	CF		CO	CF
	CO	4,4*	3,2	CO	4,3	3,4*	CO	4,3	3,4*
Friend				**Friend**			**Friend**		
	CF	2,1	1,3	CF	2,2	1,1	CF	2,1	1,2
	(G31)			(G27)			(G22)		
	Rival			Enemy			Enemy		
		CO	CF		CO	CF		CO	CF
	CO	4,3	1,4	CO	4,3	1,4	CO	3,3	2,4*
Collab.				**Collab.**			**Rival**		
	CF	2,2	3,1	CF	2,1	3,2*	CF	4,1	1,2

Note: Each player's preferences are ranked 4 (Highest) to 1(Lowest) for the outcomes of settlement (CO,CO), deadlock (CF,CF), domination (CF,CO), submission (CO,CF) for Row and settlement (CO,CO), deadlock (CF,CF), domination (CO,CF), and submission (CF,CO) for Column. Non-myopic equilibria and dominant strategies are underlined. Nash equlibria are asterisked. The G-number refers to the ID number assigned to conflict games by Brams (1994, 217-219).

An expanded set of power equality security games includes the six games in Table 8.4. These games relax the conditions of symmetrical interests and identities while maintaining the condition of equal power between the players. There is one cooperative security game (Friend-Collaborator), in which the two players pursue different appeasement strategies, and one conflict security game (Rival-Enemy) in which the two players pursue different competitive strategies. The two appeasement strategies in the Friend-Collaborator game are equally effective against each other in achieving their shared highest ranked preference for mutual cooperation (4,4) as an outcome. The Rival-Enemy game in which one player has a dominant strategy of (CF) has only one stable outcome (2,4), which is both a Nash and a non-myopic equilibrium.

The other four games are security games with asymmetrical strategies in which one player pursues a cooperative security strategy while the other pursues a conflict security strategy. Both unconditional and conditional appeasement strategies have stable outcomes of mutual cooperation against either an unconditional or a conditional competitive strategy. However, these non-myopic (CO, CO) equilibria do not overlap with a Nash equilibrium in these games. In order to make (CO,CO) a stable equilibrium, therefore, the player with the cooperative security strategy has to possess moving power or employ threat power. The former refers to the ability of a player who has the next move from a game's 'initial state' to continue to move indefinitely (cycle) while the latter requires the use of prior (pre-play) communication to make a credible threat that unless one player stays at the (CO,CO) 'initial state,' the other player will move toward or stay at a mutually disadvantageous outcome that is worse than the (CO,CO) outcome (Brams 1994: Appendix, 215-219).[5]

This analysis of power equality games yields some important insights about the requirements for an effective cooperative security strategy. It is probably not news to realists, liberals, or constructivists that players who pursue cooperative security strategies toward one another are rather likely to achieve a regional security complex characterized by a mutual cooperation (CO,CO) equilibrium while players who employ coercive security strategies are more prone to create enduring rivalries with a mutual conflict (CF,CF) equilibrium. However, there are some interesting findings for general international relations theorists regarding the outcomes associated with asymmetrical security strategies, which should engage their attention.

Under the condition of power equality, it is possible for cooperative security strategies to fare better in establishing and maintaining mutual cooperation against coercive security strategies than realist international relations theorists might anticipate. Liberal international theorists may not expect that the success of a cooperative security strategy requires a willingness to use hard power (threats and negative sanctions) in order to be effective in inducing mutual cooperation against a player employing a coercive security strategy. It may surprise constructivist international relations theorists that if a player is willing and able to employ moving power or threat power, it is not necessary to convince a player with a Rival or Enemy identity to shift to a Friend or Collaborator identity in order to achieve a stable (CO,CO) equilibrium.

---

5 Inspection of these games shows by backward induction that Row has moving power: if the Column player moves to (CO,CF), the Row player can cycle clockwise indefinitely through the game's matrix; however, Column will be blocked by Row counterclockwise when Row refuses to move from (CO, CO). Row also has threat power in repeated plays of the game and with pre-play communication: Row can threaten to move to the Pareto-inferior (2,2) (and do so in repeated plays) if Column does not stay at (4,3).

There is also an important question raised by these results. Is power equality a necessary condition for cooperative security strategies to succeed under the two-sided information assumption that states know both their own preferences and the preferences of others? That is, in a rational political universe will cooperative security strategies succeed under the condition of power disparity between states (Majeski 2004)?

Power Disparity and Security Strategies

The symmetrical games of cooperation and conflict in Table 8.5 represent situations in which one player is stronger than the other with different combinations of role identities and interests at stake. If both states pursue cooperative security strategies of appeasement and bandwagoning, respectively, it is possible to reach a stable outcome of mutual cooperation (CO,CO), which is both a non-myopic and a Nash equilibrium. Another non-myopic equilibrium (CO,CF) of domination by the stronger state over the weaker state also exists; however, it is the weaker state that must have both the incentive and the threat power to reach and maintain this outcome. The stronger state's highest preference is (CO,CO), which means that the security of the weaker state's secondary and vital interests under the stronger state's umbrella is probably not the most likely outcome. These generalizations hold no matter whether the distribution of interests is symmetrical or asymmetrical.

A (CF, CF) deadlock outcome is likely when both states pursue coercive security strategies in Table 8.5. The weak state's balancing strategy and the strong state's competition strategy lead to this outcome as both a Nash equilibrium and a non-myopic equilibrium no matter whether secondary or vital interests are at stake between them. In the case of secondary interests, the (CO, CF) outcome of domination by the Hegemon over the Balancer is also a non-myopic equilibrium, which the balancer can induce with moving power. However, this player's moving power is irrelevant, because the Balancer prefers the (4,3) outcome of deadlock to the (2,4) outcome of domination by the Hegemon (Brams 1994, 92-102). These generalizations hold no matter whether the distribution of interests is symmetrical or asymmetrical.

Table 8.6 expands the number of power disparity security games by making the mix of strategies between the two players asymmetrical. Table 8.6 shows that a (CO,CF) submission outcome is likely for weak powers who pursue bandwagoning strategies vis a vis a Hegemon, because both players rank this outcome highest (4,4) in all of their games no matter what the distribution of interests is between them. However, a mutual cooperation (CO,CO) outcome is likely between strong powers with appeasement strategies and weak powers with balancing strategies no matter whether their interests are symmetrical or asymmetrical.

Generalizing About Security Strategies in the Baltic Sea Region

Table 8.5 Power Disparity Games with Symmetrical Strategies

Cooperation Security Games					Conflict Security Games				
Symmetrical Interests					**Symmetrical Interests**				
Secondary (G34)		Vital (G50)			Secondary (G38)		Vital (G13)		
Patron		Patron			Hegemon		Hegemon		
	CO	CF		CO CF		CO CF		CO CF	
CO	<u>3,4</u>*	4,3	CO	<u>2,4</u>* 4,3	CO	3,1 <u>2,4</u>	CO	3,2 1,4	
Client			Client		Balancer		Balancer		
CF	2,2	1,1	CF	1,1 3,2	CF	1,2 <u>4,3</u>*	CF	2,1 <u>4,3</u>*	
Cooperative Role Identities					Coercive Role Identities				
Asymmetrical Interests					**Asymmetrical Interests**				
(G36)		(G35)			(G39)		(G12)		
Patron (V)		Patron (S)			Hegemon (V)		Hegemon (S)		
	CO	CF		CO CF		CO CF		CO CF	
CO	<u>3,4</u>*	4,3	CO	<u>2,4</u>* 4,3	CO	3,2 <u>2,4</u>	CO	3,1 1,4	
Client (S)			Client (V)		Balan. (S)		Balan. (V)		
CF	2,1	1,2	CF	1,2 3,1	CF	1,1 <u>4,3</u>*	CF	2,2 <u>4,3</u>*	
Cooperative Role Identities					Coercive Role Identities				

Note: Each player's preferences are ranked 4 (Highest) to 1 (Lowest) for the outcomes of settlement (CO,CO), deadlock (CF,CF), domination (CF,CO), submission (CO,CF) for Row and settlement (CO,CO), deadlock (CF,CF), domination (CO,CF), and submission (CF,CO) for Column. Non-myopic equilibria and dominant strategies are underlined. Nash equilibria are asterisked. The G-number refers to the ID number assigned to conflict games by Brams (1994, 217-219). (V) and (S) refer to Vital and Secordary interests in games with asymmetrical interests.

The qualification to this generalization is when the Patron has vital interests at stake, as when the location of the Balancer makes it a buffer state in a dispute over vital interests with another great power. Then a deadlock also becomes one of the non-myopic equilibria. When the initial state is (2,1) in G52, the nonmyopic equilibrium is mutual cooperation (3,4) when Balancer has the first move and deadlock (4,2) when Patron has the first move. When the initial state is (1,1) in G53, the nonmyopic equilibrium is mutual cooperation (3,4) when Balancer has the first move and deadlock (4,2) when Patron has the first move (see Brams 1994, 219).

Table 8.6 Power Disparity Games with Asymmetrical Strategies

Symmetrical Interests					Symmetrical Interests				
					(G20)			(G52)	
Secondary Hegemon		Vital Hegemon			Secondary Patron		Vital Patron		
	CO	CF	CO	CF		CO	CF	CO	CF
CO	3,1	<u>4,4</u>*	CO 2,2	<u>4,4</u>*	CO	<u>3,4</u>*	2,3	CO <u>3,4</u>*	1,3
Client			Client		Balancer			Balancer	
CF	2,2	1,3	CF 1,1	3,3	CF	1,2	4,1	CF 2,1	<u>4,2</u>*
Bandwagoning and Competition Strategies					Balancing and Appeasement Strategies				
Asymmetrical Interests					Asymmetrical Interests				
					(G21)			(G53)	
Hegemon (V)		Hegemon (S)			Patron (S)		Patron (V)		
	CO	CF	CO	CF		CO	CF	CO	CF
CO	3,2	<u>4,4</u>*	CO 2,1	<u>4,4</u>*	CO	<u>3,4</u>*	1,3	CO <u>3,4</u>*	2,3
Client (S)			Client (V)		Balancer (V)			Balancer (S)	
CF	2,1	1,3	CF 1,2	3,3	CF	2,2	4,1	<u>CF</u> 1,1	<u>4,2</u>*
Bandwagoning and Competition Strategies					Balancing and Appeasement Strategies				

Overall, the results from this analysis of power disparity games reveal interesting and somewhat paradoxical patterns for the creation of security equilibria between strong and weak states:

- A core assumption of neorealist international relations theory is that 'all states seek to survive' (Waltz 1979); however, when they pursue a bandwagoning strategy with a Client identity, weak states who choose a cooperative security strategy are, in effect, ranking the surrender of independent action in some degree to ally with a Hegemon as their most preferred outcome in return for security.
- A core assumption of neoliberal international relations theory is that 'the precise nature of the stakes shapes policy' (Moravcsik 2003, 164). All states should prefer mutual cooperation as their primary goal at least regarding secondary (non-security) interests; however, even weak states with vital interests at stake who choose to pursue a coercive balancing strategy of independence as their highest preference may be constrained to settle for cooperation when interacting with a strong state pursuing a cooperative security strategy regarding secondary interests.
- A core assumption of constructivist theory is that 'anarchy is what states make of it' (Wendt 1994) i.e., identities trump power structure and material interests; however, it appears that power disparity actually matters by either liberating or constraining the effects of identity, depending on whether the identity of the stronger power is Patron or Hegemon.

A mutual cooperation (CO,CO) outcome is possible between Patrons and both Clients and Balancers but impossible between Hegemons and either Clients or Balancers. This statement holds true no matter whether the distribution of interests between the strong and weak states is symmetrical or asymmetrical. However, there may be gaps between the logical outcomes predicted by these security games and the empirical outcomes of strategic interactions between pairs of states with power disparities in the Baltic Sea Region.

Security Games in the Baltic Sea Region

The dyads in the Baltic Sea Region divide logically in Table 8.7 first into the pairs in bold font with equal power (great powers, middle powers, small powers) and then into the expanded pairs with power disparities possible within this initial set of equal powers. Within this map of power relationships, the intersections along the diagonal are irrelevant because they represent each power's relationship with itself. The remaining intersections show the power relationships for each dyad above the diagonal and the security strategies for each dyad below the diagonal. Power relationships here are based on estimates of relative capabilities rather than the actual exercise of power. The latter are reflected by the security strategies each state pursues toward the others (Knudsen, Ch. 2 in this volume, 11-13).

The Ap/Ap example of security strategies in Table 8.7 is extracted from the analyses of Estonian-Russian relations by Noreen (Ch. 6 in this volume) and Karlsson (Ch. 5 in this volume). An expansion of the rows and columns in Table 8.7 to include supranational (EU) and international (NATO) organizations would also show their intersecting strategies with Sweden and Finland from the analyses of Swedish and Finnish security choices regarding membership in the EU and non-alignment with NATO by Karp (Ch. 4 in this volume). All of these case studies illustrate different kinds of patterns between members of dyads marked by power disparities.

Estonian-Russian Power Equality and Mutual Cooperation

Noreen's analysis (Ch. 6) of changes in the framing of threats by Russia and Estonia after the Cold War illustrates how changes in the international environment and domestic regimes have affected Russo-Estonian power relations. The traditional relationship of power disparity between these two states prior to World War II was characterized by an Estonian balancing strategy and a Russian competitive strategy with a domination outcome for Russia and a submission outcome for Estonia after 1940 in the form of Russia's annexation of Estonia until the end of the Cold War. After Estonia's successful achievement of independence with the collapse of the Soviet empire, the two states reverted initially to their traditional balancing and competitive strategies with Estonian efforts to join NATO over Russian objections.

However, following the Chechnya revolt in Russia and the appearance of global terrorist activities symbolized by the 9/11 attacks on the United States, each state has reframed their images of threat away from one another and toward terrorist attacks. Also, Karlsson (Ch. 5) reports a successful mutual cooperation outcome between the two states within the framework offered by an epistemic community dealing with the threat from nuclear radiation at the former Soviet nuclear submarine training center in Paldiski. Noreen explains the shift in security strategies between the two states as due primarily to a shift in the identities each state attributes to self and other in response to the appearance of new global and transnational threats in the form of terrorism, drugs, crime, and arms transfers to subnational groups with transnational goals and capabilities.

Table 8.7 Power Relationships and Baltic Security Strategies

Dyads	Rus	Ger	Pol	Swe	Nor	Fin	Den	Ice	Lat	Est	Lit
Rus	---	**GG**	Gm	Gm	Gm	Gm	Gm	Gs	Gs	Gs	Gs
Ger		---	Gm	Gm	Gm	Gm	Gm	Gs	Gs	Gs	Gs
Pol			---	**mm**	**mm**	**mm**	**mm**	ms	ms	ms	ms
Swe				---	**mm**	**mm**	**mm**	ms	ms	ms	ms
Nor					---	**mm**	**mm**	ms	ms	ms	ms
Fin						---	ms	ms	ms	ms	ms
Den							---	ms	ms	ms	ms
Ice								---	ss	ss	ss
Lat									---	ss	ss
Est	Ap/Ap									---	ss
Lit											---

G = Great Power; m = middle power; s = small power. Ap = Appeasement; Bw = Bandwagoning; Cp = Competition; Bl = Balancing security strategies can be entered below the diagonal to represent intersecting security strategies for each dyad, as in the case of Russo-Estonian relations in Row 10, Column 1.

The venues in which Estonian and Russian security strategies are formed and implemented also expanded from the Foreign Ministries of each state. The processing of the nuclear radiation issue within an epistemic community representing the members of the Council of the Baltic Sea States (CBSS) put Estonia and Russia on a formal basis of equality within a transnational organization, which mitigates the influence of their material power disparity. Within the rules and roles prescribed by membership in a transnational organization, members operate in a milieu in which hard power becomes less salient and soft power becomes more relevant (Keohane and Nye 1989; Nye 2004). Members of the epistemic community do not represent their governments and instead operate as experts who are more or less independent from their respective states (Karlsson, Ch. 5 in this volume).

Nevertheless, it still required over two years of negotiations during the mid-1990s between the Foreign Ministries of the two states in order to reach an agreement to shut down the Paldiski naval training center, transfer the facility from Russian to Estonian control, and transport nuclear fuel from site units to Russia. These negotiations were preceded by persistent efforts on the part of the Working Group on Nuclear and Radiation Safety to assess the safety conditions for treating and storing nuclear waste at Paldiski. The members of the WGNRS included experts from most of the states in Table 8.7 plus a representative from the European Commission of the EU. The success of the WGNRS efforts and the subsequent negotiations between the two states most directly involved with the status of Paldiski suggests that power disparities can be trumped by the mutual recognition of a common security problem and the constraining effects of institutional context on identities and their corresponding strategic preferences for the outcomes of settlement, domination, deadlock, and submission.

By joining the Council of the Baltic Sea States, both states came to adopt appeasement strategies in which settlement is ranked as the highest outcome for the nuclear radiation and safety issue. The game that represents the intersection of their strategies is a symmetrical game in which power equality is established between Estonia and Russia by the formation of the Council of the Baltic Sea States. The experts on the Working Group on Nuclear Radiation and Safety then laid the groundwork for state-to-state negotiations by agreeing that deadlock was the least preferred outcome, which re-enforced the structural incentives established by the formation of the Council of the Baltic Sea States for settlement as the most preferred outcome.

Together the power equality and the eventual consensus on the most preferred and least preferred outcomes created by the existence of the Council and the activities of the Working Group, respectively, led eventually to a dominant strategy of cooperation for both Estonia and Russia in order to avoid the shared worst outcome of deadlock. The need for prolonged negotiations was probably due to the necessity for experiential learning by the Russian government as they were socialized within the institutional frameworks and norms provided by the Council on the Baltic Sea States and the reports of the Working Group on Nuclear Radiation and Safety.

Table 8.8 shows the likely patterns of strategic interaction resulting in a deadlock during the early 1990s between Estonia and Russia followed by a negotiated settlement in 1995. In the Collaborator-Hegemon game Estonia's early 1990s strategy is conditional appeasement, in which settlement is the highest ranked outcome but a strategy of cooperation (CO) is contingent on Russia's strategy. Because Russia has a dominant strategy of conflict (CF), Estonia will also choose CF for a deadlock (CF, CF) outcome that is both a Nash and a non-myopic equilibrium.

The Mutual Friend Game in Table 8.8 shows the unconditional appeasement strategies associated with both sides by the mid-1990s, ranking settlement (4,4) as their most preferred outcome and deadlock (1,1) as their least preferred outcome.

Each state now has a dominant strategy of cooperation (CO) with a Nash and non-myopic equilibrium of settlement (4,4). The shifts in strategies by both states are consistent with the hypothesized learning effects via the intervening clashes between the WGNRS and 'a superpower on the retreat' (Karlsson, Ch. 5 in this volume) in obtaining relevant information necessary to assess the safety of the nuclear reactors at the Paldiski site. They also reflect the possibilities for states that have a legacy of mutual distrust on a general foreign policy level to become cooperative in particular issue areas of mutual interest despite general power disparities (Baldwin 2002).

Table 8.8 Security Strategies for Estonia and Russia

		(G24) Russia				Russia	
		CO	CF			CO	CF
Estonia	CO	4,2	1,4	Estonia	CO	4,4*	3,2
	CF	2,1	3,3*		CF	2,3	1,1
Collaborator-Hegemon Game (Conditional Appeasement-Competition Strategies)				**Mutual Friend Game (Unconditional Appeasement Strategies)**			

Note: Each player's preferences are ranked 4 (Highest) to 1 (Lowest) for the outcomes of settlement (CO,CO), deadlock (CF,CF), domination (CF,CO), submission (CO,CF) for Row and settlement (CO,CO), deadlock (CF,CF), domination (CO,CF), and submission (CF,CO) for Column. Non-myopic equilibria and dominant strategies are underlined. Nash equilibria are asterisked. The G-number refers to the ID number assigned to conflict games by Brams (1994, 217-219).

Swedish-Finnish Power Disparity and Military Non-Alignment.

According to Karp (Ch. 4 in this volume), military non-alignment as a security choice by Sweden and Finland is a puzzle. 'Within the highly institutionalized European security environment Sweden and Finland are institutional oddities. Their continued adherence to military non-alignment appears to be at odds with the structural changes brought about by the Cold War. The collapse of the Soviet Union eliminated the strategic rationale for military non-alignment in Europe and NATO enlargements in 1999 and 2004 highlight the dynamics of intensified security integration' (Ch. 4 in this volume, p. 45). Their strategy is even more curious in view of their membership in the EU and their record of support for a strong role by the United States and NATO in developing the security architecture of Europe. They are members of NATO's Partnership for Peace (PfP) and the Euro-Atlantic Partnership Council (EAPC) actively supported NATO and EU membership of their three Baltic neighbors Estonia, Lithuania, and Latvia (Ch. 4 in this volume, p. 45).

Within the framework of generalizability offered by the security games of cooperation and conflict, the solution to this puzzle depends on specifying values for the power, interests, and identities attributed to the two states and NATO.[6] A test of the solution is to contrast it with the specifications of power, interests, and identities attributed to the two states and the EU. Since the two states are willing to join one organization and not the other, examining the coherence between the two solutions offered by the game theory models should be instructive regarding their generalizability. The evidence for making these specifications is in the accounts of Swedish and Finnish security choices by Karp, which includes the power, interests, and role identities of the two states.

In both cases, the two states have the opportunity to become members of the EU and NATO, respectively, but they have only joined the EU. The EU is a 'permissive institutional environment' in which *common* security interests are the basis for a norm of consensus-building that emphasizes coordination and harmonization of *multiple* national policies around issues faced by the members. In contrast, NATO is a 'non-permissive institutional environment' in which a *collective* security interest is the basis for reaching a *single* policy (Ch. 4 in this volume). Although the power disparities between each state and the two organizations are similar, the institutional rules of the two organizations differ in important ways that affect their compatibility with the respective identities of the two states.

The EU has power disparities among its members, but the norm of harmonization and coordination mitigates the impact of these power disparities. NATO has a rule of unanimity that permits members to veto a collective policy, but the vast power disparity between the United States and the other NATO members has made it possible historically for the United States to first impose a collective policy on its members and then veto modifications favored by others (Kissinger 1965). France was the only state who consistently opposed American hegemony inside NATO during the Cold War. De Gaulle and his successors found that an exit strategy of withdrawal from NATO's organizational apparatus without also totally abandoning its alliance commitment was the only option available to it in the presence of disagreements with the superpower over a collective policy for NATO.

Like France, Sweden's cultural norms and history dispose it toward role identities in foreign affairs that permit it to pursue an independent national security strategy in coordination with other states but without losing its autonomy. Finland's cultural norms and history dispose it toward more openness in subsuming its national security strategy under a collective policy, because of historical domination or outright annexation by strong neighbors such as Sweden, Tsarist Russia, and the Soviet Union.

Therefore, Karp explains that it was relatively easy for both states to join the EU. As the EU moves further toward a federal system from a loose confederation,

---

6 In addition to the variables in the game theory models, other constraints limiting NATO membership as an option include the ebb and flow of domestic politics and public opinion inside both states. See Karp (Ch. 4 in this volume).

however, Sweden will find it increasingly difficult to manage a conflict between its national role identity and the role expectations associated with being an EU member. A prediction of continued Swedish reluctance to join NATO is also consistent with its historical national role identity as an active independent. This national role conception conflicts with the role expectations in NATO's institutional environment, which prescribes that members with differences over national security strategies should defer to American preferences for a collective security strategy (Ch. 4 in this volume).

Which game theory model best captures the identities and expectations associated with Sweden as a member of the EU and a non-member of NATO? It appears from Karp's analytical narrative that the conditional appeasement strategies for the Mutual Collaborator game in Table 8.9 fit the Swedish-EU dyad. The power disparity between Sweden and the EU is not so relevant as the permissive institutional environment and the norm of coordinating common interests while retaining national differences in foreign policy strategies. Both Sweden and the EU prefer mutual cooperation as the highest-ranked outcome while retaining and ranking mutual disagreement over either domination or submission as outcomes. This rank order is consistent with Sweden's traditional role identity of being an active independent in world affairs and also meets the EU's expectations of coordinating common interests while respecting national differences.

Table 8.9 Sweden's Security Games with the EU and NATO

	EU			NATO			NATO (G24)	
	CO	CF		CO	CF		CO	CF
CO	4,4*	1,2	CO	4,4*	1,3	CO	4,2	1,4
Sweden			Sweden			Sweden		
CF	2,1	3,3*	CF	2,1	3,2*	CF	2,1	3,3*
Mutual Collaborator			Collaborator-Patron			Collaborator-Hegemon		

Note: Each player's preferences are ranked 4 (Highest) to 1 (Lowest) for the outcomes of settlement (CO,CO), deadlock (CF,CF), domination (CF,CO), submission (CO,CF) for Row and settlement (CO,CO), deadlock (CF,CF), domination (CO,CF), and submission (CF,CO) for Column. Non-myopic equilibria and dominant strategies are underlined. Nash equilibria are asterisked. The G-number refers to the ID number assigned to conflict games by Brams (1994, 217-219).

The Swedish decision not to join NATO is consistent in Table 8.9 with either the Collaborator-Patron Game or the Collaborator-Hegemon Game, depending on whether the US role identity is specified as a Patron or a Hegemon within the institutional framework of NATO. The Collaborator-Patron game probably best describes Swedish-NATO relations after the Cold War and prior to the advent of the Bush Administration and the 9/11 terrorist attacks on the United States. In this game both players rank mutual cooperation as their highest preference, but neither one has a dominant strategy of cooperation or conflict. Mutual cooperation is the game's non-myopic equilibrium. However, the cooperation of each player is contingent on the other player also choosing cooperation, and deadlock is a Nash equilibrium for this game.

The Collaborator-Hegemon Game may better describe the relationship between Sweden and NATO during a period of US unilateralism following the US adoption of the strategy of preemption as a military doctrine to justify an American invasion of Iraq in the wake of the 9/11 attacks. In this game Sweden continues to pursue a strategy of conditional appeasement while the United States ranks domination as the highest outcome and pursues a dominant strategy of conflict. The predicted outcome is deadlock (3,3), because the Swedish strategy is conditioned by the US dominant strategy of conflict. This outcome is both a non-myopic and a Nash equilibrium.

The game theory models that appear to represent Finland's security concerns with the EU are in Table 8.10. The strategy toward the EU is a bandwagoning-for-profit variant in order to preserve the economic benefits of EU membership and still avoid cultural assimilation into a larger European identity. Its success is dependent on a continuation of the EU's permissive security environment and corresponding cooperative security strategies of collaboration rather than domination.

Table 8.10 Bandwagoning for Profit Strategy and EU Strategies

	(G38) EU (S)			(G36) EU (V)			EU (V)	
	CO	CF		CO	CF		CO	CF
Finland (S) CO	3,4*	4,2	Finland (S) CO	3,4*	4,3	Finland (S) CO	3,2	4,4*
CF	2,1	1,3	CF	2,1	1,2	CF	2,1	1,3
Client-Collaborator			**Client-Patron**			**Client-Hegemon**		

While their national identity does not require them to shun alliances, Finland (like Sweden) is likely to resist the moves toward centralization within the EU that threaten its permissive institutional environment. Finland's present strategy of military non-alignment is compatible with a European Union that is not highly integrated in the areas of foreign policy and defense. If there is not an overt threat to its security, Finland is not likely to welcome security integration and a collective defense agreement among EU members. If such a threat materializes, Finland is likely to prefer NATO membership as a security strategy over a collective EU defense commitment that may sacrifice Finland's national identity as the price for security. Consequently, Finland has opposed efforts to incorporate mutual security guarantees among EU members and the creation of autonomous military capabilities that would reduce dependence on NATO's military assets and corresponding role in European security (Ch. 4 in this volume, pp. 51-54).

Table 8.11 Bandwagoning for Safety and Balancing Toward NATO[a]

	(G50) NATO			NATO			(G13) NATO	
	CO	CF		CO	CF		CO	CF
Finland CO	<u>CO</u> 2,4*	4,3	Finland CO	<u>CO</u> 2,2	<u>4,4</u>*	Finland CO	3,2	1,4
CF	1,1	3,2	CF	1,1	3,3	CF	2,1	<u>4,3</u>*
Client-Patron			**Client-Hegemon**			**Balancer-Hegemon**		

[a] Both players have Vital interests in all three games.

Finland's current preference for a military non-alignment strategy toward the EU and NATO is partly a product of temporary inertia left over from its pragmatic Cold War strategy of non-alignment as a small power caught geographically between NATO and the Soviet Union. If and when prevailing circumstances in the European security environment provide additional incentives to join NATO, the Finnish government will be better able than Sweden to make this decision as a pragmatic choice, relatively unencumbered by a traditional role identity as an active independent (Ch. 4 in this volume; pp. 56-57). For much of its history, Finland was either annexed or dominated by Sweden and Russia. The Finns pursued a passive strategy of neutrality during the Cold War in an effort to counter a Soviet threat to their independence. However, they are also willing and able to pursue a bandwagoning strategy of joining NATO in a security environment that calls for an alliance strategy to preserve their independence.

Until and unless Russia re-emerges as an overt security threat, Finland is likely to pursue a strategy of bandwagoning for safety toward NATO in the hope that they can gain security without sacrificing their autonomy. A comparison of the Client-Patron and Client-Hegemon games in Figure 8.11 shows that the bandwagoning strategy's success depends on the pursuit of an appeasement strategy by NATO in order to avoid domination by the stronger actor. In the absence of an overt threat from Russia and with the presence of a domination strategy by NATO, Finland is likely to pursue a balancing strategy toward NATO. A balancing strategy leads to a stable (4,3) deadlock outcome, which Finland can endure in the absence of an immediate threat to its vital interests.

Conclusion

The case studies of Estonia, Sweden, and Finland offer some evidence that their Baltic security strategies of engagement with Russia and military non-alignment with the EU and NATO, respectively, are consistent with intersections of the grand strategies of appeasement, bandwagoning, competition, and balancing specified by insights from realist, liberal, and constructivist theories of international relations. Power relationships, interests, and identities interact in game theory models to specify grand strategies of appeasement, competition, balancing, or bandwagoning, which appear to represent present and future strategies by these states in the Baltic Sea Region. They encompass the range of possible security games constructed by the intersection of these strategies with the strategies of other states and actors in the region, such as Russia, the European Union, and the United States.

While the connections specified between these dyads by the game theory models appear to have some face validity, it is also important to recognize their strengths and limitations. There are two conditions present that make the products of adduction in this chapter more than an exercise in casual empiricism. First, the game theory models were constructed prior to examination of the cases. Second, the modeling and the case studies were done by independent authors. The first condition avoids the *post hoc propter hoc* error as an inductive fallacy in reasoning backward from consequents to antecedent conditions within the cases to construct the models (McGaw and Watson 1976). The second condition mitigates against selection bias as a deductive fallacy in moving from models to cases (Geddes 1991; King, Keohane, and Verba 1994). The fit is instead established by making a series of side-by-side comparisons between models and cases generated independently of each other.

In closing, there is also an important limitation apparent from the application of adduction to assess the fit between game theory models and cases. Additional evidence from the cases is necessary to assess the fit between models and cases. The case study of Estonian-Russian strategic interactions over the Paldiski naval base would appear to be an example of power disparity as an antecedent condition. However, when the existence of a transnational organization put members on a more equal basis in dealing with one another, the antecedent condition in this case appears to be power equality rather than power disparity.

Another example is the intervening and autonomous effects of national identities in specifying Swedish and Finnish strategies toward the EU and NATO. The game theory models in this chapter are constructed as structure-based explanations from the 'outside-in,' beginning with the initial distinctions in power distributions between equality and disparity. Then combinations of vital and secondary interests are attributed to each actor within the context of a given power distribution. Finally, the role identity for each player is defined by the specification of preferences over outcomes inferred from the particular combinations of power and interest distributions between self and other.[7]

However, the identities in the case studies were not always congruent with the identities predicted by the models for the cases based on their power and interest distributions. For example, Sweden's role identity as Collaborator, defined as the identity with preferences over outcomes ranked as settlement > deadlock > domination > submission, was not associated in the game theory models with the distribution of interests and power between Sweden and NATO. Therefore, the ability of states to interject their own role identities as a basis for ranking their strategic preferences independently from distributions of power and interests suggests that agent-based 'inside-out' models may be better at explaining strategic interactions between states than structure-based, 'outside-in' models. Analyses of the 'subjective games' that guide a state's strategic interactions with others may be a more effective future approach in explaining the security complexes that emerge between states (Maoz 1990; Schafer and Walker 2006; Walker and Schafer forthcoming). Subjective assessments of power relations may link identities and interests with acts of social construction in more complex, interactive patterns than the ones captured here (Ch. 2 in this volume; Smith 2001).

Appendix

The game theory used in this chapter is part of the literature on 2 x 2 ordinal games in which two players (Row and Column) have two choices that intersect to produce a matrix with four outcomes. Two players x two choices make the game a 2 x 2 game. It is an ordinal game when the players rank-order their respective preferences regarding the four outcomes from 4 (highest) to 1(lowest) rather than assigning interval (cardinal) numbers as values (utilities) associated with each preference.

Different game theories are distinguished by assumptions and rules of play, which specify the range of strategies available to each player and the best choice among available strategies within the rules of play. Classical 2 x 2 ordinal game theories assume that the players (a) decide choices simultaneously (b) in a single play of the game (c) knowing beforehand the rank order of both players' preferences (d) without being able to communicate with one another prior to making a choice. The basic rule of play under these assumptions is that each player will choose a strategy that leads to the best possible outcome under the constraints of these assumptions. Sequential game theory modifies these assumptions so that players alternate their

---

7 Wendt's (1999) constructivist theory contains the reverse argument as a causal explanation, namely, that power is only relevant in the context of interests which, in turn are specified by identities. However, his argument is still structure-based rather than agent-centered because it assumes the cultural primacy of shared beliefs as a structural cause rather than the subjective primacy of individual beliefs as an agent-centered cause under the condition of anarchy (see also Walker 2004).

choices in a game. The sequential game theory used in this chapter makes the further assumptions that the game may be repeated beyond a single play and that players may communicate with one another before making their choices (Brams 1994).

Game theory takes as givens and does not explain who the players are or why they rank or weight their preferences for the different outcomes. Instead, the focus is on explaining the choices by each player and the outcomes (equilibria) that mark the end of the game under different rules of play. Under the simpler classical rules of play, the players make simultaneous choices leading to a Nash equilibrium (if there is one) for a game. 'A Nash equilibrium is a state – or, more properly, the strategies associated with a state – from which no player would have an incentive to depart unilaterally because its departure would immediately lead to a worse, or at least not a better, state' (Brams 1994, 224). Under the more complex rules of play specified by Brams' (1994) sequential game theory, the players will make alternating choices leading to a nonmyopic equilibrium (NME). 'In a two-person game, a nonmyopic equilibrium is a state from which neither player, anticipating all possible rational moves and countermoves from the initial state, would have an incentive to depart unilaterally because the departure would eventually lead to a worse, or at least not a better, outcome' (Brams 1994, 224).

It is also important to understand that an outcome for a particular game may be both a Nash equilibrium and a nonmyopic equilibrium and that there may be more than one of each kind of equilibrium for a given game. Although it may appear that these definitions, assumptions, and rules of play generate an overwhelming number of possible games, there are only 78 strict ordinal games with two players and two choices that are structurally distinct from one another. 'Of the 78 games, 21 are no-conflict games with a mutually best (4,4) state. These states are always Nash and nonmyopic equilibria (NMEs) in these games....[T]he remaining 57 games....are divided into three main categories: (i) those with one NME (31 games), (ii) those with two NMEs (24 games), and (iii) those with three NMEs (12 games)' (Brams 1994, 215). Among these 57 games nine have indeterminate states in which the final outcome depends on which player has the next move from a particular initial state (one of the cells in the 2 x 2 game's matrix).

The outcomes for the other 48 games depend on the governing assumptions for the rules of play. The *Theory of Moves* (TOM), developed as a sequential game theory by Brams (1994) for these 57 ordinal games has six rules in its simplest form. They are stated as follows in Brams (1994, 24, 27-28):

1. Play starts at an outcome, called the *initial state*, which is at the intersection of the row and column of a 2 x 2 payoff matrix.
2. Either player can unilaterally switch its strategy, and thereby change the initial state into a new state, in the same row or column as the initial state. The player

who switches is called player 1 (P1).
3. Player 2 (P2) can respond unilaterally switching its strategy, hereby moving the game to a new state.
4. The alternating responses continue until the player (P1 or P2) whose turn it is to move next chooses not to switch its strategy. When this happens, the game terminates in a *final state*, which is the outcome of the game.
5. A player will not move from an initial state if this move (i) leads to a less preferred final state (i.e., outcome); or (ii) returns play to the initial state (i.e., makes the initial state the outcome).
6. Given that players have complete information about each other's preferences and act according to the rules of TOM, each takes into account the consequences of the other's rational choices, as well as its own, in deciding whether to move from the initial state or later, based on backward induction. If it is rational for one player to move and the other player not to move from the initial state, then the player who moves takes *precedence*; its move overrides the player who stays, so the outcome will be induced by the player who moves.

The application of TOM's rules of play is relatively straightforward to three kinds of games found in this chapter. They are: no-conflict games in which the players agree on the highest-ranked outcome; games in which at least one player has a dominant strategy; games in which neither player has a dominant strategy.

For no-conflict games in which the players agree on a (4,4) outcome, either the rules of simultaneous play associated with classical game theory or the rules of sequential play associated with TOM generate the same explanation in the form of a prediction that (4,4) will be the Nash and nonmyopic equilibria for the game. A more complicated game is when the players disagree on the highest ranked outcome; however, at least one player has a dominant strategy. 'A dominant strategy is a strategy that leads to outcomes at least as good as those of any other strategy in all possible contingencies, and a better outcome in at least one contingency' (Brams 1994, 222). Under the two-sided information assumption associated with either classical or sequential game theory, both players can see that one player will choose his/her dominant strategy no matter what the other player chooses, leaving the other player no choice but to choose his strategy based on this information. A final kind of game in this chapter is one in which neither player has a dominant strategy and there is no Nash equilibrium.

Examples of each kind of game are in Table 8.12. In each game the players have two choices of strategy: cooperation (CO) or conflict (CF). The (4,4) outcome for the no-conflict game is a Nash equilibrium because neither player can move directly from (4,4) without arriving at a cell that has a lower-ranked outcome. It is also a nonmyopic equilibrium because: once either player arrives at (4,4) after a series of alternating moves, each will choose to stay rather than move (Rules 1-5 for TOM); if one player stops before arriving at (4,4), the other player will move until (4,4) is reached (Rule 6 for TOM).

Table 8.12 Three Kinds of 2 x 2 Ordinal Games

	Column			(G13) Column			(G31) Column	
	CO	CF		CO	CF		CO	CF
CO	4,4*	1,1	CO	3,2	1,4	CO	4,3	1,4
Row			Row			Row		
CF	2,2	3,3	CF	2,1	4,3*	CF	2,2	3,1
No Conflict			**Dominant Strategy**			**No Nash Equilibrium**		

Note: Each player's preferences are ranked 4 (Highest) to 1 (Lowest) for the outcomes of settlement (CO,CO), deadlock (CF,CF), domination (CF,CO), submission (CO,CF) for Row and settlement (CO,CO), deadlock (CF,CF), domination (CO,CF), and submission (CF,CO) for Column. Non- myopic equilibria and dominant strategies are underlined. Nash equlibria are asterisked. The G-number refers to the ID number assigned to conflict games by Brams (1994, 217-219).

The second game in Table 8.12 is a conflict game (no 4,4 outcome) with a dominant strategy for Column, because Column will gain a higher-ranked outcome by choosing (CF) no matter what Row chooses. Under the two-sided information assumption Row will choose (CF) in order to obtain his/her best outcome, because s/he knows that Column will choose (CF). The same outcome is generated by TOM's rules of play above, because there is only one NME that is also a Nash equilibrium.

The third game in Table 8.12 is a conflict game without a Nash equilibrium and neither player has a dominant strategy. In the presence of assumptions allowing (a) prior communication between players before choosing strategies and (b) repeated plays of the game, the final outcome of a game is a nonmyopic equilibrium imposed by the use of moving power or threat power. One or both players may be able to exercise moving power by continuously moving to a better outcome and creating a cyclical pattern in repeated plays of the game. Or a player can exercise threat power in pre-play communication by threatening that if the other player does not choose to stay at the NME, then in repeated plays of the game the first player will change strategies and move the game to an outcome that leaves both players worse off (Brams 1994, 85-102;124-127).

In games with more than one NME, additional rules of play in TOM also determine the prediction and explanation of NMEs. Some of the games in this chapter do have more than one NME. While all nonmyopic equilibria are underlined in the matrices for these games, they are not considered in this chapter unless a Nash equilibrium and a nonmyopic equilibrium coincide. The other NMEs and their implications can be introduced later if a particular game seems especially relevant to analyze extended strategic interactions between members of a dyad over time.

Finally, two games in this chapter have two nonmyopic equilibria that are also Nash equilibria. Which of the two solutions for each game is the predicted one depends on which player has the first move from a given initial state (see the solutions to G52 and G53 in Brams 1994, 219).

Chapter 9

Looking to the Future: Security Strategies, Identity and Power Disparity

Olav F. Knudsen

Reviewing Lines of Reasoning

Our working hypothesis said that power disparity will hamper the functioning of a cooperative security system. Here we shall re-examine that hypothesis in the light of the patterns observed and look for lessons that have been learned – or ought to have been.

Has the functioning of a cooperative security system in the Baltic Sea region been hampered by power disparity, and if so, how? To what extent is there such a phenomenon as power disparity operative in the Baltic Sea region, and to what extent has it been associated with threat? Let us recapitulate the reasoning involved.

The idea of cooperative security is to gradually seek to build trust (phase 1), establishing a framework of relations of mutual trust (phase 2) within which cooperation for mutual gain can develop. As long as cooperation proceeds the way the parties expect, this experience reinforces itself and the need for cooperative security fades into the background, leading ultimately (phase 3) to the emergence of the long-term mutual trust that signifies a security community. When the population and its leaders no longer see the possibility of conflict being resolved by any but peaceful means, a security community has come into being. It is part of the cooperative-security line of thinking that if problems arise in phase 2, at least one of the parties will reactivate cooperative security by appropriate steps.

The other main thread in our reasoning concerns power disparity. Its part in the plot is that of an intervening, not an independently causal variable. It can complicate things once it is present. If power disparity is significantly present in the region at the most recent stage, without threat perceptions, even while cooperative security has reached a sustained and unshaken phase 2, then our working hypothesis must be rejected.

To gain an overall concluding perspective, we shall therefore briefly retrace from our various contributions how the region has changed in terms of the cooperative security process phases, and link that with the state of power disparity over time.

Cooperative Security in the Baltic Sea Region

It appears that the Baltic Sea Region has moved some distance in the direction of realizing an advanced stage of cooperative security, phase 2 in our scheme above. The chapter by Karlsson showed a successful early move to handle a security issue in a way that reflected the confidence-building idea of cooperative security. The early 1990s agreements to withdraw Russian forces from forward stationing in the broader East Central European region and the CFE-I Treaty also illustrated CBM reasoning in practice.

It is even possible that long-term effects of these moves showed up years later in the findings of Noreen's chapter, augmented by the 'shadow of the future' of anticipated EU memberships. The Northern Dimension policy adopted by the EU in the late 1990s indicated eagerness to extend the circle of good relations even beyond EU membership by embracing Russia in new cooperative ventures.

Noreen shows that there were significant similarities in the way the language of threat developed in Russia and Estonia after 2000, indicating possible ambitions among policy-makers in Moscow and Tallinn to develop a common understanding of not only what is threatening, but also of what is threatened in terms of values and identities. In Noreen's view, common assessments of threat are not sufficient, but may well be a precipitating condition for the development of a security community. This means that once Estonia and Latvia find themselves on speaking terms with Russia concerning their crucial minority policies and border treaties, they will also have moved closer to a security community in the Baltic Sea area.

Noreen's point is not that there is a total correspondence between decision-makers' language and their inner beliefs. He rather suggests that official statements are assumed to be credible in that they essentially correspond with practice. The underlying reasoning here is that it is difficult for political leaders to persist in saying one thing and doing another. According to the theory of cognitive dissonance, after a decision has been made, *(ceteris paribus)* '... people seek to justify their own behavior' (Jervis 1976, 406). They are concerned about their record. Rhetoric and action will tend to become aligned (Jervis 1976, 382-404, esp. 399-404; also Walker 1987, 82-3). In the present case this would mean that not calling Russia a threat would entail adjustment of behaviour to not treating Russia as a threat, and to adjusting attitudes accordingly – not preparing for conflict but rather for deeper cooperation.

A corroboration of this interpretation and a strong demonstration of political will in the region is the decision to continue the Northern Dimension programme within the EU with a third action plan beginning in 2007. In this case, a more meaningful role – in particular in Russian eyes – has been provided for Russia by the EU's inclusion in the action plan of opportunities to negotiate (Russia-EU) the specifics of the various elements of which the plan is composed.

There is also a different piece of evidence relevant to this question: the absence of military contingency planning for the region.[1] While military matters are still not openly documented, and hence impossible to verify concurrently, certain aspects of military planning are nevertheless hard to conceal if they are to have any practical significance. Contingency plans are of this kind – how to respond in case of attack, or how to undertake a military campaign in a given area. The reason for this is very simple: a concern for what we might call 'confidence maintenance' – an obvious part of the cooperative security system operative in the region in phase 2, when confidence has been considerably improved between the parties, but has not yet been entirely stabilized. If contingency planning were to be discovered, this would be a serious setback likely to lead to a renewed militarization of relations in the region. Hence, refraining from certain activities is a way to avoid triggering dangerous developments. The same logic is applicable to talking about threats.

Still, the question remains whether the movement towards security community that we have uncovered is sustainable, and how deep or superficial it is. Data gathered by Knudsen in 2000 in Estonia are at variance with at least some interpretations of Noreen's findings. Knudsen found that some Estonian political leaders showed a deeply sceptical attitude to Nordic ideas of cooperative security, attitudes which also seemed to be widely shared (Knudsen 2004, 20-21). Tromer concludes similarly when she says (Tromer 2006, 373) that

> The absence of reference to Russia in the Baltic states' national security guidelines compared with its presence between the lines of the same documents, and in nearly every conversation on the Baltic states' security, reflects a "do not provoke the bear" attitude. It also reflects a concern not to upset EU partners and not to expose the Baltic states to renewed accusations that they are playing the Russian card in order to keep the USA [sic] engagement in Europe. Finally, an explicit mention of Russia might open a Pandora's box of internal debates, including debates on the usefulness of the ESDP.

Hence, Noreen's conclusions need to be seen in a broader perspective. We shall return below to the connected matter of how governments are likely to assess Russia's policy direction at this juncture. If the practices of cooperative security have survived in spite of – or alternatively due to an absence or a decline of – threatening power disparities, then the implications are very different. We must therefore take this into account to understand what it is we are observing. We want to know (a) to

---

1   Statements by Jamie Shea (NATO Secretariat, Director of Policy Planning) and Dmitri Trenin (Carnegie Moscow Center) at the conference "NATO: Baltic, European and Global", Swedish Institute of International Affairs, June 1st, 2006. This author has further independent corroboration. At a point in the late 1990s when Polish NATO membership was being prepared, the author was contacted for consultation about the political situation in the Baltic states by a NATO country's planning staff officer. Shortly before the appointment came up, the officer canceled, saying a decision had just been made to terminate all planning regarding Poland's eastern border and the southeastern Baltic region.

what extent the region has been marked by power disparity since 1991; (b) what potential the region holds for future power disparities.

Power Disparity, Cooperative Security and Role Identities

To what extent are power relations in the Baltic Sea region marked by disparities, and to what extent have they carried political significance, during this period? Although the potentially leading centres of power in the region are three – Russia, Germany and the EU – the question must first of all be addressed to Russia's position and role, since the others have not been associated with danger or threat at all.

Power disparity after 1991?

Looking back to the early post-Cold War days, the most widespread feeling at the time was probably a tremendous relief, not least among the Nordic countries, at the unexpected turn of events. Suddenly, the Soviet shadow disappeared; no substance remained of old fears. This sense of relief deeply infused subsequent Nordic policies, as we saw in Ch. 3. One might rephrase this position as one of denying the existence of any power disparity between the fallen giant and its Nordic neighbours. Nordic policies for the post-Cold War era were henceforth based on the assumption that Russia needed development assistance above all. Considerations of power were scarce in policy declarations from the Nordics at the time.

The collapse of the Soviet Union clearly entailed a disruption of the country's ability to act coherently abroad – most clearly illustrated by the First Chechen War. The years leading up to that war were the years of Russian withdrawal from the Baltic Sea region, a process of change that was taken by many – if not necessarily all – of Russia's neighbours to signify a new era of peace in the region. While some concern remained, especially in Finland and Norway, regarding residual strategic ambitions on the Russian side, the conduct of the Russian military and the state of the Russian armed forces convinced most observers that Russia was a spent force for decades to come (Baev 1996, 2002). From this perspective, the glass was at least half full.

Still, difficulties experienced by the Baltic states in dealing with Russia during 1992-94 evoked a different reality, suggesting that the glass was rather half empty at best, and that power may have something to do with the region's relationships after all.

When the attempts of Estonia, Latvia and Lithuania to be accepted as members of NATO failed in their first round during 1996-97 it was probably not least due to the strident opposition of the Russian Government and the misgivings of many NATO members – first among them Germany – at the prospect of perhaps triggering new East-West friction. Power assessments necessarily played a role when these positions were taken.

1997, 1998 and 1999 were years marked by rhetorical confrontation in the region and apprehension linked to NATO's expansion and the Kosovo war. Russia responded to the 1997 rejection of NATO membership for the Baltic states by outlining a new concept, a 'non-bloc zone', for the Baltic Sea region, to include not just the Baltic states but also Finland and Sweden; Russia defining herself as the pre-eminent power of the area (Knudsen 1998). Signs of a more relaxed attitude in the Baltic Sea region to these developments were nevertheless visible in the Finnish and Swedish joint diplomacy to tone down Russian aspirations. Finnish and Swedish support for 'lethal' military assistance to the Baltic states had begun even earlier, but now accelerated, especially from Sweden. Before long, the Swedish government started arguing in favour of Baltic membership in NATO for the second round of membership expansion, something they had previously declared to be an incorrect stance for Sweden as a non-member of NATO (Karlsson and Knudsen 2001). The virtual collapse of the Russian economy in August 1998 and the coincidental governmental instability continuing into 1999 underlined the shaky foundations of Moscow's capacity to act.

Once Putin was securely in charge, assessments started changing. In the ensuing years, as the story goes, Putin's gamble on a new post-9/11 relationship with the United States led him to 'release' the Baltic states and accept their candidacy for NATO membership. In this case it is possible to exaggerate the significance of Putin's change of heart, however. President Bush repeatedly stated before the summer of 2001 that regardless of Russia's opposition, the US Government wanted NATO membership for the Baltic states. In any case, Putin's turn to the US after 9/11 opened the way for a friction-less new phase in the history of the Baltic Sea region when Lithuania, Latvia and Estonia became members of NATO – and, along with Poland – also of the EU.

Whether this concern over NATO membership has anything to do with Russia's power standing is debatable. The high political overtones of the issue may be seen as indicative of the continuing salience of military aspects of relations in the region, continuing even into the new Millennium. Russia is being taken into account not because of what it does, but because of assessments of what it could do – its capacity to be a nuisance (see also Neumann 2005).

In non-military matters, the region's relationships were probably less clear-cut. The appearance of power was dispersed by contextual effects. Recall that according to one of our arguments above, contextualized power is likely to become diffused because the relevant capabilities and/or perceptions of capabilities are not coinciding or otherwise reinforcing across contexts. To give an example, if power relations in cyberspace contexts are different from power in trade contexts, then there is no aggregate effect of power from these contexts. Actually, as Eriksson points out (Ch. 7 in this volume, p. 145),

> In terms of role identity, the general observation made here is that established offline identities largely correspond to identities in cyberspace.

In other words, the general power hierarchy in international politics has *not* been turned up-side-down by the information revolution.

Sometimes, however, power in different issue areas are indeed disconnected; the logic of one activity having no bearing on the logic of another or of general politics, as shown (e.g.) in the case of shipping politics and international high politics (Knudsen 1979). In Ch. 5, Karlsson shows how even power disparity *within* an issue-area becomes irrelevant when the issue-area is dominated by scientific expertise (this volume, p. 94). Evidently escape routes from power disparity do exist.

In the 1990s the Nordic governments drew on similar reasoning to shape a 'counter-power' strategy for Russia that would never have been workable with the USSR: They compartmentalized their handling of Russian official conduct. Nordic ministerial routines were helpful instruments for subdividing issues concerning Russia into 'portions' small enough to be handled separately: (a) bilateral Russian-Nordic relations, (b) multilateral Russian-Nordic-Baltic relations, (c) Russian-EU relations, (d) Russian-Baltic and Russian-non-EU relations. These relations were further compartmentalized by issue area, so that trade relations, fisheries relations, defence relations (etc) in the bilateral sphere were tailored to specific, clearly defined and delimited contexts. Within each of these contexts, specific policies were developed for the Baltic Sea region and for dealing with Russia. In Ch. 8 Eriksson shows that policy development was key to gaining a position of power in cyberspace politics. In Eriksson's view (this volume, 147, 148), power in cyberspace is not an immediate effect of how the national network society is developing, but is rather the result of how a national government develops a policy, organization and expertise concerning information warfare (IW).

To put it in different terms, considerations of power were defined away, so to say, in Nordic relations with Russia during the 1990s and early 2000s. This tied in rather well with Russia under Yeltsin, which was suitably decentralized.[2] It went less well with Russia under Putin. As Bobo Lo sees it (2003, 3):

> If the Yeltsin administration's conduct of international relations revealed the primacy of competing sectional agendas over a consensus vision of the 'national interest', then today it is appropriate to speak about a genuinely 'presidential' foreign policy ...

However, Putin's policy is 'wannabe'; it only succeeds if others accept the pose. This was notable when the other Baltic Sea states confronted Russia over the environmental risks of oil transports in the Baltic Sea. In this power struggle over the environment from 2001-2005, Russia gambled on a great-power posture and lost spectacularly.[3]

---

2 'Over the course of the [1990s] decade, the number of foreign policy actors grew steadily, as did the range of competing policy agendas. Even within government, the MFA found itself regularly contradicted or, worse still, ignored by other ministries and agencies.' (Lo 2003, 21)

3 The IMO decided to accept a Finnish-Swedish proposal backed by all other Baltic littoral states except Russia, to declare the Baltic Sea as a whole a particularly sensitive sea

In this connection Walker (this volume, p. 171) argues that membership in a transnational or international organization can intervene to mitigate the effects of power disparity on the strategies of weaker actors by constraining the strategies of stronger actors.

Yet in the case just cited, three different international bodies – the Council of the Baltic Sea States, HELCOM, and the International Maritime Organization – failed to provide the resolution so obviously needed and so actively sought by the other governments entreating with Russia. In the first two years of interaction over this issue, Russian maritime authorities cooperated with the other regional governments in trying to find a solution. Then, suddenly, the question was transferred to the Russian MFA and discussions on a compromise were broken off (Knudsen 2006). In this case, lifting the issue to a high-politics sphere made it easier for the Russian government to politicize it.

A related tactic is to link issues and make their resolution conditional, either via their contexts or by political design. The potentiality for linkage is where power relations are most likely to show up. The experience of Ukraine in the gas export and transit question in early 2006 has been used by many observers as an example of linkage by political design to draw far-reaching conclusions about the direction Russia is taking. Actually, the political message involved here is not crystal clear, unless seen simply as a vague warning to 'stay in line' with Russia. Indeed, the political advantages to be harvested from energy resources are easily overestimated. Such pressures are usually bounded by short-term circumstances. To manipulate energy supplies – and do it often – would in the long run be self-defeating unless the supplier is a long-term monopolist. Russian energy policy is indeed often marked by short term considerations, but even Russia is likely to encounter negative consequences by persisting on this course (see, e.g., Larsson 2006).

Such conduct is still not the daily routine of the Baltic Sea region. Even if not yet a security community, expectations of violence are near zero. Under such conditions, power can more easily be kept contextualized – tied to specific circumstances and concrete issues – and hence dispersed. Even occasionally great disparities in power in given issue areas may appear less significant since they are not the same in other areas.

In sum, the post-Cold War period in the Baltic Sea region did not begin with a high level of assessed power disparity. The assessments started out low, then were contextualized and continued even into the 2000s to be marked by modest levels of expectation for Russia's ability to impact on its surroundings. In a coincidence of efficient Nordic MFA organization and temporary Russian MFA disorganization, aspirations on Russia's part to play a great power role were largely neutralized. Lately, however, this may be changing, as the IMO decision illustrates – even though the lesson from that case was rather negative for Russia.

In terms of our working hypothesis, indications are that cooperative security has not really been put to the test in the Baltic Sea region. The hard question at this point

---

area (PSSA) and passed associated measures taking effect July 1st, 2006 (Knudsen 2006).

is whether we are '… witnessing a seismic shift in Russian foreign policy, or merely a sophisticated reinterpretation of standard themes' (Lo 2003, 5). Even the simple formulation of the former possibility reminds us that we cannot in the future exclude change leading to significantly different assessments of power in the region.

Future power disparities?

Even if military capabilities are irrelevant to most of today's regional issues, their potential is not entirely discounted by Russia's own decision-makers, for instance in the words of Defence Minister Sergei Ivanov (2006):

> Everyone knows that when it comes to war and conflict-prevention, Russia always goes first for political, diplomatic, economic and other nonmilitary means. But maintaining a robust military capability is clearly in our national interests (*sic*).

Whatever relevance this statement might have for the Baltic Sea region would seem to lie in the potential for deeper disagreement to cause tension in the area. Does the Baltic Sea region harbour issues that might lead Russia to pursue them even with military means? If so, this might under certain circumstances trigger a reassessment of power relations in the region. The consequence could well be that the aura of military power would carry over even to issues of non-military relevance. In this case the potential for dispersed power to consolidate could be considerable – and power disparities could again gain political salience.

In fact, the question of Kaliningrad's territorial status is one such issue. While not currently disputed, its continued use for military purposes might raise such questions. Likewise, the military uses to which the Baltic states, as NATO members, put their territories make up another cluster of similarly laden issues. Should unexpected developments put these issues in focus, there are indeed reasons to expect Russian military capabilities to have relevance to power relations in the region.

Nevertheless, barring such focusing events, the relevance of military factors in the politics of the Baltic Sea region appears to be very limited. Yet before the discussion is closed we need to introduce a final complicating factor: the lack of congruence between Russian self-conceptions of their country as a great power and others' conceptions of Russia as less of a great power and more of a 'nuisance power' in the Baltic Sea region. The identities of other regional actors as 'small states' are also under scrutiny.

Identities and self-conceptions

We have wanted to learn how role identities like 'small state' and 'great power' have developed during the post-Cold War period. One thing is the way analysts classify countries, but to what extent do government leaders themselves explicitly identify their country by such labels?

As has already been suggested, national self-conceptions in the Baltic Sea region were in many cases fundamentally changed and severely tested during the 1990s. Russia being the most prominent case, Dmitri Trenin argues that his homeland in the first decade of the 21st century has moved beyond its simple post-imperial trauma to developing a case of 'delayed nationalism' or 'delayed adoption of nation-state status'.[4] Used to seeing their country as an empire, Russians have been wary of nationalist ideas (Lo 2003). More recently Russian elites – in Trenin's analysis – have nonetheless approached this new phase in their self-understanding under Putin, that of nationalism. The new trend reinforces their longer-standing preoccupation with great-power status.[5]

The tendency is not just a purely Russian matter. It has consequences for the way Russia relates to their neighbours in the Baltic Sea region, not least because the Russian self-conception is not mirrored there. Interestingly, the smaller countries in the region are not very likely to refer to themselves as 'small states' in their official rhetoric.[6] Sweden is the most consistent case, with not a single self-reference as a small country or small state in web-posted speeches by the Foreign Minister or Prime Minister during the past 5 years. Only Latvia matches that pattern.[7] From time to time the MFA officials of Estonia, Finland, Denmark, and Lithuania refer to themselves as small states, though only in certain contexts (e.g., UN and EU debates of a general character) and apparently never in security policy fora and certainly not in bilateral relations with Russia.

Walker (Ch. 8 in this volume) argues that national role identities may also have effects that are independent and autonomous from power disparity on the selection of a security strategy by either the weaker state or the stronger state in a relationship. Avoiding self-identification as a small state is an obvious way to deal with power disparity. By labelling oneself, one steps into a role that has an unpleasant counterpart. Staying out of that role is therefore to some extent liberating. Ultimately, of course, one cannot always as a weaker party avoid contexts where weakness counts. However, identity is self-chosen and thus in a small state more likely to be linked to other kinds of foreign policy roles ('mediator' and 'bridge-builder' have a proud tradition as self-identification in all the Nordic countries).

Karp finds identity preservation to be a key concern to the region's non-aligned states. Here, in the face of security integration, Finland and especially Sweden seem to have picked their chief security-policy role conception: staying out of alliances. Defining this choice, not as a matter of policy to deal with power disparity, but as maintaining a preferred security identity, they sidestep the 'reality' that successively

---

4 Dmitri Trenin, presentation at the conference 'NATO: Baltic, European and Global', June 1st, 2006.

5 The literature documenting and analyzing this tendency is extensive; Hedenskog et al. 2005 make a systematic effort to cover the phenomenon in all its aspects.

6 Based on searches of official websites for the Ministries of Foreign Affairs.

7 MFA only.

has been closing in on them. As Karp puts it in her chapter (this volume, pp. 48-50),

> Power disparities need not translate into abandoning identity. Even in the security field, where low national capacities make a compelling case for military alignment, small states can maintain considerable autonomy and institutional choice. They need neither rush to embrace institutions nor suffer the drawbacks of marginalization. If small states can successfully negotiate between the demands for structural adaptation and identity preservation, larger states can be expected to use their much greater capacity to develop policies that reflect conditionality.

Identities have positive valuation for their carriers. Yet they need to be matched by the expectations of others to become more than mere idiosyncracies. So far, its neighbours' responses to Russia's attempts at role-taking in the Baltic Sea region have left Moscow high and dry.

Ways Out?

Are Baltic regional affairs, in power terms, simply moving in circles, or is there some degree of learning involved? No clear-cut reply can be given to that question.

On the one hand, the trend where identity is concerned gives some cause for worry, since Russian preoccupations in foreign affairs seem to prioritize the ideational sphere over the practical, whereas the Nordics and Baltics – not to mention the EU – insist on taking the other line: the practical over the ideational. On the other hand, the role-taking of the Nordic and Baltic states also demonstrate considerable smartness on their part in avoiding the high-politics contexts where power disparity is inescapable, and sticking to issue-specific contexts where decisions are more easily made on the merits of the case itself. Russia's attempt to break this strategy by shifting the IMO decision to the MFA – perhaps an indication of Putin's preference for centralization – nevertheless failed.

Evidently, the preference in Moscow is for the new profile of Putin's Russia to be the long-term Russian policy style. At the same time a dismal fact of life in the Baltic Sea region is simply that the countries here are all too small to really matter to Russia. They cannot make much trouble for Russia, and the issues that really count in Moscow are found elsewhere.

Thus, better prospects for the future require a shift of thinking and self-identification on the part of Russia, and probably a good bit more collective smartness on the part of the neighbours.

References

Sources by individual authors

Aalto, P. (2003), 'Revisiting the security/identity puzzle in Russo-Estonian relations', *Journal of Peace Research* 40:5, 573-591.

Adler, E. (1992), 'The Emergence of Cooperation: National Epistemic Communities and the International Evolution of the Idea of Nuclear Arms Control', in Haas (ed.).

—— and Barnett, M. (eds) (1998), *Security Communities* (Cambridge: Cambridge University Press).

—— (2002), 'Constructivism and International Relations', in Carlsnaes et al. (eds), 94-118.

Alderson, K. (2001), 'Making Sense of State Socialization', *Review of International Studies* 27, 415-433.

Alexeev, D. (2004), 'NATO Enlargement: A Russian Outlook', Conflict Studies Research Centre: *Russian Series* 04/33: Defence Academy of the United Kingdom.

Ambrosio, T. (2003), 'From Balancer to Ally? Russian-American Relations in the Wake of 11 September', *Contemporary Security Policy* 24:2, 1-28.

Andersson, J. (2006), *Armed and Ready? The EU Battlegroup Concept and the Nordic Battlegroup,* Report No. 2 (Stockholm: Swedish Institute for European Policy Studies).

—— (ed.) (2005), *Sverige och Europas försvar* (Stockholm: Utrikespolitiska Institutet).

Andrén, N. (ed.) in collaboration with Brodin, K. (1977), *The Future of the Nordic Balance* (Stockholm: SSLP, Ministry of Defence [Sekretariatet för säkerhetspolitik och långsiktsplanering inom totalförsvaret, Försvarsdep.].

Archer, C. (1984), 'Deterrence and Reassurance in Northern Europe', *Centrepiece 6* (Aberdeen: Centre for Defence Studies).

—— (1996), 'The Nordic Area as a Zone of Peace', *Journal of Peace Research* 33:4, 451-467.

—— and Jones, C. (1999), 'The Security Policies and the Concepts of the Baltic States – Learning from their Nordic Neighbours?' in Knudsen (ed.), *Stability and Security*, 167-183.

Archer, T. (2003), 'Keeping Out of It: The Hangover of Finnish Neutralism and the Limits of Normative Commitments', in *Yearbook of Finnish Foreign Policy 2003* (Helsinki: Finnish Institute of International Affairs).

Arquilla, J. and Ronfeldt, D. (eds) (2001), *Networks and Netwars: The Future of Terror, Crime, and Militancy* (Santa Monica: RAND).

Arteus, G. and Nevakivi, J. (eds) (1997), *Security and Insecurity: Perspectives on Finnish and Swedish Foreign Policy* (Stockholm: Försvarshögskolan).

Asmus, R. (2002), *Opening NATO's Door. How the Alliance Remade Itself for a New Era* (New York: Columbia University Press).

Åström, S. (1989), 'Swedish Neutrality: Credibility Through Commitment and Consistency', in Sundelius (ed.), 15-33.

Axelrod, R. (1984), *The Evolution of Cooperation* (New York: Basic Books).

Bachrach, P. and Baratz, M. (1962), 'Two Faces of Power', *American Political Science Review* 56: 947-952.

—— (1963), 'Decisions and Non-Decisions: An Analytical Framework', *American Political Science Review* 57: 632-642.

Baev, P. (1996), *The Russian Army in a Time of Troubles* (London: Sage Publications).

—— (2002), 'The Plight of the Russian Military: Shallow Identity and Self-defeating Culture', *Armed Forces and Society* 29:1, 129-46.

Bailes, A. et al. (eds) (2006), *The Nordic Countries and the European Security and Defence Policy* (Oxford, UK: Oxford University Press).

Baldwin, D. (1969), 'Foreign Aid, Intervention, and Influence', *World Politics* 21-3 (April): 425-47.

—— (1971), 'The Power of Positive Sanctions', *World Politics* 24:1, 19-38.

—— (1989), *Paradoxes of Power* (Oxford: Blackwell).

—— (ed.) (1993), *Neorealism and Neoliberalism. The Contemporary Debate* (New York: Columbia University Press).

—— (1997), 'The Concept of Security', *Review of International Studies* 23:1, 5-26.

—— (2002), 'Power and International Relations', in Carlsnaes et al. (eds), 177-91.

Barak, S. (2004), 'Between Violence and "e-Jihad": A British View', in Nicander and Ranstorp (eds).

Baylis, J. and Rengger, N. (eds) (1992), *Dilemmas Of World Politics: International Issues in a Changing World* (Oxford: Clarendon Press).

Beer, F. and Landtsheer, C. (eds) (2004), *Metaphorical World Politics* (East Lansing: Michigan State University Press).

Bendix, R. (1959), *Max Weber: An Intellectual Portrait* (London: Methuen & Co. Ltd).

Bendrath, R. (2003), 'The American Cyberangst and the Real World – Any Link?' in Latham (ed.).

Bengtsson, R. (2004), 'The EU as a Security Policy Actor. Russian and US Perceptions', *Research Report* 36. (Stockholm: The Swedish Institute of International Affairs).

Berg, E. (2003), 'A lively and active foreign policy', Estonian Ministry of Foreign Affairs, <www.vm.ee>, accessed 20.05 2004.

Bildt, C. (1998), 'Sveriges Säkerhet i det nya Europa', http://www.bildt.net/index.asp?artid=268.

—— (2003), 'Vad vill Sverige? Nya säkerhetspolitiska perspektiv i Nordeuropa', http://www.bildt.net/dbdocuments/cb000020.pdf.
Bitzinger, R. (1990), 'The Threat, the Conventional Balance and "Common Security": the emerging "Alternative View" in Europe', *Defence Analysis* 6:1, 35-48.
Bjereld, U. (2005), 'Allt fler svenskar säger nej till medlemskap i Nato', *Dagens Nyheter*. DN Debatt, 23 May.
Bjurner, A. (2003), 'Sweden: A Changed Environment', in Ojanen (ed.), 41-45.
Booth, K. (1991), 'War, security and strategy: towards a doctrine for a stable peace', in Booth (ed.), 375-376.
—— (ed.) (1991), *New Thinking about Strategy and International Security* (London: Harper Collins).
—— and Wheeler, N. (1992), 'The Security Dilemma', in Baylis and Rengger (eds), 29-60.
Borch, C. (1995), 'Norway and NATO', *ODIN*, online information about Norway. Document retrieved from http://www.odin.dep.no/odin/engelsk/norway/foreign/032005-990413/index-dok000-b-n-a.html.
Borchgrave, A. de et al. (2000), *Cyber Threats and Information Security Meeting the 21st Century* (Washington, DC: Center for Strategic and International Studies).
Brams, S. (1994), *Theory of Moves* (Cambridge, UK: Cambridge University Press).
Browning, C. (1999), *Coming Home or Moving Home? 'Westernizing' Narratives in Finnish Foreign Policy and the Reinterpretation of Past Identities* (Helsinki: Finnish Institute of International Affairs).
Brundtland, A. (1966), 'The Nordic Balance: Past and Present', *Cooperation and Conflict* 2.
—— (1985), 'Norwegian Security Policy: Defense and Nonprovocation in a Changing Context', in Flynn (ed.).
Bueno de Mesquita, B. (1996), 'Beliefs About Power and the Risks of War: A Power Transition Game', in Kugler and Lemke (eds), 271-286.
Bukkvoll, T. (2003), 'Putin's Strategic Partnership with the West: The Domestic Politics of Russian Foreign Policy', *Comparative Strategy* 22:3, 223-242.
Butfoy, A. (1997), *Common Security and Strategic Reform* (Basingstoke: Macmillan).
Buzan, B. (1991a) *People, States and Fear. Second Edition. An Agenda for International Security Studies in the Post-Cold War Era*. (London: Harvester Wheatsheaf).
—— et al. (1991b), *The European Security Order Recast* (London: Pinter).
—— et al. (1998), *Security: A New Framework for Analysis* (Boulder, CO: Lynne Rienner Publishers, Inc.).
—— and Wæver, O. (2003), *Regions and Powers: The Structure of International Security* (Cambridge: Cambridge University Press).
Camilleri, J. and Falk, J. (1992), *The End of Sovereignty? The Politics of a Shrinking and Fragmenting World* (Aldershot, UK: Edward Elgar).
Carlsnaes, W. et al. (eds) (2002), *Handbook of International Relations* (London: Sage Publications).
—— (2002), 'Foreign Policy', in Carlsnaes et al. (eds), 331-349.

Castells, M. (2000), *The Information Age: The Rise of the Network Society*, Vol. 1, 2nd edition (Malden, MA: Blackwell).

Checkel, J. (1997), *Ideas and International Political Change: Soviet/Russian Behavior and the End of the Cold War* (New Haven, CT: Yale University Press).

—— (1998), 'The Constructivist Turn in International Relations Theory', *World Politics* 50, 324-348.

—— (1999), 'Norms, Institutions, and National Identity in Contemporary Europe', *International Studies Quarterly* 43, 83-114.

—— (2001), 'Social Learning and European Identity Change', *International Organization* 55:3 (Summer), 553-588.

—— (2005), 'International Institutions and Socialization in Europe: Introduction and Framework', *International Organization* 59:Fall, 801-826.

Chhikvishvili, V. (2003), 'Стенограмма Радио Интервью Посла России в Грузии В.И.Чхиквишвили 17 Июля 2003 год / Report from a radio interview with the Russian ambassador in Georgia V.I. Chhikvishvili 17 July 2003 The Ministry of Foreign Affairs of the Russian Federation, (23.07 2003) <http://www.ln.mid.ru>, accessed 23.05 2006.

Chizhov, V. (2004), 'Выступление заместителя Министра иностранных дел России В.А.Чижова на конференции 'Расширяющаяся Европа: новая повестка дня' по теме 'Черноморское и кавказское соседство Европы', Братислава, 19 марта 2004 года / Statement by Deputy Minister of Foreign Affairs of The Russian Federation Mr. Chizhov V. at the conference 'Broadening Europe: New Agenda; The Black Sea and the Caucasus-European neighbourhood', Bratislava 19 March', The Ministry of Foreign Affairs of the Russian Federation, (20 March 2004) <http://www.ln.mid.ru>, accessed 07.05 2005.

Christiansen, Jorgensen, K. and Wiener, A. (eds) *The Social Construction of Europe* (London: Sage).

Cordesman, A. (2002), *Cyber-Threats, Information Warfare, and Critical Infrastructure Protection: Defending the U.S. Homeland* (Westport, CT: Praeger).

Cowles, M. et al. (eds) (2001), *Transforming Europe: Europeanization and Domestic Change* (Ithaca and London: Cornell University Press).

Cox, R. et al. (1973), *The Anatomy of Influence. Decision Making in International Organization* (New Haven: Yale University Press).

Daalder, I. (2003), 'The End of Atlanticism', *Survival* 45:2 (Summer), 147-166.

Dahl, A. (1999), *Svenskarna och NATO* (Stockholm: Timbro).

Dahl, R. (1957), 'The Concept of Power', *Behavioral Science* 2, 201-215.

—— (1961), *Who Governs: Democracy and Power in an American City* (New Haven, CT: Yale University Press).

—— (1991), *Modern Political Analysis*, 5th edition. (Englewood Cliffs, N.J.: Prentice Hall.

—— and Stinebrickner, B. (2003), *Modern Political Analysis*, 6th edition. (Upper Saddle River, N.J.: Prentice Hall).

Darst, R. (2001), *Smokestack Diplomacy: Cooperation and Conflict in East-West Environmental Politics* (Cambridge: Massachusetts Institute of Technology Press).

Denning, D. (1999), *Information Warfare and Security*. Reading, MA: ACM Press Books.

—— (2001), 'Is Cyber Terror Next?' in *Essays after September 11* (New York: Social Science Research Council) <http://www.ssrc.org/sept11/essays/denning.htm>

Deutsch, K. et al. (1957), *Political Community in the North Atlantic Area: International Organization in the Light of Historical Experience* (Princeton, NJ: Princeton University Press).

—— (1978), *The Analysis of International Relations*, Second Edition (Englewood Cliffs, NJ: Prentice-Hall).

Dewitt, D. (1994), 'Common, Comprehensive and Cooperative Security', *The Pacific Review* 7:1, 1-15.

Diehl, P. and Goertz, G. (2000), *War and Peace in International Rivalry* (Ann Arbor, MI: University of Michigan Press).

Dobbins, J. (2005), 'NATO's role in nation-building', *NATO Review* Summer, http://www.nato.int/docu/review/2005/issue2/english/art1_pr.html.

Dörfer, I. (1997), *The Nordic Nations in the New Western Security Regime* (Washington, D. C.: The Johns Hopkins University Press).

Downs, G. (ed.) (1994), *Collective Security Beyond the Cold War* (Ann Arbor: University of Michigan Press).

Duffield, J. et al. (1999), 'Correspondence, Isms and Schisms: Culturalism versus Realism in Security Studies', *International Security*, 24:1 (Summer), 156-180.

Dunnigan, J. (2003), *How to Make War*, 4th edition. (New York: Quill).

Eggert, K. and Yusin, M. (1996), 'Secret Yeltsin-Clinton Correspondence', Izvestia, 6 July, *Current Digest of the Post-Soviet Press* 48:27, 2.

Elman, C. (1996), 'Horses for Courses: Why Not Neorealist Theories of Foreign Policy?' *Security Studies* 6:7-53.

—— and Elman, M. (eds) (2003), *Progress in International Relations Theory: Engaging the Field* (Cambridge, Mass: MIT Press),

Emerson, R. (1962), 'Power-Dependence Relations', *American Sociological Review* 21: 31-41.

Eriksson J. (ed.) (2001), *Threat Politics: New Perspectives on Security, Risk and Crisis Management* (Aldershot, UK: Ashgate Publishing).

—— (2001a), 'Cyberplagues, IT and Security: Threat Politics in the Information Age', *Journal of Contingencies and Crisis Management* 9:4, 211–22.

—— (2001b), 'Securitizing IT', in Eriksson (ed.).

—— (2004), *Kampen om hotbilden: Rutin och drama i svensk säkerhetspolitik* [The Politics of Threat Images: Routine and Drama in Swedish Security Policy] (Stockholm: Santérus).

—— and Giacomello, G. (2006a), 'The Information Revolution, Security and International Relations: (IR)relevant Theory?', *International Political Science Review* 27(3).

—— and Giacomello, G. (eds) (2006b), *International Relations and Security in the Digital Age* (London: Routledge).
Etzioni, A. (1965), *Political Unification: A Comparative Analysis of Leaders and Forces* (New York: Holt, Rinehart & Winston).
Evangelista, M. (1995), 'Transnational Relations, Domestic Structures, and Security Policy in the USSR and Russia', in Risse-Kappen (ed.).
—— (1999), *Unarmed Forces: The Transnational Movement to End the Cold War* (Ithaca: Cornell University Press).
Everard, J. (2000), *Virtual States: The Internet and the Boundaries of the Nation-State* (London: Routledge).
Fearon, J. and Wendt, A. (2002), 'Rationalism v. Constructivism: A Skeptical View', in Carlsnaes et al. (eds), 52-72.
Finnemore, M. and Sikkink, K. (1998), 'International Norm Dynamics and Political Change', *International Organization* 54:4 (Autumn), 887-917.
Fischer, D. (1997), *History of the International Atomic Energy Agency. The First Forty Years* (Vienna: IAEA).
Flockhart, T. (2006), '"Complex Socialization": A Framework for the Study of State Socialization', *European Journal of International Relations* 12:1, 89-118.
Flynn, G. (ed.) (1985), *NATO's Northern Allies: The National Security Policies of Belgium, Denmark, the Netherlands, and Norway* (Totowa, NJ: Rowman & Unwin).
Forno, R. (2002), Quotes on 'Electronic Pearl Harbor', online 25 July 2002 <http://www.soci.niu.edu/~crypt/other/harbor.htm>.
Fountain, J. (2001), *Building the Virtual State: Information Technology and Institutional Change* (Washington DC: Brookings Institution).
Fox, A. (1959), *The Power of Small States. Diplomacy in World War II* (Chicago, IL: University of Chicago Press).
—— (1977), *The Politics of Attraction* (New York: Columbia University Press).
Frankel, B. (ed.) (1996), *Realism: Restatement and Renewal* (London: Frank Cass).
Fredén, L. (2006), *Återkomster. Svensk säkerhetspolitik och de baltiska ländernas första år i självstendighet* (Stockholm: Atlantis).
Freedman, D. (2000), 'How to hack a bank', *Forbes.com*. <http://www.forbes.com/asap/2000/0403/056.html>
Frey, F. (1985), 'The Distribution of Power in Political Systems' (paper presented at the World Congress of the International Political Science Association, Paris).
Friedrich, C. (1937), *Constitutional Government and Politics: Nature and Development* (New York: Harper & Brothers).
Gambles, I. (ed.) (1995), 'A Lasting Peace in Central Europe? The Expansion of the European Security Community', *Chaillot Papers* 20 (Paris: Institute for Security Studies, Western European Union).
Garfield, A. (2004), 'Terrorism and Asymmetric Conflict: A British Perspective', in Nicander, L. and Ranstorp, M. (eds), 28–40.
Geddes, B. (1991), 'How the Cases You Choose Affect the Answers You Get', in Stimson (ed.).

Gellman, B. (2002), 'Cyber Attacks by Al Qaeda Feared', *Washington Post*, 27 June, p. AO1.
George, A. (1993), *Bridging the Gap: Theory and Practice in Foreign Policy*, (Washington, D.C.: United States Institute of Peace Press).
—— and Bennett, A. (2005), *Case Studies and Theory Development in the Social Sciences* (London: MIT Press).
Gerth, H. and Mills, C. (1948/1998), *From Max Weber: Essays in Sociology* (London: Routledge and Kegan Paul / Routledge reprint).
Giacomello, G. (2004a), 'Bangs for the Buck: A Cost-Benefit Analysis of Cyberterrorism', *Studies in Conflict and Terrorism* 27: 387–408.
—— (2004b), *National Governments and the Internet: A Digital Challenge?* (London: Routledge).
—— and F. Mendez (2001), '"Cuius Regio, Eius Religio, Omnium Spatium?" State Sovereignty in the Age of the Internet', *Information and Security* 7: 15–27.
Gibson, W. (1984), *Neuromancer* (New York: Ace).
Gnesotto, N. (ed.) (2004), *EU Security and Defence Policy: The First five Years (1999-2004)* (Paris: EU Institute for Security Studies).
Godzimirski, J. (1998), 'Russian Security Policy objectives in the Baltic Sea and the Barents Area', *Norwegian Atlantic Committee Security Policy Library*, No. 12 (Oslo: DNAK).
Goldmann, K. (1988), *Change and Stability in Foreign Policy* (Princeton: Princeton University Press).
—— (2002), 'Internationalisation and the Nation-State: Four Issues and Three Non-Issues', *European Journal of International Relations* 41:3.
—— and Sjöstedt, G. (eds) (1979), *Power, Capabilities, Interdependence* (Beverly Hills: Sage Publications Inc).
Goldstein, J. and Keohane, R. (1993), *Ideas and Foreign Policy: Beliefs, Institutions, and Political Change* (Ithaca, NY: Cornell University Press).
Goodby, J., et al (2002), *A Strategy for Stable Peace: Toward a Euroatlantic Security Community* (Washington, D.C.: United States Institute of Peace Press).
Goroshko, L. (2004), 'Russian computer crime statistics', Computer Crime Research Center, 30 July 2004 <http://www.crime-research.org/news/30.07.2004/530/>
Goverde, H. et al. (eds), *Power in Contemporary Politics* (London: Sage).
Green, D. and Shapiro, I. (1994), *Pathologies of Rational Choice* (New Haven, CN: Yale University Press).
Greenwood, J. (1997), *Representing Interests in the European Union* (Basingstoke: Macmillan).
Grieco, J. (1988), 'Anarchy and the Limits of Cooperation: A Realist Critique of the Newest Liberal Institutionalism', *International Organization* 42:3, 485-507.
—— (1993), 'Understanding the Problem of International Cooperation: The Limits of Neoliberal Institutionalism and the Future of Realist Theory', in Baldwin (ed.), 301-338.
—— (1996), 'State Interests and Institutional Rule Trajectories', in Frankel (ed.).

Gryaznevich, V. (2005), 'The Scandal Over the Russian-Estonian Boarder Agreement', Factiva Database, (26 July 2005), <www.factiva.com>, 10.12 2005.

Guillaume, C. (2004), 'Russian Foreign Policy Discourse during the Kosovo Crisis: Internal Struggles and the Political Imaginaire', *Questions de Recherche* 2. (Paris: Institut d'Etudes Politique).

Guzzini, S. (1993), 'Structural Power: The Limits of Neorealist Power Analysis', *International Organization* 47-3 (Summer): 443-478.

—— (2000), 'The Use and Misuse of Power Analysis in International Theory', in Palan (ed.), 53–66.

Haab, M. (1998), 'Estonia', in Mouritzen (ed.), 91-109).

Haas, P. (1990), *Saving the Mediterranean: The Politics of International Environmental Cooperation* (New York: Columbia University Press).

—— (ed.), (1992a), *Knowledge, Power, and International Policy Coordination* (Columbia: University of South Carolina Press).

—— (1992b), 'Introduction: Epistemic Communities and International Policy Coordination', in Haas (ed.).

Haftendorn, H. (1991), 'The Security Puzzle: Theory-Building and Discipline-Building in International Security', *International Studies Quarterly* 35:2, 3-17.

Hagström, L. (2005), *Japan's China Policy: A Relational Power Analysis* (London: Routledge).

Haikio, M. (1997), 'Changes in Finnish Security Policy: The Koivisto Presidency, 1981-1994', in Arteus and Nevakivi (eds), 83-96.

Hallenberg, J. (2000), 'Swedish Foreign and Security Policy', in Miles (ed.).

—— (2000), *The Extension of the European Security Community to the Periphery: France in the Mediterranean and Finland and Sweden in the Baltic Countries* (Stockholm: Swedish National Defence College).

—— et al (eds), (2003), *Transitions. In Honour of Kjell Goldmann* (Stockholm: Stockholm University, Department of Political Science).

Hansen, B. and Heurlin, B. (1998), *The Baltic States in World Politics* (Richmond, UK: Curzon).

Hansen, L. and Waever, O. (eds), (2002), *European Integration and National Identity* (London and New York: Routledge).

Haugaard, M. (2000), 'Power, Ideology and Legitimacy' in Goverde et al. (eds), 59-76.

Hedenskog, J. et al. (eds), (2005), *Russia as a Great Power: Dimensions of Security Under Putin* (London: Routledge).

Heikka, H. (2005), 'Finland: Still in Search of a Mission Statement', *CFSP Forum* 3:1, 14-16.

Heinemann-Grüder, A. (2002), 'Small-States - Big Worries. Choice and Purpose in the Security Policies of the Baltic States' (Bonn International Center for Conversion).

Heisler, M. and Quester, G. (1999), 'International Security Structures and the Baltic Region: The Implications of Alternative Worldviews', in Knudsen (ed.), 55-77.

Henry, R. and Peartree, C. (eds) (1998), *The Information Revolution and International Security* (Washington, D.C.: Center for Strategic and International Studies).

Hermann, C. (1990), 'Changing Course - When Governments Choose To Redirect Foreign Policy', *International Studies Quarterly* 34:1, 3-21.

Hermann, M. (ed.) (2004), *Advances in Political Psychology,* Volume 1. (Amsterdam: Elsevier).

Herrmann, R. (2002), 'Linking Theory to Evidence in International Relations', in Carlsnaes et al. (eds), 119-136.

Himanen, H. (2003), 'Finland: From Neutrality to Engagement', in Ojanen, (ed.), 19-26.

Hirschman, A. (1970), *Exit, Voice and Loyalty. Responses to Decline in Firms, Organizations, and States* (Cambridge, MA: Harvard University Press).

Hoffmann, S. (1968), 'Obstinate or Obsolete? The Fate of the Nation-State and the Case of Western Europe', in Nye (ed.), *International Regionalism; Readings* (Boston: Little, Brown & Company).

Hopf, T. (1998), 'The Promise of Constructivism in International Relations Theory', *International Security* 23:171-200.

—— (ed.) (1999), *Understandings of Russian Foreign Policy* (University Park: The Pennsylvania State University Press).

—— (1999), 'Introduction. Russian Identity and Foreign Policy After the Cold War', in Hopf (ed.), 1-13.

—— (2002), *Social Construction of International Politics: Identities and Foreign Policies, Moscow, 1955 & 1999* (London: Cornell University Press).

Howard, P. (2004), 'The Language of International Socialization' (paper presented at the Annual meeting of the International Studies Association, Montreal, Canada).

Howorth, J. (2000), *European Integration and Defence: The Ultimate Challenge?* Chaillot Paper 43 (Paris: Institute for Security Studies, Western European Union).

—— and Keeler, J. (2003), 'The EU, NATO and the Quest for European Autonomy', in Howorth and Keeler (eds).

—— and Keeler, J. (eds), (2003), *Defending Europe: The EU, NATO and the Quest for European Autonomy* (New York: Palgrave Macmillan).

Hudson, V. (2005), 'Foreign Policy Analysis: Actor Specific Theory and the Ground of International Relations', *Foreign Policy Analysis* 1:1, 1-30.

Hubel H. (ed.), *EU Enlargement and Beyond: The Baltic States and Russia* (Berlin: Arno Spitz GmbH).

Huldt, B. (2003), 'Comments on the Swedish Position', in Ojanen (ed.), 46-51.

—— et al. (eds), (2001), *Finnish and Swedish Security: Comparing national policies*, (Stockholm and Helsinki: Swedish National Defence College and Finnish Institute of International Affairs).

Ikenberry, G. (1992), 'A world economy restored: expert consensus and the Anglo-American postwar settlement', in Haas (ed.).

Ilves, T. (1999), Address to the 4th Annual Stockholm Conference on Baltic Security and Cooperation, (Stockholm: Embassy of the United States of America), 31-34.

—— (2000), 'Developments in the Main Directions of Estonia's Foreign Policy', address to the Riigikogu, 12 October, Estonian Ministry of Foreign Affairs, <www.vm.ee>.

—— (2001), 'Main Guidelines of Estonia's Foreign Policy', address to the Riigikogu, 25 October, Estonian Ministry of Foreign Affairs < www.vm.ee>.

Ivanov, I. (2000), 'Russia and the World at the turn of the Millennium', The Ministry of Foreign Affairs of the Russian Federation, (24.10 2000), <www.mid.ru>.

—— (2003a), 'Remarks by Minister of Foreign Affairs of Russia', Münich, December 10, 2003, The Ministry of Foreign Affairs of the Russian Federation, <www.mid.ru>, accessed 13.09 2005.

—— (2003b), 'Speech by Russian Minister of Foreign Affairs in the Brazilian MFA Rio Branco Institute, Brasilia, December 19, 2003', the Ministry of Foreign Affairs of the Russian Federation, <www.mid.ru>, accessed 15.09 2004.

Ivanov, S. (2000), 'Статья Министра иностранных дел России И.С.Иванова, 'Внешняя политика России на современном этапе'/ Article by Minister of Foreign Affairs of the Russian Federation [Ivanov, S. 'Contemporary Foreign Policy of Russia' ', the Ministry of Foreign Affairs of the Russian Federation, (2000-07-13), <http://www.ln.mid.ru>, accessed 04.05 2005.

—— (2001), 'Speech at the 37th International Security Conference on the Theme "Global and Regional Security at the Start of the 21st Century", 13.02 2001', the Ministry of Foreign Affairs of the Russian Federation, <www.mid.ru>.

—— (2006), Article by Deputy Prime Minister and Minister of Defense of the Russian Federation Sergey Ivanov, published in *The Wall Street Journal* on 11 January 2006.

Jackson, W. (2002), 'Report: Cyberterrorism still more of a threat than a reality', *Government Computer News* 7 August 2002. <http://www.gcn.com/vol1_no1/daily-updates/19237-1.html>

—— (2002), 'Encircled Again: Russia's Military Assesses Threats in a Post-Soviet World', *Political Science Quarterly* 117:3, 373-400.

Jakobson, M. (1984), *Finland Survived: An Account of the Finnish-Soviet Winter War, 1939-1940* (Helsinki: Otava).

—— (1998), *Finland in the New Europe* (Washington, D. C.: Praeger).

Jalonen, O. (ed.) (1993), *Approaches to European Security in the 1990s*, Research Report No. 49 (Tampere: Tampere Peace Research Institute).

Jervis, R. (1976), *Perception and Misperception in International Politics* (Princeton: Princeton University Press).

Joenniemi, P. (1996), 'Norden: A Community of Asecurity?', *COPRI Working Paper* 6.

—— (2002), 'Finland in the New Europe: a Herderian or Hegelian project', in Hansen and Wæver (eds).

Jonsson, L. (2004), *Vladimir Putin and Central Asia. The Shaping of Russian Foreign Policy* (New York: I.B. Tauris).

Kapstein, E. (1992), 'Between Power and Purpose: Central Bankers and the Politics of Regulatory Convergence', in P. Haas (ed.).

Karlsson, M. (2004a). *Transnational Relations in the Baltic Sea Region*, Södertörn Academic Studies 21 (Huddinge: Södertörns högskola).
—— (2004b), 'Epistemic Communities and Cooperative Security: The Case of Communicable Disease Control in the Baltic Sea Region', *Journal of International and Area Studies* 11:1, 79-100.
—— and Knudsen, O. (2001), 'Sweden and the Baltic States', in Huldt et al. (eds), 180-203.
Kassianova, A. (2001), 'Russia: Still Open to the West? Evolution of the State Identity in the Foreign Policy and Security Discourse', *Europe-Asia Studies* 53:6, 821-839.
Katzenstein, P. (ed.) (1996), *The Culture of National Security* (New York: Columbia University Press).
—— et al. (1998), 'International Organization and the Study of World Politics', *International Organization* 52: 645-685.
Kauppila, L. (1999). 'The Baltic Puzzle. Russia's Policy Towards Estonia and Latvia 1992-1997', *Pro Gradu*, January, (Helsinki: University of Helsinki).
Keal, P. (1983), *Unspoken Rules and Superpower Dominance* (New York: St. Martin's Press).
Keohane, R. (ed.), (1986), *Neorealism and Its Critics* (New York: Columbia University Press).
—— and Nye, J. (1977 / 1989), *Power and Interdependence* (Boston, MA: Little, Brown).
—— (1984), *After Hegemony. Cooperation and Discord in the World Political Economy* (Princeton: Princeton University Press).
—— and Nye, J. (1974), 'Transgovernmental Relations and World Politics', *World Politics* 27:1, 39-62.
—— and Nye, J. (1998), 'Power and Interdependence in the Information Age', *Foreign Affairs* 77:5, 81–94.
King, G. et al (1994), *Designing Social Inquiry* (Princeton, NJ: Princeton University Press).
Kissinger, H. (1965), *The Troubled Partnership* (New York: McGraw-Hill).
—— (1994), *Diplomacy* (New York: Simon and Schuster).
Knorr, K. (1970), *Military Power and Potential* (Lexington, MA: D.C. Heath. Lexington Books).
Knudsen, O. (1979), 'Capabilities, Issue-Areas, and Inter-State Power', in Goldmann and Sjöstedt (eds), 85–114).
—— (1988), 'Of Lambs and Lions: Relations Between Great Powers and Their Smaller Neighbours', *Cooperation and Conflict* 23:4, 111-122.
—— (1992), 'Two Soviet Neighbours: Did Accommodation Work?' *Journal of Peace Research* 29:1, 53-69.
—— (1992a), *Sharing Borders with a Great Power: An Examination of Small State Predicaments,* NUPI Report 159 (Oslo: Norwegian Institute of International Affairs).

—— (1992b), 'Two Soviet Neighbors: Did Accommodation Work?' *Journal of Peace Research.* 29-1: 53-69.
—— *(1998),* 'Cooperative Security In The Baltic Sea Region', *Chaillot Papers* No. 33. (Paris: Institute for Security Studies, Western European Union, November).
—— (ed.), (1999), *Stability and Security in the Baltic Sea Region: Russian, Nordic and European Aspects* (London: Frank Cass).
—— (1999), 'Introduction' in Knudsen (ed.)
—— (1999), 'Security on the Great Power Fringe: Dilemmas Old and New', in Knudsen (ed.).
—— (2003), '"Cooperative Security" - Slogan and Norm: Some Policymaking Complications', in Hallenberg et al (eds).
—— (2004), '"Institutions" vs "Power": Baltic Perspectives on Regional Security', *Baltic Sea Area Studies: Northern Dimension of Europe. BaltSeaNet Working Papers volume 13 (Gdansk-Berlin: Wydawnictvo Uniwersytetu Gdanskiego; Nordeuropa-Institut der Humboldt-Universität zu Berlin).*
—— (2004), 'Contemplating Secession: Emergent Identity and Power Disparity - The Case of Greenland', (paper presented at the Annual Convention of the International Studies Association, Montreal, March).
—— (2006), 'Environmental Constraints and Market Forces in a Disputed Regime: The Case of Russian Oil Exports in the Baltic Sea' (paper presented at the Annual Convention of the International Studies Association, San Diego, CA, March.
Konnander, V. (2005), 'What Prospects for Russia in the Baltic Sea Region? Cooperation or Isolation?', in Hedenskog et al. (eds).
Kozyrev, A. (1994a), 'The Lagging Partnership', *Foreign Affairs* 73:3, 59-71.
—— (1994b), 'Russia and NATO: A Partnership for a United and Peaceful Europe', *NATO Review* 42:4, 3-6.
Krasner, S. (1995), 'Power politics, institutions, and transnational relations', in Risse-Kappen (ed.).
Krause, K. and Williams, M. (eds) (1997), *Critical Security Studies: Concepts and Cases* (London: UCL Press).
Krieger, L. (1968), 'Authority'. *Dictionary of the History of Ideas. Studies of Selected Pivotal Ideas,* Volume I. (New York: Charles Scribner's Sons), 141-162.
Krohn, A. (ed.) (1996), *The Baltic Sea Region: National and International Security Perspectives* (Baden-Baden: Nomos Verlag).
Kugler, J. and Lemke, D. (eds) (1996), *Parity and War : Evaluations and Extensions of The War Ledger* (Ann Arbor: University of Michigan Press).
Kuus, M. (2002a), 'European Integration in Identity Narratives in Estonia: A Quest for Security', *Journal of Peace Research* 39:1, 91-108.
—— (2002b), 'Sovereignty for Security? The Discourse of Sovereignty in Estonia', *Political Geography* 21:3, 393-412.
—— (2002c), 'Toward Cooperative Security? International Integration and the Construction of Security in Estonia', *Millennium-Journal of International Studies* 31:2, 297-317.

Kux, S. (2005), 'European Union-Russia Relations: Transformation Through Integration' in Motyl A. et al. (eds).
Labs, E. (1992), 'Do Weak States Bandwagon?' *Security Studies* 1:3, 383-416.
Lake, D. and Morgan, P. (eds) (1997), *Regional Orders. Building Security in a New World* (University Park, PA: Pennsylvania State University Press).
Larrabee, S. (2003), *NATO's Eastern Agenda in a New Strategic Era* (Santa Monica: RAND).
Larsson, R. (2006), *Rysslands energipolitik och pålitlighet som energileverantör. Risker och trender i ljuset av den rysk-ukrainska gaskonflikten 2005-2006* [Russia's Energy Policy and Reliability as Supplier of Energy. Risks and Trends in the Light of the Russian-Ukrainian Gas Conflict 2005-2006.] Report FOI-R-1905-SE. (Stockholm: FOI – Totalförsvarets Forskningsinstitut).
Lasswell, H. and Kaplan, A. (1950), *Power and Society; A Framework for Political Inquiry* (New Haven, CT: Yale University Press).
Latham, R. (ed.) (2003), *Bombs and Bandwidth: The Emerging Relationship between IT and Security* (New York: The New Press).
Laudan, L. (1977), *Progress and its Problems: Towards a Theory of Scientific Growth* (Berkeley: University of California Press).
Lavrov, S. (2005), 'Main Points of the Address by the Foreign Minister of the Russian Federation S. Lavrov at the Stanford University, San Francisco, 20 September 2005', The Ministry of Foreign Affairs of the Russian Federation, <www.mid.ru>, accessed 05.06 2006.
—— (2006), 'Speech by Minister of Foreign Affairs of the Russian Federation Sergey Lavrov at the Tenth World Russian People's Council (Sobor), Moscow, April 4, 2006', The Ministry of Foreign Affairs of the Russian Federation, <www.mid.ru>, accessed 05.06 2006.
Layne, C. (1993), 'The Unipolar Illusion: Why New Great Powers Will Emerge', *International Security,* 17:4, 5-51.
Leeds, C. (1999), 'Worldframes and cultural perspectives with specific focus on Scandinavia and Russia', in Knudsen (ed.), 78-96.
Lehti M. and Smith D. (eds) (2003), *Post-Cold War Identity Politics: Northern and Baltic Experiences* (London: Frank Cass).
Lemke, D. (1996), 'Small States and War: An Expansion of Power Transition Theory' in Kugler and Lemke (eds), 77-91.
—— and Kugler, J. (1996), 'The Evaluation of the Power Transition Perspective' in Kugler and Lemke (eds), 3-34.
Libicki, M. (1997), *Defending Cyberspace and Other Metaphors* (Washington, D.C.: National Defense University).
Lipschutz, R. (ed.) (1995), *On Security* (New York: Columbia University Press).
Lo, B. (2002), *Russian Foreign Policy in the Post-Soviet Era. Reality, Illusion, and Mythmaking* (Houndmills, Basingstoke: Palgrave Macmillan).
—— (2003), *Vladimir Putin and the Evolution of Russian Foreign Policy* (London: Chatham House Papers / Blackwell Publishing).

Lonsdale, D. (1999), 'Information Power: Strategy, Geopolitics, and the Fifth Dimension', *The Journal of Strategic Studies* 22:2/3, 137–57.

Losyukov, A. (2001), 'Moscow's Policy: Neither a Western Nor an Eastern Tilt', *Diplomat Magazine,* The Russian Ministry of Foreign Affairs, (03.04 2001), <www.mid.ru>, 13.09 2003.

Luik, J. (1994), 'Statement at the Swedish Institute of International Affairs, Stockholm, 2 March', Estonian Ministry of Foreign Affairs, <www.vm.ee>.

Lukes, S. (1974), *Power: A Radical View* (London: Macmillan).

—— (2005), *Power: A Radical View,* Second Edition (London: Palgrave Macmillan).

Lyashenko, V. (1993), *The Report of the Representative of the RF Department of Defence on the Radiation and Nuclear Safety at the Meeting of the Working Group,* Moscow, 20 April 1993, CBSS - Working Group on Nuclear and Radiation Safety (WGNRS) 1994b, annex 3.

Made, V. (2003), 'Estonia and Europe: A Common Identity of an Identity Crisis?' in Lehti and Smith (eds), 183-198.

Majeski, S. (2004), 'Asymmetric Power among Agents and the Generation and Maintenance of Cooperation in International Relations', *International Studies Quarterly* 48:455-470.

Malmborg, M. af (2001), 'Sweden in the EU', in Huldt et al. (eds), 38-59.

Maoz, Z. (1990), *National Choices and International Processes* (Cambridge, UK: Cambridge University Press).

Maremäe, E. et al. (eds), *Historical Survey of Nuclear Non-Proliferation in Estonia, 1946-1995* (Tallinn: Estonian Radiation Protection Centre).

Martin, L. and Keohane, R. (1995), 'The Promise of Institutionalist Theory', *International Security* 20:1 (Summer), 39-51.

Martirosyan, T. (2004), 'Armenia's Foreign Policy: Complementary or Conformable?' http://www.ui.se (accessed 2005-06).

Matviyenko, V. (2001), 'Statement at the 31st Session of the General Conference of UNESCO, 18-10-2001', The Ministry of Foreign Affairs of the Russian Federation, <www.mid.ru>.

Matz, J. (2001), *Constructing a post-Soviet international political reality: Russian foreign policy towards the newly independent states 1990-95* (Uppsala: Acta Universitatis Upsaliensis).

Maude, G. (1976), *The Finnish Dilemma* (London: Oxford University Press).

McGaw, D. and Watson, G. (1976), *Political and Social Inquiry* (New York: John Wiley).

Mearsheimer, J. (1990), 'Back to the Future: Instability in Europe After the Cold War', *International Security* 15:1, 5–56.

—— (2001), *The Tragedy of Great Power Politics* (New York: Norton).

Mercer, J. (1995), 'Anarchy and Identity', *International Organization* 49:2, 229-52.

Meri, L. (2000), Interview in *Politique Internationale*, no. 86 1999/2000. http://vp1992-2001.president.ee/eng/.

Miles, L. (1997), *Sweden and European Integration* (Aldershot, UK: Ashgate Publishing).
—— (ed.) (2000), *Sweden and the European Union Evaluated* (London and New York: Continuum).
Milliken, J. (1999), 'The study of discourse in international relations: A critique of research and methods', *European Journal of International Relations*, 5:2, 225-254.
Mills, C. (1956), *The Power Elite* (New York: Oxford University Press).
Mingst, K. (1995), 'Uncovering the Missing Links: Linkage Actors and Their Strategies In Foreign Policy Analysis', in Neack, L. et al. (eds), *Foreign Policy Analysis: Continuity and Change in Its Second Generation* (Englewood Cliffs: Prentice Hall).
Miniotaitė, G. (2001), 'The Baltic States: In Search of Security and Identity', *COPRI Working Paper* 14.
Mintz, A. (ed.), (forthcoming), *Advances in Foreign Policy Analysis Yearbook* (New York: Palgrave Macmillan).
Moon, B. (1983), 'The Foreign Policy of the Dependent State.' *International Studies Quarterly* 27, 315-340.
Moon, C-I. (1988), 'Complex Interdependence and Transnational Lobbying: South Korea in the United States', *International Studies Quarterly* 32:1, 67-89.
Moravcsik, A. (1998), *The Choice for Europe: Social Purpose and State Power from Messina to Maastricht* (Ithaca: Cornell University Press).
—— (2003), 'Liberal International Relations Theory', in Elman and Elman (eds).
Morozov, V. (2003), 'The Baltic States in Russian Foreign Policy Discource: Can Russia become a Baltic Country?' in Lehti and Smith (eds), 219-252.
—— (2004), 'Russia in the Baltic Sea Region. Dessecuritization or Deregionalization?' *Cooperation and Conflict* 39:3, 317-331.
Möttölä, K. (2001), 'Finland, the European Union and NATO: Implications for Security and Defence', in Reiter and Gartner (eds), 113-144.
Motyl, A. et al. (eds) (2005), *Russia's Engagement with the West: Transformation and Integration in the Twenty-First Century* (Armonk, NY: M.E. Sharpe).
Mouritzen, H. (1988), *Finlandization: Towards a General Theory of Adaptive Politics*, (Aldershot, UK: Avebury).
—— (ed.) (1998), Bordering Russia: Theory and Prospects for Europe's Baltic Rim (Aldershot, UK: Ashgate Publishing).
—— (2001), 'Security Communities in the Baltic Sea Region: Real and Imagined', *Security Dialogue* 32:3, 297-310.
Mowlana, H. (1997), *Global Information and World Communication: New Frontiers in International Relations* (London: Sage).
Mutimer, D. (1997), 'Beyond Strategy: Critical Thinking and the New Security Studies', in Snyder (ed.), 77-101.
Nagel, J. (1975), *The Descriptive Analysis of Power* (New Haven, CT: Yale University Press).

Neumann, I. (1992), 'Identity and Security', *Journal of Peace Research* 29:2, 221-6.

—— (1996), 'Self and Other in International Relations', *European Journal of International Relations* 2:2, 139-174.

—— (2002), 'Returning Practice to the Linguistic Turn: The Case of Diplomacy', *Millennium-Journal of International Studies* 31:3, 627-651.

—— (2005), 'Russia as a Great Power', in Hedenskog et al. (eds).

Nicander, L. and M. Ranstorp (eds), (2004), *Terrorism in the Information Age – New Frontiers?* Acta Series B29 (Stockholm: Swedish National Defence College).

Noreen, E. (1983), *The Nordic Balance: A Security Policy Concept in Theory and Practice*, Report 23 (Uppsala: Uppsala University, Department of Peace and Conflict Research).

—— (2001), 'Verbal Politics of Estonian Policy-makers: Reframing Security and Identity', in Eriksson(ed.), 84-99.

—— and Sjöstedt, R. (2004), 'Estonian Identity Formations and Threat Framing in the Post-Cold War Era', *Journal of Peace Research* 41: 733-750.

Norris, P. (2001), *Digital Divide: Civic Engagement, Information Poverty, and the Internet Worldwide* (Cambridge: Cambridge University Press).

Nossal, K. (1995), 'Seeing Things? The Adornment of "Security" in Australia and Canada', *Australian Journal of International Affairs* 49:1.

Nye, J. (1987), 'Nuclear Learning and U.S.–Soviet Security Regimes', *International Organization* 41, 371-402.

—— (1990), *Bound to Lead: The Changing Nature of American Power* (New York: Basic Books).

—— (1998), 'Foreword' in Henry and Peartree (eds).

—— (2004a), *Soft Power: The Means to Success in World Politics* (New York: Public Affairs).

—— (2004b), *Power in the Global Information Age: From Realism to Globalization* (London: Routledge).

O'Day, A. (ed.), (2004), *Cyberterrorism* (Aldershot, UK: Ashgate Publishing).

Ojanen, H. et al. (2000), *Non-Alignment and European Security Policy: Ambiguity at Work* (Helsinki: The Finnish Institute of International Affairs).

—— (ed.) (2003) *Neutrality and Non-Alignment in Europe Today*, FIIA Report 6. (Helsinki:: The Finnish Institute of International Affairs).

Ojuland, K. (2002), 'Address by Estonian Foreign Minister at the Danish Institute of International Affairs, Copenhagen, 12 April', Estonian Ministry of Foreign Affairs, <www.vm.ee>.

Organski, A. (1958), *World Politics* (New York: Knopf).

—— and Kugler, J. (1980), *The War Ledger* (Chicago: University of Chicago Press).

Oye, K. (1986), *Cooperation Under Anarchy* (Princeton, NJ: Princeton University Press).

Palan, R. (ed.), *Global Political Economy: Contemporary Theories* (London and New York: Routledge).

Palme Commission (1982), *Common Security: A Blueprint for Survival*, The Independent Commission on Disarmament and Security Issues (Simon and Schuster: New York).

Park, A. (1995), 'Russia and Estonian Security Dilemmas', *Europe-Asia Studies* 47:1, 27-45.

Parker, C. and Stern, E. (2002), 'Blindsided? September 11 and the Origins of Strategic Surprise', *Political Psychology* 23:3, 601-630.

Peou, S. (2001), 'Security-Community Building for Better Global Governance', in Rittberger (ed.).

Petersen, P. (1992), 'Security Policy in the Post-Soviet Baltic States', *European Security* 1:1, 13-49.

Petrova, A. (2001), 'NATO Expansion: a Threat to Russia, Public Opinion Foundation, Database, Russia, (04.10 2001), <www.fom.ru/report/map/>, accessed 23.06 2004.

—— (2004), 'Russians Feel Threatened by NATO Expansion', Public Opinion Foundation, Database, Russia, (19.04 2004), <www.fom.ru/report/map/>.

Pfaltzgraff, R. and Shultz, R. (eds), *War in the Information Age: New Challenges for US Security Policy* (Washington, D.C. and London: Brassey's).

Polikanov, D. (2001), *Information Challenges to National and International Security* (Moscow: PIR Center).

Pond, E. (2004), *Friendly Fire – The Near-Death of the Transatlantic Alliance* (Washington, D.C.: Brookings Institution Press).

Pouliot, V. (2006), 'The Alive and Well Transatlantic Security Community: A Theoretical Reply to Michael Cox', *European Journal of International Relations* 12:1, 119-127.

Pursiainen, C. and Sinikukka, S. (2002), *Et tu Brute! Finland's NATO Option and Russia*, UPI Report 1/2002 (Helsinki: The Finnish Institutue of International Affairs).

Putin, V. (2000a), 'Interview with French TV Channels TF-1 and France-3, RFI Radio Broadcasting Corporation and ORT TV Channel, Moscow, October 23, 2000', The Ministry of Foreign Affairs of the Russian Federation, <www.mid.ru>, accessed 13.09 2004.

—— (2000b), 'Statement in Connection with the Explosion of Pushkin Square, Moscow, 11.08 2000', The Ministry of Foreign Affairs of the Russian Federation, <www.mid.ru>, accessed 13.09 2004.

—— (2001a), 'Interview granted by the President to the Finnish Newspaper Helsingin Sanomat, September 1, 2001', The Ministry of Foreign Affairs of the Russian Federation, <www.mid.ru>, accessed 13.09 2004.

—— (2001b), 'Interview to National Public Radio, the US Radio Station, New York, 19.11 2001', The Ministry of Foreign Affairs of the Russian Federation, <www.mid.ru>, accessed 13.09 2005.

—— (2001c), 'Remarks by President Vladimir Putin of Russia in the Bundestag of the Federal Republic of Germany Berlin, September 25, 2001', The Ministry of Foreign Affairs of the Russian Federation, <www.mid.ru>.

—— (2002), 'Interview with President Vladimir Putin by the Indian newspaper The Hindu and Television Channel Star TV, The Kremlin, Moscow, November 28, 2002', The Ministry of Foreign Affairs of the Russian Federation, <www.mid.ru>, accessed 15.09 2004.

—— (2003a), 'Interview with the Italian News Agency ANSA, Newspaper Corriere della Sera and the Television Company RAI, the Kremlin, Moscow, November 3, 2003', The Ministry of Foreign Affairs of the Russian Federation, <www.mid.ru>, accessed 05.06 2006.

—— (2003b), 'Joint Press Conference of Russian President Vladimir Putin and British Prime Minister Tony Blair, Novo-Ogaryovo, April 29, 2003', The Ministry of Foreign Affairs of the Russian Federation, <www.mid.ru>, accessed 15.09 2004.

Putnik, H. (2003), 'The former Soviet Naval Nuclear Training Center at Paldiski', in Maremäe et al. (eds).

Rapoport, A. and Chammah, A. (1970). *Prisoner's Dilemma* (Ann Arbor: University of Michigan Press).

——, Guyer, M. and Gordon, D. (1976), *The 2 x 2 Game* (Ann Arbor: University of Michigan Press).

Reiter, D. (1996), *Crucible of Beliefs: Learning, Alliances and World Wars* (London: Cornell University Press).

Reiter, E. and Gartner, H. (eds) (2001), *Small States and Alliances* (Heidelberg: Physica-Verlag).

Ries, T. (1988), *Cold Will: The Defence of Finland*, (London: Brassey's).

—— (1999), *Finland and NATO* (Helsinki: Department of Strategic and Defence Studies, National Defence College Finland), http://www.mil.fi/perustietoa/julkaisut/finland_and_nato/index.dsp.

—— and Skorve, J. (1986), *Investigating Kola: A Study of Military Bases Using Satellite Photos* (Oslo: Norwegian Institute of International Affairs).

Risse-Kappen, T. (1994), 'Ideas Do Not Float Freely: Transnational Coalitions, Domestic Structures, and the End of the Cold War', *International Organization* 48, 185-214.

—— (1995a), *Cooperation Among Democracies: The European Influence on U.S. Foreign Policy* (Princeton: Princeton University Press).

—— (1996), 'Collective Identity in a Democratic Community: the Case of NATO', in Katzenstein (ed.), 357-399.

—— (ed.), (1995b), *Bringing Transnational Relations Back In: Non-State Actors, Domestic Structures and International Institutions* (Cambridge: Cambridge University Press).

Riste, O. (1965), *The Neutral Ally. Norway's Relations with Belligerent Powers in the First World War* (London: Allen & Unwin).

Rittberger, V. (ed.), *Global Governance and the United Nations System* (New York: United Nations University Press).

Rogozin, D. (2002), 'Интервью Председателя Комитета Госдумы по Международным Делам Д. О. Рогозина "Я- Государственный Эгоист", опубликованное в еженедельнике "Век" 15 февраля 2002 года' /Interview with the Head of the State Duma's Committee on Foreign Affairs D. O. Rogozin, 15 February 2002 The Ministry of Foreign Affairs of the Russian Federation, (2002-02-18), <http://www.ln.mid.ru>, accessed 04.05 2005.

Rose, R. (1997), 'Baltic Trends: Studies in Co-operation, Conflict, Rights and Obligations', *Studies in Public Policy* 288 (Glasgow: University of Strathclyde).

—— (2000), 'New Baltic Barometer IV: A Survey Study' *Studies in Public Policy* 338. (Glasgow: University of Strathclyde).

Rosecrance, R. (1999), *The Rise of the Virtual State: Wealth and Power in the Coming Century* (New York: Basic Books).

Rosenau, J. (1993), *Turbulence in World Politics: A Theory of Change and Continuity* (New York, London: Harvester Wheatsheaf).

Ruggie, J. (1997), 'Consolidating the European Pillar: The Key to NATO's Future', *Washington Quarterly* 20:1, 109-125.

—— (1998), 'What Makes the World Hang Together? Neo-Utilitarianism and the Social Constructivist Challenge.' *International Organization*, 52:855-885.

Russell, B. (1938), *Power. A New Social Analysis* (London: Allen & Unwin).

Russett, B. and Starr, H. (1992), *World Politics: The Menu for Choice*, Fifth edition. (Oxford: Freeman).

—— et al. (2000), *World Politics: The Menu for Choice,* Sixth edition. (Boston: Bedford/St. Martin's).

Ruth, A. (1984) 'The Second New Nation: The Mythology of Modern Sweden', *Daedalus*, 113:1, 71.

Rynning, S. (2006), *NATO Renewed: The Power and Purpose of Transatlantic Cooperation* (New York: Palgrave).

Saarelainen, J. (1999), *Aspekter på rysk informationskrigföring [Aspects of Russian Information Warfare]*. Series: Taktisk forskningsserie 1/99. (Stockholm: National Defence College).

Safonov, A. (2001), '"The Chief One on Terrorism", interview Granted to the Newspaper Moskovskiye Novosti, 25.10 2001', The Ministry of Foreign Affairs of the Russian Federation, <www.mid.ru>, accessed 13.09 2005.

Sakwa, R. (1996), *Russian Politics and Society*, Second edition (London: Routledge).

—— (2005), 'The 2002-2004 Russian Elections and Prospects for Democracy', *Europe-Asia Studies* 57:3, 369-398.

Saytarly, T. (2004), *Russia: Computer Crimes Statistics* (Computer Crime Research Center), <http://www.crime-research.org/news/13.03.2004/131>

Schafer, M. (1999), 'Cooperative and Conflictual Policy Preferences: The Effect of Identity, Security, and Image of the Other', *Political Psychology* 20:4, 829-844.

—— and Walker, S. (2006), *Beliefs and Leaders in World Politics: Methods and Applications of Operational Code Analysis* (New York: Palgrave Macmillan).

Schimmelpfennig, F. (2000), 'International Socialization in the New Europe: Rational Action in an Institutional Environment', *European Journal of International Relations* 6:1, 109-139.

—— (2003), *The EU, NATO and the Integration of Europe: Rules and Rhetoric* (Cambridge: Cambridge University Press).

Schwartau, W. (1997), 'An Introduction to Information Warfare', in Pfaltzgraff, R. and Shultz, R. (eds).

—— (2002), *Pearl Harbor Dot Com* (Seminole, FL: Interpact Press).

Schweller, R. (1994), 'Bandwagoning for Profit. Bringing the Revisionist State Back In', *International Security* 19:1, 72-107.

—— (2003), 'The Progressiveness of Neoclassical Realism', in Elman and Elman (eds), 311-347.

Sergounin, A. (1998), 'The Russia Dimension', in Mouritzen (ed.), 15-71.

Sherstyuk, V. (2003), 'Information Security of the Russian Federation', *Military Thought* March-April.

Shevtsova, L. (2005), 'Political Leadership in Russia's Transformation', in Motyl et al (eds).

Shore, S. (1998), 'No Fences Make Good Neighbours: The Development of the Canadian-US Security Community, 1871-1940' in Adler and Barnett (eds), 333-267.

Sigal, L. (2000), *Hang Separately: Cooperative Security between the United States and Russia, 1985-1994* (New York: The Century Foundation Press).

Simonsen, S. (2001), 'Compatriot Games. Explaining the "Diaspora Linkage" in Russia's Military Withdrawal from the Baltic States', *Europe-Asia Studies* 53:5, 771-792.

Singer, J. (1963), 'Inter-Nation Influence: A Formal Model.' *American Political Science Review* 57:2, 420-430.

Sinijärv, R. (1995), *Remarks by Mr. Riivo Sinijärv at the Council of the Baltic Sea States Ministerial Meeting*, 19 May 1995, Gdansk, Estonian Ministry of Foreign Affairs [website], http://www.vm.ee/eng/nato/aken_prindi/1349.

Sivonen, P. (2001), 'Finland and NATO', in Bo Huldt et al. (eds), 92-104.

Smith, D. (2003). 'Minority Rights, Multiculturalism and EU Enlargement: The Case of Estonia', *Journal of Ethnopolitics and Minority Issues in Europe*, 1-38.

Smith, G. (1998), 'An Electronic Pearl Harbor? Not Likely', *Issues in Science and Technology*, online, Fall. <http://issues.org/15.1/smith.htm>

Smith, M. (2004), *Europe's Foreign and Security Policy: The Institutionalization of Cooperation* (Cambridge: Cambridge University Press).

Smith, S. (2001), 'Social Constructivism and European Studies', in Christiansen et al. (eds).

Snidal, D. (1986), 'The Game Theory of International Politics', in Oye (ed.).

—— (2002), 'Rational Choice and International Relations', in Carlsnaes et al. (eds), 73-94.

Snyder, C. (ed.) (1997), *Contemporary Security and Strategy* (Basingstoke: Macmillan).

Snyder, J. (2003), '"Is" and "Ought": Evaluating Empirical Aspects of Normative Research', in Elman and Elman (eds), 349-377.

Softa, J. (2004), 'Contending Threat Framing in the Digital Age', (paper presented at the 5th Pan-European IR conference, The Hague, September 9–11, 2004).

Solomon, H. (1998), 'From Marginalized to Dominant Discourse: Reflections on the Evolution of New Security Thinking', in Solomon and van Aardt (eds).

—— and van Aardt, M. (eds), (1998), *'Caring' Security in Africa: Theoretical and Practical Considerations in New Security Thinking,* Monograph No. 20, (Pretoria: South African Institute for Security Studies).

Spruds, A. (2002), 'Perceptions and Interests in Russian-Baltic Relations', in Hubel (ed.), 345-370.

Starr, B. (1999), 'Cyberwarfare: Foreign Government Hackers May Be Getting Help from within the U.S. Government', *ABC News*, March 5, 1999. <http://www.abcnews.com>.

Stein, A. (1990), *Why Nations Cooperate: Circumstance and Choice in International Relations* (Ithaca, NY: Cornell University Press).

Stein, J. (2002), 'Psychological Explanations of International Conflict', in Carlsnaes et al (eds), 292-308.

Steinberg, J. (2003), 'An Elective Partnership: Salvaging Transatlantic Relations', *Survival* 45:2 (Summer), 113-146.

Stimson, J. (ed.) (1991), *Political Analysis* (Ann Arbor, MI: University of Michigan Press).

Sundelius, B. (1989), 'Committing Neutrality in an Antagonistic World', in Sundelius, B. (ed.), 1-13.

—— (ed.), *The Committed Neutral: Sweden's Foreign Policy* (Boulder, CO: Westview Press).

Svennevig, T. (1998), 'Russland ved Østersjøen', *Atlanterhavskomitéens Serier* no. 207 (Oslo: DNAK).

Talbott, S. (2002), *The Russia Hand. A Memoir of Presidential Diplomacy* (New York: Random House).

Theiler, T. (2003), 'Societal Security and Social Psychology', *Review of International Studies* 29:2, 249-268.

Thies, C. (2003), 'Sense and Sensibility in the Study of State Socialisation: A Reply to Kai Alderson', *Review of International Studies* 29:4, 543-550.

Thomas, T. (1996), 'Russian Views on Information Based Warfare', *Airpower Journal* Special Edition <http://www.airpower.maxwell.af.mil/airchronicles/apj/apj96/spec96/thomas.html>

—— (1998), 'Dialectical Versus Empirical Thinking: Ten Key Elements of the Russian Understanding of Information Operations', *Journal of Slavic Military Studies* 11:1.

Tiido, H. (2002), 'Security, 2001, 14 March, 2002', Estonian Ministry of Foreign Affairs, <http://www.vm.ee>, accessed 12.10 2005.

Tiilikainen, T. (1998), *Europe and Finland: Defining the Political Identity of Finland in Western Europe* (Aldershot, UK: Ashgate Publishing).

Trägårdh, L. (2002), 'Sweden and the EU: Welfare State Nationalism and the Spectre of "Europe"', in Hansen and Wæver (eds), 130-181.

Trenin, D., and Lo, B. (2005), *The Landscape of Russian Foreign Policy Decision-Making* (Moscow: Carnegie Moscow Center).

Tromer, E. (2006), 'Baltic Perspectives on the European Security and Defence Policy' in Bailes et al (eds).

Tuomioja, E. (2003), 'Europe needs to Work as a Whole on Defence', *Financial Times*, October 28.

—— (2004), 'Shaping the EU's Future Role in the World', *Ministry of Foreign Affairs of Finland*, October 26.

Vaahtoranta, T. and Forsberg, T. (2000), *Post-Neutral or Pre-Allied? Finnish and Swedish Policies on the EU and NATO as Security Organizations, UPI Working Papers* 29 (Helsinki: Finnish Institute of International Affairs).

Vanhanen, M. (2004a), *Review of Foreign and Security Policy*, April 4, (Helsinki: Ministry of Foreign Affairs), 23 April.

—— (2004b), *Speech in the Debate on the Security and Defence Policy Report in Parliament* (Helsinki: Prime Minister's Office), 20 December.

Vasquez, J. (1997), 'The Realist Paradigm and Degenerative Versus Progressive Research Programs: An Appraisal of Neotraditional Research on Waltz's Balancing Proposition', *American Political Science Review* 91:4, 899-912.

Vatis, M. (2001), 'Cyber Attacks During the War on Terrorism: A Predictive Analysis', Institute for Security Technology Studies, Dartmouth College, 22 September 2001 <www.ists.dartmouth.edu/ISTS/counterterrorism/cyber_ad1.pdf>

Väyrynen, R. (2003), 'Comments on the Finnish Positions', in Ojanen (ed.), 27-29.

Vogt, H. (2004), 'The Art of Caution: The Iraq Crisis and Finnish Foreign Policy Continua', in *The Yearbook of Finnish Foreign Policy 2004* (Helsinki: The Finnish Institute of International Affairs), 63-76.

Volkova, Y. (2006), 'RF calls on Estonia to Grant Political Rights to Ethnic Minorities, 7 March 2006', Factiva Database, ITAR- TASS World Service, <http://global.factiva.com>, accessed 20.03 2006.

Wæver, O. (1995), 'Securitization and Desecuritization', in Lipschutz, R. (ed.), 46-86.

——, et al (1993), *Identity, Migration and the New Security Agenda in Europe* (London: Pinter).

—— (1998), 'Insecurity, Security and Asecurity in the West European Non-War Community', in Adler and Barnett (eds), 69-118.

Wagnsson, C. (2000), *Russian Political Language And Public Opinion On The West, Nato And Chechnya: Securitisation Theory Reconsidered*, New edition. (Stockholm: Stockholm University & the Department for Strategic Studies, Swedish National Defence College).

Wahlbäck, K. (1986), *The Roots of Swedish Neutrality* (Stockholm: The Swedish Institute).

Walker, R. (1997), 'The subject of security', in Krause and Williams (eds), 61-81.

Walker, S. (2004), 'Role Identities and the Operational Codes of Political Leaders', in Hermann (ed.).

―― (ed.) (1987), *Role Theory and Foreign Policy Analysis* (Durham, NC: Duke University Press).

―― and Schafer, M. (forthcoming), 'Operational Code Analysis and Foreign Policy Decision-Making', in Mintz (ed.).

Wallace, W. (ed.) (1990), *The Dynamics of European Integration* (London: Pinter).

Wallensteen, P. (1994), *Towards a Security Community in the Baltic Region: Patterns of Peace and Conflict*, Baltic University Secretariat (Uppsala: Uppsala University).

Walt, S. (1987), *The Origins of Alliances* (Ithaca, NY: Cornell University Press).

―― (1998), 'International Relations: One World, Many Theories', *Foreign Policy* Spring, Issue 110, 29-46.

―― (1999), 'Rigor or Rigor Mortis? Rational Choice and Security Studies', *International Security* 23:4 (Spring), 5-48.

Waltz, K. (1959), *Man, the State, and War* (New York: Columbia University Press).

―― (1979), *Theory of International Politics* (New York: Random House).

―― (1993), 'The Emerging Structure of International Politics', *International Security*, 18:2, 45–73.

Weiss, L. (1998), *The Myth of the Powerless State: Governing the Economy in a Global Era* (Cambridge: Polity Press).

Weiss, T. (ed.) (1993), *Collective Security in a Changing World* (Boulder, CO: Lynne Rienner).

Wendt, A. (1994), 'Collective Identity Formation and the International State', *American Political Science Review* 88: 384-396.

―― (1999), *Social Theory of International Politics* (Cambridge: Cambridge University Press).

Wight, M. (1978), *Power Politics*. Edited by Hedley Bull and Carsten Holbraad. (Leicester: Leicester University Press).

Williams, M. and Neumann, I. (2000), 'From Alliance to Security Community: NATO, Russia, and the Power of Identity', *Millennium: Journal of International Studies* 29:2, 357-387.

Winnerstig, M. (2001), 'Sweden and NATO', in Bo Huldt et al. (eds), 76-91.

Wolfers, A. (1962), *Discord and Collaboration: Essays on International Politics* (Baltimore: The Johns Hopkins Press).

Yakovenko, A. (2003), 'Statement regarding likely adoption by Estonian Parliament of Aliens Law Amendments. 17.12. 2003', The Ministry of Foreign Affairs of the Russian Federation, <www.mid.ru>, accessed 03.05 2005.

Zhdannikov, V. (1994), 'Russia Concerned About Possibility of NATO Expansion', Sevodnya, 6 January, p.1. *Current Digest of the Post-Soviet Press* vol 46: 1.

Zimmerman, W. (2002), *The Russian People and Foreign Policy. Russian Elite and Mass Perspectives, 1993-2000* (Washington: Princeton Paperbacks).

Media and Institutional Publications, incl. Databases and Websites

Aftonbladet, 20 November 1999.

Agence Europe (2004a), 'EU/Russia - Protocol on extending PCA to ten accession countries signed, due to joint declarations', *Factiva database* (28.04 2004) <http://global.factiva.com>, accessed 10.10 2005.

BBC Monitoring Former Soviet Union (2004), 'Kremlin insider gives upbeat account of EU-Russia talks. Interview with President Putin's aide Sergey Yastrzhembskiy, 22 May, 2004', Factiva Database, <http://global.factiva.com>, accessed 03.12 2005.

BBC News (1998), 'World: America's CIA chief fears "cyber attacks"', 25 June. <http://news.bbc.co.uk/1/hi/world/americas/119657.stm>

CBSS. Council of the Baltic Sea States (1992a), *Copenhagen Declaration*, Conference of Foreign Ministers of the Baltic Sea States, Copenhagen, 5-6 March 1992.

—— (1992b), *Terms of Reference for the Council of the Baltic Sea States*, Conference of the Foreign Ministers of the Baltic Sea States, Copenhagen, 5-6 March 1992.

CBSS-CSO. (1993), *The First Year of the Council Activity*, Report of the Committee of Senior Officials, 16 March 1993.

—— (2003), *Members of the WGNRS*.

CERT Coordination Center (2005), CERT/CC Statistics 1988-2004. CERT-CC. <http://www.cert.org/stats/cert_stats.html>

Computer Security Institute (2004), *CSI/FBI Computer Crime and Security Survey*. Computer Security Institute.

CSCE. Conference on Security and Cooperation in Europe (1992), *CSCE Helsinki Document 1992. The Challenges of Change*, <http://www.osce.org/documents/mcs/1992/07/4046_en.pdf>

Dagens Nyheter, 17 December 2003.

—— 21 March 2004.

Doktrina informatsionnoj bezapastnosti Rossiskoj Federatsii [The Information Security Doctrine of the Russian federation] (2000), Moscow: The Russian Presidential Commission on Information Security. Available at http://www.scrf.gov.ru/documents/decree/2000_pr-1895.shtml

DSBTF (2001), *Protecting the Homeland. Report of the Defense Science Board Task Force on Defensive Information Operations*. 2000 Summer Study Volume II. (Department of Defense, Washington, D.C. <http://www.iwar.org.uk/iwar/index.htm>

'e-russia' (2001), <http://www.e-russia.ru/program>

Eesti Varbariigi Kaitseministeerium (2003), Avalik Arvamus ja Riigikaitse 2000-2003 (Public Opinion and Defence Forces 2000-2003), Estonian Ministry of Defence, <www.mod.gov.ee>, accessed 23.06 2004.

Estonia Today. (1995), 'The Paldiski Nuclear Facilities: A precedent in international co-operation', 8 September 1995, Estonian Ministry of Foreign Affairs [website], http://www.vm.ee.

Estonian Ministry of Environment. (1995), *Environmental Action Plan for Paldiski*, Tallinn, 20 January 1995.

Estonian Ministry of Foreign Affairs (2001), *National Security Concept of Estonia*, adopted by the Parliament. Tallinn.

—— (2004), 'Estonia Today. Support for NATO Membership', Estonian Ministry of Foreign Affairs, (February) <www.vm.ee>.

—— (2004), *National Security Concept of the Republic of Estonia*. Tallinn. <http://www.vm.ee/eng/kat_177/4665.html>

—— (2005a), 'Estonia and Russia. Important Visists and Meetings. 06 October, 2005', Estonian Ministry of Foreign Affairs, <www.vm.ee>, accessed 20.03 2006.

—— (2005b), 'Estonia Today. Support for NATO Membership', Estonian Ministry of Foreign Affairs, (April 2005) <www.vm.ee>, accessed 10.10 2005.

EU (2003), *European Security Strategy* (Brussels and Paris: The EU Commission). Available on 5 June 2006 at < http://www.iss-eu.org/solana/solanae.pdf>

European Commission. (1999a), *Review of Existing and Future Requirements for Decommissioning Nuclear Facilities in the CIS*, a report produced for the European Commission, Directorate General XI, EUR 18945 EN.

—— (1999b), *Radioactive Waste Management in the Central and Eastern European Countries. Directorate-General for Environment, Nuclear Safety and Civil Protection*, compiled and edited by S. Webster, DGXI-C2, EUR 19154 EN.

European Constitution, http://ue.eu.int/igcpdf/eng/04/cg00/cg00087-re01.eng04.pdf

European Union (2004), *EUROBAROMETER EB 61 - CC-EB 2004.1. Comparative Highlights*, Brussels, 11.

Federal News Service (2006), 'Press Conference with Effective Policy Fund President Gleb Pavlovsky on President Vladimir Putin's Address to the Federal Assembly', Factiva database, (11.05 2006) <http://global.factiva.com>, accessed 08.06 2006.

Federal News Service Russia (2004), 'Press Conference with State Duma Committee for Foreign Affairs, Chair Konstantin Kosachev, May 19, 2004', Factiva Database, <http://global.factiva.com>, accessed 03.12 2005.

Government of Finland (2004), *Finnish Security and Defence Policy 2004* (Helsinki: Prime Minister's Office: Publications 18).

Helsingin Sanomat (International Edition), 22 January 2006.

—— (International Edition), 12 September 2005.

—— (International Edition), 23 March 2004.

—— (International Edition), 28 February 2005.

IAEA (2003a), *Annual Report 2002* (Vienna: IAEA).

—— (2003b), *Nuclear Power Reactors in the World*, Reference Data Series No. 2, April (Vienna: IAEA).

IDC (2003), *IDC's Information Society Index* (International Data Corporation). http://www.idc.com/groups/isi/main.html

IFSH (1996), *The European Security Community (ESC): the Security Model for the Twenty-First Century*, Institute for Peace Research and Security Policy at the University of Hamburg (IFSH), (Baden-Baden: Nomos).

Information Technology in Public Administration of Estonia (2003), (Tallinn: Ministry of Economic Affairs and Communications, Department of State Information Systems and the Estonian Informatics Centre).

ITU (2003), *ITU Digital Access Index: World's First Global ICT Ranking*. International Telecommunication Union http://www.itu.int/newsarchive/press_releases/2003/30.html

Kontseptsija informatsionnoj bezopastnosti setej svjazi obsjtjevo poljzovannija vzaimouvjazannoj seti svjazi Rossiskoj Federatsii [The Russian Federation's Concept of Information Security in Common Communication Networks] (2003), Moscow: The Ministry of Information Technology and Communications.

Ministry of Defence (2004), *All set for Swedish led EU Battle Group*, Stockholm, November 22.

Ministry of Foreign Affairs of Russia (2000), 'Foreign Policy Concept of the Russian Federation', The Ministry of Foreign Affairs of the Russian Federation, (10.07 2000), <www.mid.ru>.

—— (2001a), 'Russian Federal Assembly State Duma Council, Message to Congress of United States of America and American People, 13-09-2001', The Ministry of Foreign Affairs of the Russian Federation, <www.mid.ru>.

—— (2001b), 'Situation in the Chechen Republic (Factsheets), 29-08-2001', The Ministry of Foreign Affairs of the Russian Federation, <www.mid.ru>.

—— (2003), 'List of Main Claims and Recommendations as Regards the Rights of National Minorities Offered by International Organizations and NGO to Estonia (Reference paper), 18.12 2003', The Ministry of Foreign Affairs of the Russian Federation, <www.mid.ru>, accessed 03.04 2005.

—— (2004), 'Russian MFA Information and Press Department Commentary Regarding the Human Rights Situation in Latvia and Estonia', The Ministry of Foreign Affairs of the Russian Federation, <www.mid.ru>, 03.04 2005.

—— (2001), 'Statement by Official Spokesman of the Ministry of Foreign Affairs of Russia, Apropos Media Reports about the Appointment of Usama bin Ladin Commander-in-Chief of Taliban Armed Militias in Afghanistan', The Ministry of Foreign Affairs of the Russian Federation, (2001-08-30), <www.mid.ru>, accessed 2006-05-21.

Ministry of the Interior of Russia (2004), "Sostojanie prestupnosti v Russiskoj Federatsii za janvar – dekabr 2004 goda" [Crime in the Russian Federation from January 2004 to December 2004] http://www.mvd.ru/files/3157.pdf

NATO (1999), *Strategic Concept*, press release (Brussels: NATO Headquarters). Available on 5 June 2006 at http://www.nato.int/docu/pr/1999/p99-065e.htm

NIS Nuclear Trafficking Abstracts Database http://www.nti.org/db/nistraff/index.html

PBS Online (2002), 'Frontline hackers' <http://www.pbs.org/wgbh/pages/frontline/shows/hackers/whoare/notable.html>

PCCIP (2002), Fact Sheet. President's Commission on Critical Infrastructure Protection (accessed 20 June 2002), <http://www.info-sec.com/pccip/web/backgrd.html>

Principles of Estonian Information Policy. Tallinn: Estonian Informatics Centre (accessed: 16 March 2003), <http://www.ria.ee/english/principles.html>

Public Opinion Foundation (2001), 'Russia and NATO', Public Opinion Foundation, Database, Russia, (04.10 2001), <www.fom.ru/report/map/>, accessed 23.06 2004.

—— (2002), 'NATO Expansion', Public Opinion Foundation, Database, Russia, (05.12 2002), <www.fom.ru/report/map/>, accessed 23.06 2004.

—— (2003), 'Problems and Threats', Public Opinion Foundation, Database, Russia, (16.01 2003), <www.fom.ru/report/map/>, accessed 23.06 2004.

—— (2004), 'NATO Expansion', Public Opinion Foundation, Database, Russia, (15.04 2004), <www.fom.ru/report/map/>, accessed 23.06 2004.

Regeringskansliet Stockholm (2002a), *Sveriges Säkerhetspolitiska Linje*, February 11.

—— (2002b), *Statement of Government Policy in the Parliamentary Debate on Foreign Affairs*, February 13.

—— (2004), *Statement of Government Policy in the Parliamentary Debate on Foreign Affairs*, February 11.

RIA Novosti (2006), 'Russian FM Lavrov on border talks with Latvia, Estonia', Factiva database, (7 June 2006), <http://global.factiva.com>, accessed 08.06 2006.

Rossiiskaya Gazeta (1997), 'Russian National Security Blueprint, 1997', FBIS-SOV-97-364, 30 December 1997 <http://www.fas.org/nuke/guide/russia/doctrine/blueprint.html>, accessed 20.10 2005.

Russian National Security Concept (2000), signed by President Vladimir Putin on January 10, 2000, <www.russiaeurope.mid.ru/russiastrat2000.html>, accessed 22.10 2005.

Sankt Petersburg Times (2005), 'For Stance on Baltic Borders', Factiva database, (12 July), <www.factiva.com>, accessed 20.06 2006.

'Sostojanie prestupnosti v Rossiskoj Federatsii za janvar - dekabr 2004 goda' (Moscow: Ministry of Internal Affairs), <http://www.mvd.ru/files/3157.pdf>

State Programme. Approved by the Government of Estonia (2000), '*Integration in Estonian Society 2000-2007*', (14 March, 2000), www.riik.ee/saks/ikomisjon/programme.htm , 23 May 2006.

Swedish Government (2004), *Sweden's Cooperation in the Euro-Atlantic Partnership Council (EACP), and Partnership for Peace (PfP)*. Government Communication 2003/04:84, 11 March 2004.

U.S. Government (2002), *National Strategy for Homeland Security* (Washington D.C., Office for Homeland Security), Available on 5 <http://www.whitehouse.gov/homeland/book/nat_strat_hls.pdf>

—— (2003), *The National Strategy to Secure Cyberspace* (Washington, DC: The White House).

—— Department of Defense (2000), 'Military Critical Technologies, Part III: Developing Critical Technologies, Section 10: Information Technology' (Dulles, VA: Defense Threat Reduction Agency), <http://www.dtic.mil/mctl/>

UN (1998), General Assembly Resolution 53/70, U.N. GAOR, 53rd Sess., UN Doc. A/RES/53/70 (New York: United Nations).

"Vistuplenie predstavitelja Rossii A.N. Anatonova v Pervom Komitete 55-j sessii GA OON pri predstavlenii proekta rezoljutsii "Dostizjenija v sfere informatizatsii i telekommunizatsii v kontekste mezjdunarodnoj bezopastnosti" 19 oktjabrja 2000 goda", [Presentation by the Russian representative A.I. Antonova in the first committe of the 55th meeting of GA OON in the UN, during the discussion of a draft resolution for 'Actions concerning information and communications technology in an international security context', 19 October 2000]. Accessed May 26, 2005.

http://www.ln.mid.ru/Ns-dmo.nsf/arh32569F10031EB934325699C003C102A?OpenDocument

Webster's Third International Dictionary of the English Language (1976), Unabridged, Volume 1 A to G (Chicago, IL: Encyclopedia Britannica, Inc.).

WEF (2004), *Network Readiness Index*. The World Economic Forum. <http://www.weforum.org/pdf/Global_Competitiveness_Reports/Reports/GITR_2004_2005/Networked_Readiness_Index_Rankings.pdf>

WGNRS (1993a), *Interim report of the Working Group on Nuclear and Radiation Safety*, Helsinki, 26 February 1993.

—— (1993b), *Progress report and recommendations of the working group to the CBSS CSO on the decommissioning of the Paldiski training reactor facilities*, General Headquarters of the Russian Navy, 16 April 1993, in WGNRS 1994b, annex 2.

—— (1993c), *Statement on the visit of the WG to the Paldiski Training Center on the Pakri Peninsula in Estonia on 9 September 1993*, in WGNRS 1994b, annex 1.

—— (1994a), *Action plan of the working group on nuclear and radiation safety for 1994/95*, 15 April 1994, in WGNRS, 1994b, annex 5.

—— (1994b), *Report of the Working Group on Nuclear and Radiation Safety*, Tallinn, 24-25 May 1994.

—— (1995), *Status Report of the Chairman*, Novgorod, 26 January 1995.

—— (1999), *Activity Report from the Working Group on Nuclear and Radiation Safety (WGNRS)*, Chairman's report to the Committee of Senior Officials, 28 April 1999.

—— (2000), *Chairman's report to the Committee of Senior Officials*, Chairman of the Working Group on Nuclear and Radiation Safety, Raimo Mustonen, 17 April 2000.

—— (2001), *Annual Report of the Working Group on Nuclear and Radiation Safety*, 27 April 2001.

Index

accommodation
    and power disparity 21–2
    and small states 21
actors
    and conception of power 3–4
    and definition 3
Afghanistan, and Russian warnings 108
agents, and definition 3
Ahtisaari, Martti 55
al-Qaeda 131
American Citibank, and cyberattack on 134
Amsterdam Treaty (1997), and Petersberg Tasks 62
anarchy, and government relationships 3
appeasement, and grand strategy 151, 152
Armenia, and complementarity ('Maastricht neutrality') 21
assertion, and small states 20
authority, and power 12
avoidance
    and great power confrontations 23–7
    and power relations 26
    and small states 20

balance of power 23–7
balanced closure 20
balanced openness 20–1
balancing, and grand strategy 151, 152
Baldwin, David 90
    and balance of power 24–5
Balladur plan 34
BALTBAT 34
BALTDEFCOL 34
Baltic Ring Electricity Cooperation 90
Baltic Sea region
    and change processes in 6–7
    and Cold War 29–30, 150
    and cooperative security 43
        absence of military contingency planning 179
        development of 178–9
        scepticism towards 179
    and definition of 5–6
    and Germany, 'Russia first' approach 36
    and national self-conceptions 184–6
    and NATO membership 35–6
    and post-Cold War security developments 30–7
    and power disparity 1, 89
        historical perspective 2
        nuclear power 90
        post-1991 180–4
    and prospects for 186
    and regional security complex 149
    and Russia
        military capabilities 184
        strategy of 36–7, 181
        weak interest in 112
    and security community 121, 151
    and security thinking 38–42
        causal beliefs 40–2
        Common Security 42–3
        cooperative security 43
        principled beliefs 39–40
        understanding of security 44
        worldviews 38–9
    see also Baltic states; entries for individual countries; Nordic countries; nuclear and radiation safety; Russia
Baltic states
    and defence cooperation 34
    and 'euroatlantic structures' 35
    and European Union, membership of 35, 41–2
    and institutional integration 61
    and membership of CSCE 34
    and national self-conceptions 185
    and NATO 35, 41–2, 180, 181
    and Nordic countries, defence assistance from 33, 181
    and OSCE regional table 34
    and Popular Fronts 30

and post-Cold War security
    developments 30–7
and Russia 180
    border negotiations 34–5
    confrontational approach 36
    negative perception of 41–2
    troop withdrawal 30, 31–2
    understanding of security 44
and security thinking 38–42
    causal beliefs 40–2
    structural context 61
    worldviews 38–9
and Soviet Union
    blockade by 30
    ex-Soviet citizens 31, 101–2,
        117–18, 118–19
    recognition of independence by 30
and Swedish diplomacy on behalf of
    31–2
and threat perceptions
    cognitive factors 113, 121
    domestic influences on 112–13
    traditional approaches to 111–14
see also Baltic Sea region; entries for
    individual countries
BALTNET 34
BALTRON 34
bandwaggoning 20 n31, 21 n37
    and grand strategy 151, 152
bargaining power, and power disparity 92–3
Berlin Plus agreement 65, 66
Beslan tragedy 110
Bildt, Carl 31, 59, 69
Blix, Hans 59
Brams, S 173
Bush, George W 181
Buzan, B 149

capabilities
    and information warfare capability
        141–4
    and power 10, 11, 126–7
    and power estimation 25–6
caste system 17, 18
causal beliefs, and influence on security
    thinking 40–2
causality, and power 13
Central and Eastern Europe, and European
    security community 37–8

Centre Party (Finland) 55, 56
Centre Party (Sweden) 60
Chechnya 33, 109, 180
Checkel, J 38, 116
Chernobyl 77, 83
China, and digital power 141
    and information warfare capability 142,
        146
Christian Democrats (Sweden) 60
CIS, and accommodation with Russia 23
Clinton, Bill 32
cognitive dissonance 178
Cold War
    and Baltic Sea region 29–30
    and end of 30, 180
collaboration, and small states 21
Common Security 42–3
    and causal beliefs 40
    and cooperative security 43
competition, and grand strategy 151,
    152
complementarity 21
Computer Emergency Readiness Team
    Coordination Center (USA) 132
Conference for Security and Cooperation in
    Europe (CSCE)
    and Baltic states admitted 34
    and Helsinki Summit (1992) 31
    and Paris Summit (1990) 30
    see also Organization for Security and
        Cooperation in Europe (OSCE)
confidence-building, and cooperative
    security 5
conflict resolution, and government
    relationships 3
conflicting preferences, and power 10
confrontation
    and avoidance of 9, 11, 13, 26
    and power 9–10
    and responses to 14–15
        great power 23–7
        small states 19–21
constructivism, and international politics 46
context, and identity 16
cooperation
    and game theory, power equality games
        156–60
    and government relationships 3
cooperative security

and Baltic Sea region
    development in 178–9
    scepticism towards 179
and Baltic states 34
and Common Security 43
and confidence-building 5
and definition of 5
and nature of 1
and power disparity 2, 177
and process of developing 177
and threat 2
Copenhagen Summit (EU, 1993) 32
Council of the Baltic Sea States (CBSS) 36, 183
    and establishment of 76
    and nuclear and radiation safety 77
    see also Working Group on Nuclear and Radiation Safety
cyberspace, *see* digital power disparity

Dahl, R 10, 11, 14
deadlock, and grand strategy 151
deference, and power 14 n19
denial-of-service attacks, and digital power 132
Denmark
    and accommodation with Germany 21
    and Baltic states, defence assistance to 33
    and 'base and ban' decisions 40–1
Denning, Dorothy 131
dependence, and power 12–13
digital power disparity 145–7
    and cyberwar/cyberterrorism 130–4
    and denial-of-service attacks 132
    and digital gap 136, 145
    and domains of 134–5
    and fear-mongering 130–2
    and information dominance 129
    and information warfare capability 129, 141–4, 145–6, 182
    and interstate relations 132–4
    and military strategic perspective 129
    and network society 129
        rankings of 140–1
        vulnerability of 140–1
    and non-state agents 143, 144–5
    and power disparity 128–30, 143–4, 181–2

and role identities 135–7, 145
and threat perceptions 130–1
    realistic 146–7
and variable scope of 137–40
and weak/strong powers 144–5
discourses, and practices 99–100
domination, and grand strategy 151

Ekeus, Rolf 59
environmental movements, in Baltic states 30
epistemic communities
    and definition of 73
    and influence of 73–4
    and Paldiski case 74, 75
        game theory analysis 163–6
    and power disparity 91–3, 95
        empirical evidence 93–5
    see also Working Group on Nuclear and Radiation Safety
estimation, and power 25–6
Estonia
    and digital power 133
        cybersecurity 133
        cyberthreats 135
        information warfare capability 142, 143
        limited attention to 139–40, 145
        network ranking 140–1
    and European Union
        membership of 101
        motives for joining 104
    and integration policy 102, 118
    and national identity, language 100–1
    and NATO 180
        membership of 101, 181
        motives for joining 104
    and Popular Front 30
    and post-Cold War history
        formal independence 101
        proto-independence 100–1
        state building phase 101
    and Russia 99–100
        border negotiations 34–5, 102
        integration policy 102
        power disparity 97
        relations with 163–4
        role identities 97

Russian-speaking minority 31, 101–2, 117–18
security community 111, 119
stress on cooperation 104
threat perceptions 98, 102–3
troop withdrawal 32, 101
and Soviet blockade of 30
and threat perceptions 100–4
cognitive factors 113, 121
domestic influences on 112–13
identity formation 115
international socialization 119–20
Russia 98
soft threats 103
terrorism 103, 110–11
traditional approaches to 111–14
trends in 109–11
see also Baltic states; Paldiski nuclear submarine training facility; Working Group on Nuclear and Radiation Safety

Euro-Atlantic Partnership Council 51, 166

European Union
and Baltic states 35, 41–2
and cooperative security 1
and Copenhagen Summit (1993) 32
and NATO 63, 67, 69
Berlin Plus agreement 65, 66
and Northern Dimension policy 178
and power politics 20
and Russia 117, 178
Estonia's Russian-speaking minority 118–19
Russia-EU agreement 33
and security integration 49, 54
crisis management 59–60, 64
dynamics of 66
European integration 66
intergovernmentalism 67
international environment 66–7
rapid reaction forces 65
solidarity 63
Sweden and Finland 62–4
tightening of 65
and small states 20
and United States 67

Finland
and accommodation with Soviet Union 21, 22
and cooperative security 1
and European Union 67–8
as core of security policy 52
crisis management 62, 64
cultural connectedness 53
defence integration 63
game theory analysis 169–70
impact of weakened 68
membership of 52, 167
military capability of 63
NATO/EU distinction 63, 64
opportunities presented by 62
rapid reaction forces 65
resistance to majority decision-making 62–3
as safe security option 68
security integration 54, 68
solidarity clause 63
and institutional environment 49
European Union 62–4
NATO 64–5
permissive 61–2
and military nonalignment 36 n15, 45
accommodation of neutralism 53
adaptation 49–50
Cold War experiences 51
game theory analysis 166–7, 169–70
impact of EU membership 65–6, 67–8
maintenance of 61
motives for 48, 51, 52
national identity 185–6
as pragmatic policy choice 52
viability of 55
and national identity 53, 54–5
and NATO 35–6, 65, 67, 70, 167
attitude of political parties 55–6
game theory analysis 169–70
low cost of non-membership 54
open-door stance towards 68
political debate over 55–6, 68
relationship with 51
support for strong 64
and nuclear power 90
and security integration 48
and security policy 70–1

Defence White Paper (2004) 55
failure to solve national security 68–9
future development of 69–70
identity 49, 50–1, 53, 70
identity/interests interplay 46–7
identity/structure interplay 45–6, 50–1, 63–4
impact of weakened EU 68
instrumentalist perspective 52
neutrality 51, 53
normative anchoring 53–4
normative perspective 53
political parties 55–6
post-9/11 68
realist explanation of 52
and worldview 39
Finnish-Soviet Treaty (1948) 51

game theory 8, 149 n1, 154
and Baltic Sea region strategies 171
Estonian-Russian power equality 163–6
Swedish/Finnish military non-alignment 166–70
and explanation of 172–6
and security strategy
limitations of models 171–2
power disparity games 160–3
power equality games 156–60
strength of models 171
and world politics
as conceptual framework 155
as formal model 155–6
as metaphor 154–5
Geijer, Erik Gustaf 57
Germany
and Baltic Sea region, 'Russia first' approach 36
and nuclear power 90
and reunification of 1, 2, 30
and Russia 36
Gorbachev, Mikhail 29, 30, 84
government relationships
and anarchical mode 3
and cooperative mode 3
grand strategy, *see* security strategy
great powers
and confrontation avoidance between 23–7
and role identity 16
Green Party (Sweden) 60

Haas, Peter M 73
Haftendorn, H, and security 6
Halonen, Tarja 55, 56
Hammarskjöld, Dag 59
Hamre, John 130, 134
Hanson, Per Albin 57
hard power, and security strategy 149
hegemonic stability, and power disparity 92
HELCOM 36, 183
Helsinki Summit (1975) 30
Helsinki Summit (1992) 31
Herrmann, R 16
Huldt, B 59
Hungary, and collaboration with Germany 21

ideas
and causal beliefs 40–2
and definition of 38
and principles beliefs 39–40
and worldviews 38–9
identity
and conceptions of 4 n3
as context-bound 16
and integration processes 2, 47
and interests 46–7
and international socialization 115–17, 120
and national self-conceptions 184–6
and power disparity 4, 15–16, 48, 186
and power relations 4, 15–16
and role conception of 15–16
and security integration 49
and security policy 114–16
and structure 45–6
see also role identities
Ilves, Toomas Hendrik 41–2
Independent Commission on Disarmament and Security Issues, *see* Palme Commission
India, and information warfare capability 146
INF (US-Soviet) missile treaty (1988) 29
influence, and power disparity 14

information revolution, and state power
  and common approach to 123
  and conceptual framework 125–8
    definition of power 125
    domain of power 125–6
    means 128
    power resources 126–7
    scope of power 125
    soft power 127
  and cyberspace 125
  and digital divide 127
  and international relations approach to 123–4
  and national network society 127
  and national security 123
  and network society 127
  see also digital power disparity
integration, *see* security integration
intentionality, and power 12
interests
  and identity 46–7
  and norms 46
intergovernmental institutions
  and European Union security integration 67
  and government relationships 3
internalization, and international socialization 116
International Atomic Energy Agency (IAEA) 80
International Data Corporation 140
International Maritime Organization 183
international organizations, and power disparity 183
international relations
  and power 10
  and role identities 15–16, 126
international socialization 115–17
  and explanatory power of 119–20
  and identity 120–1
International Telecommunications Union 140
internet, and expansion of 123
Ivanov, S 109, 184

Jervis, R 178

Kaliningrad 184
Knudsen, O, and security 6

Kola Peninsula 29
Kosovo crisis 107, 181
Kozyrev, Andrei 106

Latvia
  and ex-Soviet citizens 31
  and national self-conception 185
  and NATO 180, 181
  and Popular Front 30
  and Russia
    border negotiations 34–5
    troop withdrawal 32
  and Soviet blockade of 30
  see also Baltic states
Left Party (Sweden) 60
legitimacy, and authority 12
'Lenin, Vladimir' 134
Leningrad Nuclear Power Plant 83
Liberal Party (Sweden) 60
Lindh, Anna 58–9
Lipponen, Paavo 55
Lithuania
  and ex-Soviet citizens 31
  and NATO 180, 181
  and nuclear power 90
  and Popular Front 30
  and Russia
    border negotiations 34–5
    troop withdrawal 32
  and Soviet blockade of 30
  see also Baltic states
Lo, Bobo 182, 184
Lukes, S 10, 17, 18

Maastricht Treaty 59
  and complementarity 21
Mearsheimer, John 10
Meri, Lennart 100
military power, and balance of power 24–5
Moderate Party (Sweden) 60
Montreux Treaty 22
Moravcsik, A 162

National Coalition Party (Finland) 55, 56
national network society 127
  and rankings of 140–1
  and vulnerability of 140–1
nationalism, and Russia 185
NATO

and Baltic states 35, 41–2, 180, 181
and cooperative security 1, 43
and crisis management 64–5
and European Union 63, 67, 69
    Berlin Plus agreement 65, 66
and expansion of
    post-9/11 35
    post-Cold War 32–3
as permissive institution 65
and small states 20, 21–2
network society 127
    and rankings of 140–1
    and vulnerability of 140–1
neutral state, as role identity 16
neutrality
    and difficulty in maintaining 20
    and small states 19
Niinistö, Sauli 56
non-alignment
    as role identity 16
    and small states 19
    see also Finland; Sweden
Nordic countries
    and Baltic states
        defence assistance to 33
        influence of principled beliefs 39–40
    and Cold War 29–30
    and Russia, 'counter-power' strategy 182
    and security thinking 38–42
        causal beliefs 40–2
        Common Security 42–3
        cooperative security 43
        post-Cold War 180
        principled beliefs 39–40
        understanding of security 44
        worldviews 38–9
    see also entries for individual countries
norms, and interests 46
Norway
    and accommodation with Soviet Union 22
    and Baltic states, defence assistance to 33
    and 'base and ban' decisions 40–1
    and Svalbard 20–1
nuclear and radiation safety
    and focus on Eastern European countries 76–7
    and power disparity
        empirical evidence 93–5
        epistemic communities 91–3
    see also Working Group on Nuclear and Radiation Safety
Nye, Joseph 127

observability, and power 13–14
Organization for Security and Cooperation in Europe (OSCE)
    and limited success of 34
    and regional tables 34
    see also Conference for Security and Cooperation in Europe (CSCE)

Paldiski International Expert Reference Group (PIERG) 89
Paldiski nuclear submarine training facility 32, 74, 87–8
    and epistemic community 75
        role of 75
    and expert support for Estonia 88–9
    and lack of information about 84–5
    and limited access to 87–8
    and nuclear risk assessment 85
    and Russian Navy 86–7
    and Russian withdrawal from 74–5
    and transfer to Estonia 75, 88, 89
    see also nuclear and radiation safety; Working Group on Nuclear and Radiation Safety
Palme, Olof 42, 57, 59
Palme Commission 57–8
    and Common Security 42–3
Paris CSCE Summit (1990) 30
Partnership for Peace 33, 51, 166
Pentagon, and cyberattacks on 134
Petersberg Tasks 62
Poland, and democratization of 29
Popular Fronts, and Baltic states 30
power
    and appearance of 11
    and authority 12
    and capabilities 10, 11, 126–7
        information warfare 141–4
    and causality 13
    and conflicting preferences 10
    and confrontation 9–10
        avoidance of 9, 11, 13

and contextual nature of 4, 181–3
and deference 14 n19
and definition of 3–4, 125
and dependence 12–13
and domain of 125–6
  digital power 134–5
and estimation/measurement of 25–6
and identity 4, 15–16
and intentionality 12
and means 128
and observability 13–14
as possession 18
and power structures 13
and relational approach to 10–11
and role identities 15–16, 126
  digital power 135–7
and role of 4
and scope of 125
  digital power 137–40
as social relationship 4
as socially constructed 4
and soft power 127, 151
as subjective phenomenon 26
and unobservable aspects of 9, 11–12, 13–14
see also digital power disparity; power disparity
power disparity
  and Baltic Sea region 1, 89
    historical perspective 2
    nuclear power 90
    post-1991 180–4
    Russian military capability 184
  and bargaining power 92–3
  and confrontation 14
    possible responses to 14–15
  and continuing significance of 1
  and cooperative security 2, 177
  and definition of 89
  and effects of 1, 2
  and epistemic communities 73–4, 91–3, 95
  and great power confrontations 23–7
  and hegemonic stability 92
  and identity 4, 15–16, 48, 186
  and influence 14
  and integration processes 6–7
  and international organizations 183
  and international socialization 119

  and national self-conceptions 185
  and relative gains theory 92
  and role identity 97
  and small states 19–23
    empirical record 21–3
    possible strategies 19–21
  and threat 1, 2
  and time dimension of 17–18
  see also digital power disparity
power relations, and time dimension of 17–18
power structures 13
practices, and discourses 99–100
Primakov, Yevgenii 106–7
principal-agent relationships 3
principled beliefs, and influence on security thinking 39–40
prisoner's dilemma 154–5
Putin, Vladimir 105, 108, 181

rational choice, and international politics 46
regional security complex
  and definition of 149
  and security strategy 149–50
relationships, see government relationships
relative gains theory, and power disparity 92
resistance
  and power 10
  and small states 20
role identities
  and digital power 135–7, 145
  and international relations 15–16
  and national self-conceptions 184–6
  and power 15–16, 126
  and power disparity 97
  and security strategy 153–4, 171–2
Romania, and collaboration with Germany 21
Rosenau, James 10
Russell, Bertrand 12
Russia
  and accommodation by neighbouring states 23
  and Baltic Sea region 1–2
    military capabilities 184
    strategy towards 36–7, 181
    weak interest in 112
  and Baltic states 180

acceptance of NATO membership 181
confrontational towards 36
Near Abroad doctrine 101
Russian minority in 101
troop withdrawal 30, 31–2
understanding of security 44
and digital power 132–3
  cyberthreats 135, 138
  digital gap 136, 145
  information warfare capability 142, 143, 146
  network ranking 140–1
and energy policy 183
and Estonia
  border negotiations 34–5, 102
  power disparity 97
  relations with 163–4
  role identities 97
  Russian minority in 32, 101–2
  Russian-speaking minority 117–18
  security community 111, 119
  threat perceptions 98–9, 102–3
  troop withdrawal 32, 101
and European Union 117, 178
  Estonia's Russian-speaking minority 118–19
  Russian-EU agreement 33
and national self-conception 185
and nationalism 185
and NATO
  changing attitudes towards 105–7
  opposition to expansion of 33, 41, 105, 180
  perceived as threat 98, 105, 106, 107
and Nordic countries 182
and nuclear power 90
  potential use of 90–1
and oil transport dispute 182–3
and pro-Western direction of 120
and threat perceptions 98–9, 105–9, 134–5
  digital gap 136
  domestic influences on 112–13
  identity formation 116
  impact of events 113–14
  international socialization 119–20
  NATO 98, 105, 106, 107
  realist explanation of 111–12
  scope of digital power 138
  terrorism 107–9, 110, 112, 114
  traditional approaches to 111–14
  trends in 109–11
  United States 105
and Ukraine 183
and United States 181
  cyber-relationship 133–4, 134–5
  digital power 136–7
  perceived as threat 105
  see also Paldiski nuclear submarine training facility; Soviet Union; Working Group on Nuclear and Radiation Safety
Ruth, A 58

sanctions
  and grand strategy 151
  and power 14
Savisaar, Edgar 74
Schröder, Gerhard 36
security
  and balancing of objectives 47
  in Cold War era 29–30
  and collective identity 114–15
  and definition of 6
  and Nordic/Baltic thinking about 38–42
    causal beliefs 40–2
    Common Security 42–3
    cooperative security 43
    principled beliefs 39–40
    understanding of security 44
    worldviews 38–9
  and post-Cold War reassessment of 38, 43
  and small states 20
security community 5, 7
  and Baltic Sea region 121, 151
  and definition of 37
  and Estonian-Russian relations 111, 119
  and expansion of European 37–8
  and nascent phase of 44
security complex theory 6
security integration 46 n2
  and conditionality of 61–70
  and identity 2, 47, 49
  and incentives/disincentives 61
  and power disparity 6–7
  and security choices 47

and security community 37
and state structures 2
and theorizing of 71
security strategy
  and approaches to 152–3
    constructivist 153
    neoliberal 152–3
    neorealist 152
  and Baltic Sea region 150–1, 171–2
  and coexistence of different 150
  and conflict 149
  and cooperation 149
  and game theory 154–6, 171
    as conceptual framework 155
    Estonian-Russian power equality 163–6
    explanation of 172–6
    as formal model 155–6
    limitations of models 171–2
    as metaphor 154–5
    power disparity games 160–3
    power equality games 156–60
    strength of models 171
    Swedish/Finnish military non-alignment 166–70
  and grand strategy
    Baltic Sea region 171
    families of 152
    typology of 151–2
  and regional security complexes 149
  and role identities 153–4, 171–2
settlement, and grand strategy 151
Shore, Sean M 41
Sinijärv, Riivo 75
Skrunda long-distance radar 32
small states
  and integration/identity trade-offs 48
  and power disparity 19–23
    empirical record 21–3
    possible strategies 19–21
  as role identity 16
Social Democratic Party (Finland) 55, 56
Social Democratic Party (Sweden) 57, 60
social identity theory 115–16, 120–1
soft power 127
  and definition of 151
  and security strategy 149
sovereignty, and information revolution 123
Soviet Union

and blockade of Baltic states 30
and fall of 30, 180
and Norway 22
and nuclear and radiation safety 77
and Turkey 22
see also Russia
Stability Pact of Paris (1995) 34
state structures, and integration processes 2
states
  and balancing of objectives 47, 49
  and influence of epistemic communities 73
  and institutions 47
  and permissive institutional environment 62
  and promotion of norms and interests 46
  and security integration 47
  and security policy 47
Stockholm Group 31
strategy, *see* security strategy
structuration
  and power 13
  and power disparity 17
structure, and identity 45–6
submission, and grand strategy 151
Suez Canal crisis (1956) 150
Sun Tzu 142
Svalbard, and balanced openness 20–1
Svalbard Treaty (1925) 21
Sweden
  and accommodation with Soviet Union 22
  and Baltic states
    defence assistance to 33, 181
    diplomacy on behalf of 31–2
  and cooperative security 1
  and digital power 132–3, 145
    cybersecurity 133
    cyberthreats 135, 138–9
    information warfare capability 142, 143
    network ranking 140–1
  and European Union 58, 67–8
    crisis management 59–60, 62, 64
    defence integration 63
    membership of 59, 167
    military capability of 63
    NATO/EU distinction 63, 64
    opportunities presented by 62

Index 225

potential difficulties in 167–8
potential marginalization within 69
rapid reaction forces 65
resistance to majority decision-
  making 62–3
security integration 59–60
solidarity clause 63
and institutional environment 49
  European Union 62–4
  NATO 64–5
  permissive 61–2
and international activism 57–8, 61
  non-alignment as buttress of 58–9
and military nonalignment 36 n15, 45
  adaptation 49–50
  buttress for international role 58–9
  core of foreign policy 59
  criticisms of 69
  domestic values 56
  game theory analysis 166–9
  impact of EU membership 59–60,
    65–6, 67–8
  interpretative adjustments 59
  maintenance of 61
  motives for 48, 51
  national identity 61, 185–6
and national identity 56–7
  development of 57
  foreign policy as part of 61
  preservation of 59, 60
  Swedish 'model' 57
and NATO 35–6, 65, 67, 70, 167
  game theory analysis 166–9
  political debate over 60
  relationship with 51, 69
  reluctance to join 168
  support for strong 64
and nuclear power 90
and role identity 16, 167
  self-conception 185
and security integration 48
and security policy 70–1
  future development of 69–70
  identity 49, 50–1, 70
  identity/interests interplay 46–7
  identity/structure interplay 45–6,
    50–1, 63–4
  post-9/11 68
Swedish People's Party (Finland) 55

Switzerland, and role identity 16
Sydow, Björn von 58–9

terrorism
  and cyberterrorism 131, 135
  and threat perceptions
    Estonia 103
    Russia 107–9, 112, 114
    trends in 109–11
threat images
  and development of
    cognitive factors 113, 121
    domestic influences on 112–13
    identity formation 114–16
    impact of events 113–14
    international socialization 115–17,
      119–20
    realist explanation of 111–12
    traditional approaches to 111–14
  and digital power 130–1, 133, 135
    digital gap 136
    realistic assessment of 146–7
    scope of digital power 138–40
  and Estonia 100–4
  and Russia 105–9
  and terrorism
    Estonia 103
    Russia 107–9, 112, 114
    and trends in 109–11
time, and power disparity 17–18
Trenin, Dmitri 185
Tuomioja, Erkki 55
Turkey, and Soviet Union 22

Ukraine 183
uncertainty, and power estimation 25
United Nations Security Council 26
United States
  and Baltic states 32
  and Commission on Critical
    Infrastructure Protection 135
  and digital power 132–3
    cyberattacks on 134
    cyberterrorism 135
    cyberthreats 130–1, 135, 138–9
    exploiting digital gap 137
    information warfare capability 142,
      143
    network ranking 140–1

and European Union 67
and NATO 167
  expansion of 33, 35, 181
and Russia
  cyber-relationship 133–4, 134–5
  digital power 136–7
unobservables, and power 9, 11–12, 13–14

Vanhanen, Matti 54, 68
Väyrynen, Paavo 77
Visegrad Group 32
voice opportunities 20
Vuorinen, Antti 79, 81

Waever, O 149
Waltz, K 23, 25, 162
Weber, M 10
Wendt, A 4, 16, 162
Western Europe, and security community 37–8
Western European Union 101
Working Group on Nuclear and Radiation Safety (WGNRS)
  and Baltic Sea region, controversy over definition 82–4
  as epistemic community 79–80
    knowledge-based 80
    policy-oriented 82
    as transnational network 80
  and establishment of 77–8
  and first assignment of 82

and game theory analysis 163–6
and information difficulties 84–5
and institutional context 81–2
and membership of 78–9
  interactions between 81
and ministry representation on 79
and organization of 80–1
and Paldiski case 95
  expert support for Estonia 88–9
  lack of information from Russia 84–5
  limited access to base 87–8
  nuclear risk assessment 85
  Russian Navy contacts 86–7
and power disparity
  empirical evidence 93–5
  epistemic communities 91–3
and Russia
  concerns over nuclear safety of 83–4
  definition of Black Sea region 83
  non-cooperation of 84–5
  nuclear risk assessment 85
and tasks of 78
World Economic Forum 140
worldviews, and influence on security thinking 38–9

Yeltsin, Boris 32, 101, 182

zero-sum relationship 40 n23, 42, 44, 92, 94, 183

For Product Safety Concerns and Information please contact our EU
representative GPSR@taylorandfrancis.com
Taylor & Francis Verlag GmbH, Kaufingerstraße 24, 80331 München, Germany

www.ingramcontent.com/pod-product-compliance
Lightning Source LLC
Chambersburg PA
CBHW060602230426
43670CB00011B/1930